Problems of Psychoanalytic Technique in Freud and Lacan

Problems of Psychoanalytic Technique in Freud and Lacan contributes to the everyday work of contemporary psychoanalysts through a critical examination of psychoanalytic technique.

Bruno Bonoris revisits and questions key concepts, including free association, evenly suspended attention, transference, interpretation, and construction, with reference to Freud, Lacan, and the work of contemporary philosophers, psychologists, and psychoanalysts. The book considers four fundamental questions about the notion of "text" in order to rethink psychoanalytic technique, elucidating essential technical concepts while also introducing important modifications. Bonoris recovers the pragmatic spirit of early literature on psychoanalytic technique, oriented toward everyday clinical problems, using simple but powerful language with the added conceptual rigor of Lacan's ideas.

Problems of Psychoanalytic Technique in Freud and Lacan is essential reading for students of, and trainees in, psychoanalysis and psychoanalytic studies. It is also of interest to readers who wish to learn more about psychoanalysis and psychodynamic therapies.

Bruno Bonoris is a psychoanalyst based in Buenos Aires, Argentina. He is Professor of Psychology at the University of Buenos Aires and a doctoral researcher in psychology (UBA) and philosophy (Université Paris 8).

"Far from Lacanian purely theoretical discussions and closed language, in *Problems of Psychoanalytic Technique*, Bonoris thinks about daily psychoanalytic practice through a more clinical than theoretical lens. He invites us to rethink what a psychoanalyst does in the office."

Jorge N. Reitter, author of *Heteronormativity and Psychoanalysis: Oedipus Gay*

"*Problems of Psychoanalytic Technique* inscribes itself in the antipodes of the project to naturalize psychoanalysis. Bonoris elucidates the modalities through which a particular subject is instituted within the psychoanalytic clinic, conceiving it as an integrally a formal entity under which there is, literally, nothing."

Nicolás Garrera-Tolbert, PhD, lecturer of Philosophy, St Francis College, USA

Problems of Psychoanalytic Technique in Freud and Lacan

What Does a Psychoanalyst Do?

Bruno Bonoris

Translated by Juana Issel in collaboration with Carolina Isabel Jalil and Jamie Keesling

Routledge
Taylor & Francis Group

LONDON AND NEW YORK

Designed cover image: Getty Images | kyoshino.

First published 2025
by Routledge
4 Park Square, Milton Park, Abingdon, Oxon OX14 4RN

and by Routledge
605 Third Avenue, New York, NY 10158

Routledge is an imprint of the Taylor & Francis Group, an informa business

© 2025 Bruno Bonoris

Translated by Juana Issel in collaboration with Carolina Isabel Jalil and Jamie Keesling.

Published in Spanish by Coloquio de Perros 2022

British Library Cataloguing-in-Publication Data
A catalogue record for this book is available from the British Library

ISBN: 978-1-032-69639-3 (hbk)
ISBN: 978-1-032-69633-1 (pbk)
ISBN: 978-1-032-69642-3 (ebk)

DOI: 10.4324/9781032696423

Typeset in Times New Roman
by Taylor & Francis Books

To Juana and Elina

Contents

Foreword

The cultural place and significance of psychoanalysis are once again immensely precarious. A rampant, wild, unchecked, prevailing naturalism corrodes contemporary life to its most remote corners. Indeed, certain trends in psychoanalytic research today deliberately choose to inscribe themselves within the alleged prestige of such a form of scientistic reductionism and aim to relaunch, imbued with the latest findings of cognitive and neuroscience, the dream of Freud's 1895 Project. In doing so, they obliterate the transformative power of psychoanalysis and erase its specificity, since they conceive of the nature of its "object" as firmly anchored in the biological realm. Certainly, attempts are made to rectify some of Freud's rudimentary epistemic commitments and the vitalism pervading his metapsychology's energetics. The fact remains, though, that the naturalistic and vitalistic approaches to contemporary psychoanalysis reject (without discussion) the fundamental thesis defended by Jacques Lacan that the eminent object of psychoanalysis is a subject understood as a speculative construction resulting from the analyst's act.[1]

Written under the horizon of Lacan's thesis, the present book inscribes itself in the antipodes of the project to naturalize psychoanalysis: its approach is decidedly Lacanian. Indeed, Lacan's thesis—systematically neglected, misinterpreted, or simply disbelieved, even by most of his self-proclaimed followers—informs Bonoris's overall approach to psychoanalysis and his systematic, subtle reflection on psychoanalytic technique. For Bonoris, the subject is integrally a formal entity, an intellectual hypothesis or conjecture under which, or around which, there is, literally, nothing. If Bonoris's first book examines the historical conditions of the emergence of psychoanalysis,[2] his second book, *Problems of Psychoanalytic Technique in Freud and Lacan*, elucidates the modalities or functions through which a particular subject is instituted in the specific context of the psychoanalytic clinic. These functions, for Bonoris, only exist within psychoanalysis understood as a symbolic device that is re-created ("habilitated") each time by the analyst's acts (ultimately sustained by his "desire"): through his knowledge (*savoir*), the analyst institutes a practical field—that is, a way of operating with the symptom. Hence Bonoris's "methodological" decision to address "the issue of psychoanalytic technique" entirely within the domain of knowledge (*savoir*) and, in parti-cular, as a question that refers essentially to the analyst's relation to knowl-edge. Thus, habilitating, desiring, and, specially, reading and writing become the eminent "analytic functions" through which the subject of each particular case is created.[3] The significance of these functions for psychoanalytic praxis is superlative, and the clinical consequences of this approach are far-ranging. Notice, for instance, that the psychoanalytic subject, so construed, has no body, no organs, and no brain. Furthermore, no natural properties inhere in it, from which it follows that it has no biological sex. In short, it is not a "psycho-physical" individual. Thus, an important merit of Bonoris's book lies in its contribution to the criticism of naturalistic, vitalistic, and individualistic tendencies in mainstream psychoanalysis.[4]

The pervasiveness of the Freudian tradition is not only recognizable in the attempts to reinscribe psychoanalysis in the domain of the natural sciences. It is also apparent in its "humanist" version, vaguely informed by the post-modern dismissal of truth and objectivity. In this view, there is no clear boundary between the "poem" and the "matheme," and psychoanalysis is—so it is repeated ad nauseam—both an "art" and a "science." This view is usually accompanied by a reading of the history of psychoanalysis in which Lacan's work plays the role of a purifying force, a purely gestural means of detoxifying Freudian psychoanalysis from its homophobic, misogynist, trans-phobic, and Eurocentric sins, making it politically palatable for the "public."

In the United States, partly owing to practical and market-related motiva-tions, the seduction of the scientistic version of psychoanalysis is particularly effective. Consequently, its rejection is, at most, partial and often happens within an impossibly vague and ever-expanded eclecticism (through which conscientious analysts aspire to defend themselves against the accusation of dogmatism, sectarianism, and authoritarianism—a fair recrimination, after all, given what we know about the social dynamics of most psychoanalytic insti-tutes). Ironically, though, such eclecticism is vehemently imposed on all those who dare to reject it and hold a stance fiercely critical of the past and present state of our discipline. Further, paradoxically, the alleged "open-mindedness" of psychoanalysis as practiced by the "new generations" is an expression of intel-lectual laziness at best and of an overt rejection of the analytic value and function of knowledge and truth at worst. As a result, psychoanalysis is no longer seen as a rigorous device and a promising means to treat the con-temporary forms of human suffering emerging from our symbolic constitution.

To all this, it may be objected that there is, at least in some small circles where psychoanalysis is still practiced, some promising signs of "resistance" to what I have called the "naturalistic/vitalistic" and the "humanist" versions of psychoanalysis. I agree. There is a certain revision of Freud through the prism of gay, queer, Foucauldian, and feminist studies that has been devel-oping for decades. However, is this a systematically critical examination of the foundations of Freud's psychoanalysis, or is it an attempt to rid it of its untenable "moral" and "political" commitments? In my view, any indictment we may hand down against psychoanalysis must be the result of a systematic criticism of the different epistemic, ontological, and ethical commitments of the various psychoanalytic theories and their interpretations. As a precondition, the belief that psychoanalysis is possible only by professing one's adherence to Freud's paradigmatic theses and concepts must be debunked. For some of us, Lacan's work expresses the necessity of such a re-founding of our theory and praxis. This is the task of those analysts who desire to fundamentally renew psychoanalytic theory and clinic. My hope is that anglophone readers will appreciate Bonoris's book as a valuable contribution to this collective enterprise.

Nicolás Garrera-Tolbert, PhD, LP
New York City, Winter 2024

Notes

1 I owe this crucial insight to Alfredo Eidelsztein's reading of Lacan. Cf., for instance, his "The Concept of Subject in Lacan's Theory" (in *The Origin of the Subject in Psychoanalysis: Rethinking the Foundations of Lacanian Theory and Clinic*, forthcoming, Routledge, 2024).
2 *El nacimiento del sujeto del inconsciente* [*The Birth of the Unconscious's Subject*] (Buenos Aires: Letra Viva, 2024).
3 That the psychoanalytic subject is not only instituted but genuinely *created* (ex nihilo) by the analyst's acts is a thesis defended by Alfredo Eidelsztein in his book *El origen del sujeto en psicoanálisis. Sobre el Big-Bang del sujeto y del lenguaje* (Buenos Aires: Letra Viva, 2016) [in *The Origin of the Subject in Psychoanalysis. Rethinking the Foundations of Lacanian Theory and Clinic*; op. cit.].
4 Among these tendencies one should count "relational psychoanalysis," as it merely duplicates the individualistic stance by positing an *inter*subjectivity that conceives of the subject as emerging and deriving "from an interactive, *interpersonal* field" (Mitchell, Stephen, *Relational Concepts in Psychoanalysis. An Integration* [Cambridge, MA and London: Harvard University Press, 1988], p. 17; my italics). The difference with Lacanian psychoanalysis as I'm presenting it is that, for Lacan, the subject is *nothing but a pure relation of signifiers*, i.e., a *purely linguistic phenomenon*. In Lacan's theory, the person as a psycho-physical unity is dissolved.

Chapter 1

Dreaming

Cut and Beginning

One winter afternoon in 2019, a colleague called me in a hurry to tell me he had to cancel his presentation in a graduate course we were teaching. He asked me to step in for him. We had to switch the order of our lessons. My presentation was supposed to be a month later, but he was asking me to give it in just a few days. I agreed, no problem. Although I was uneasy about the short time frame, I began to prepare what I wanted to say. That same night I had the following dream:

> I am in a big, polygonal classroom, surrounded by massive windows inviting the intrusion of light. I lean over the desk resting on my hands, looking closely at a landscape which strikes me as extraordinary. Relatives, friends, and colleagues are sitting in front of me. There are also people I do not know. Carlos Kuri, who was sitting beside me at the desk, stands up and starts talking to the audience. "On this day, doctoral student Bruno Bonoris will present his thesis entitled 'The Problem of Interpretation in Psychoanalysis: From Truth Hermeneutics to Archaeology of Knowledge'." The audience claps enthusiastically. I gaze at them, dumbstruck. It is strange, I think: this topic concerns me, it has to do with me, but the truth is that I have nothing to say. I despair. I look around the desk for some backup text, but there is nothing there. I then check to see if there are any notes left in my bag. Nothing. I look at the floor in search of a lost note. Nothing. I look up, begging for some truth to take over my body. Nothing. It is a fact: I do not know. I approach Carlos Kuri, I apologize, and tell him there must have been some mistake with the dates. I do not know what I am doing here, I insist. There is no mistake, the date is today, he says. Then, I woke up.

Where do you want to begin? The dream brings the presentation of my doctorate thesis many years closer. Recently, in November of 2018, I presented my master's thesis and, a few months later, after some editing and rewriting, I published it under the title *El nacimiento del sujeto del inconsciente* (The birth of the subject of the unconscious). What came immediately after that happened naturally, in the strange intersection of desire and duty. I enrolled in a doctorate course to

DOI: 10.4324/9781032696423-1

continue the research that had been left on standby, "in progress," like all research. In my published thesis, I had been dedicated to thinking of the episte-mological and historical conditions that made the creation of the psychoanalytic unconscious possible, focusing my attention on the Cartesian *cogito* and the birth of modern science. Just as Lacan had noted in "Science and Truth,"[1] it is unthinkable that the Freudian unconscious appeared without the foreclosure of truth in the field of knowledge and without the production of what is real as *the impossible*; a transmutation bordering the symbolic. Truth and knowledge, real and reality, separated by a wall which should be crossed or, at least, moved. The body, a privileged site for disputes over knowledge, also experienced the con-sequences of these alterations. It was emptied of its truth, thrust into the morti-fying dimension of mere extension, sectioned by the surgical knives of budding medical science. It was silenced. The body is the main battlefield in the fight over truth. This was what Freud's hysterical women revealed. The truth of sexuality returned in their symptoms. The muddy field of the sexual. This is the question which remained unanswered and which I now want to answer: why is the unconscious sexual?

Interesting question. However, in the dream, the topic of your thesis is different. Yes, it seems to be a Foucauldian title. Where could I have gotten that from? It is a mixture of hermeneutics of the subject and the archaeology of knowledge. Not very original, truth makes the difference. Technical issues, particularly interpreta-tion, have been bothering me for a while. It is a parallel investigation I have been conducting with Tomás Pal. This year, we will teach a course on free association. I also remember a conversation I had with Omar Acha after a presentation he gave on one of Lacan's texts. Rather than a conversation, it was actually a question: would you not consider that Foucault's archaeology is an interesting method to rethink the reading of analytic texts? I do not remember well what he said, I simply know that he did not seem convinced. Evidently, it is a theoretical forcing, just an intuition. In any case, I find the question valid, arising from the difficulties we psychoanalysts face once we are left without our hermeneutical apparatus: the Oedipus complex. How do psychoanalysts read if they do not have a reading key? What does it mean to interpret outside of a hermeneutics?

I am in a big, polygonal classroom, surrounded by massive windows inviting the intrusion of light. Where does that come from? I think I was at the National Library in Buenos Aires. The dream reminds me of some of my visits there when I was in primary school: the thrill of wandering around that fortress of knowledge, the excitement of finding unfindable texts. I am so old. We did not have Google then; the library was our infinite archive. I felt like a proper researcher. I also remember the opening sessions. Giving a presenta-tion in the Jorge Luis Borges room was a tremendous pleasure. Friends and family came to see me. At some point, my dad came and, when I was done presenting, he approached me and said, "I didn't understand a thing but … you spoke so well!" Those words moved me. Now I think, regarding the truth, that what matters is not only what is said, but how it is said, as well as when and where. Besides, how much of the truth *is* about the desire of transmission and not just what is transmitted? After the presentation, we found those massive windows and the profuse influx of light. Very nice memories.

The light. Yes, I have a thing about lights. Every time I visit a friend's house I start fiddling with the lights. I turn one on, turn another off, dim that one, and so on. My friends usually tease me, "So, Bruno, which light would you like?" At night, I like dim lights, warm, and sometimes intermittent, like Christmas lights. During the day—sunlight. I cannot study without lots of light, which is why I used to have a hard time studying at night. Although nighttime is not so bad for writing. Reading is for the daytime; writing, for the nighttime.

The library and the light. The Enlightenment debate? Ha! What you say reminds me of the original back cover of Lacan's *Écrits*: Lacan said there that there was only one debate, always the same one—the Enlightenment debate. Later, Miller discarded that back cover and replaced it with an extract from a magazine which says, among other things, that "there are individuals, that is all." Lacan speaking of individuals—the guy who dedicated decades to studying the divided subject. This Millerian maneuver seems to me fitting of the obscurantism Lacan himself denounced in that first back cover. In some way, I feel that I am dealing, together with some colleagues, with this Enlightenment debate. There are no great intentions. It is about providing a rational argument-based debate which will open a dialogue with other fields. The word "rational" chills me. What I want to say is that I am sick of the twisted Lacanian language, of the obscurantism of experiential ineffability. It is likely that there is something along those lines happening with technical issues. What do we Lacanian analysts do? What happens within the office? Why do we sometimes feel that the concepts lose all kinds of practical reference, and other times that theory *overrides* experience with unstoppable force? Is it about the texts we read and the way we read them? At the same time, in what way do clinical problems become conceptual questions? How can we see a problem when we are so convinced of what we are doing? Can any knowledge be derived from practice, or is it rather a non-knowledge that is extracted?

I feel like writing about this, but I am looking for another type of writing, more essayistic, freer, dispensing with textual support. Writing in the intersection between concept and sense. In the future, I might loosen up. Lower my guard.

Texts might be done away with as long as they are used. Losing that support at the time of saying. Yes, definitely … I just noticed for the first time that photo of the typewriter on fire. How remarkable! I have been coming to this office for months and I had never seen it. The ways of repression.

I am here to change my relationship with writing. Now I can see that, the purpose of my calling you. To you.

And Carlos Kuri? The most enigmatic part of the dream; I do not know what to say about him because I do not know him. In fact, I do not even recall his face. I know some things about him and about the group of analysts from Rosario. Many have written in *Conjetural* magazine. In there, there is powerful psychoanalysis, but the truth is that I have not read many of them. I remember now that I read one of Kuri's books for my research for the scientific and technical scholarship of the University of Buenos Aires (UBACyT).

Which book? I cannot remember the name.

Which book?

Yes! *Nada nos impide, nada nos obliga* (Nothing stops us, nothing compels us).

Note

1 Cf. Lacan (1966).

Reference

Lacan, J. (1966). Science and Truth. In J. Lacan, *Écrits: The First Complete Edition in English*. Trans. B. Fink, pp. 726–745. New York and London: W.W. Norton.

Chapter 2

Conjecturing

Experience and Theory

Also, Theory

The work of the analyst can be described in many ways. Throughout the history of psychoanalysis there have existed, successively and simultaneously, diverse, and even opposing, ways of understanding analytic practice, from both the theoretical and clinical perspectives. The difference between theory and experience is relevant to the extent that concepts—and not only technical ones—*inform* the analyst's actions and the development of a treatment, even if this difference should be revised. I say "inform" instead of "determine" because such concepts open a range of possibilities and limitations.[1] They reveal an orientation. The analyst's work is affected by a number of factors beyond theoretical knowledge and analytic experience as analyst and analysand, such as neurosis, life crises, biases, and lack of theoretical training, to name a few. In other words, the analyst's act is affected by everything Lacan aptly called countertransference.[2] A strong theoretical model does not guarantee good analysis, but its absence foretells a bad one. To learn how to analyze, it is not necessary to be in the room, to lie on the couch or sit behind it, or to observe clinical intake meetings. It is not necessary to crash into a wall to know the wall is there—it is enough to have blueprints and to know how to interpret them.

There are, however, those who claim not to need such blueprints—who claim to have read enough to know that psychoanalysis has little to do with reading. "Close the libraries!" they demand from their lofty positions. "Close the libraries!" they shout from within analytic circles. Theoretical knowledge, they say, is useful for teaching but not for analysis. According to such minds, the analyst necessarily leads a double life—partially in contact with theory (the professor) and partially in contact with experience (the analyst). I do not underestimate the question of theoretical knowledge relevant to the analyst, but the inquiry implies that there is at least some theory that is necessary beyond the know-how attained through personal experience as an analysand and through clinical experience as an analyst.

DOI: 10.4324/9781032696423-2

It is a fact: in the useless yet endless debate about theory versus experience, the latter comes out victorious. In Miller's words:

> for practicing analysts, theory is in the past. They experience tenderness towards it; it is their youth, when they did not know how to do it. But later they go back—because they managed, in their own way, to achieve the analytic attitude—[…] theory is, essentially, a commentary on experience.[3]

The analytic attitude is achieved by analyzing oneself, or, rather, concluding a self-analysis. Theory is a "childhood disease" that benefits those still young and lacking in analytic experience.[4] Later, equipped with the analytic attitude, they *go back* to experience (back to what there was *before*). Theory comes after experience. It is *essentially* a commentary.

"Psychoanalysis is an experience," we blurt out, with an odd expression on our faces, a sign of assurance in the face of a problem ignored. I agree with Lacan: an experience is formed only if we start from a question and a supposition, in other words, if a hypothesis is established. It is from there that something can begin to take shape as fact because "a fact [*fait*] [is] always made up of [*fait de*] discourse."[5] There is no *raw* experience, no analytic fact beyond the theoretical-discursive scheme of which it is part. If psychoanalysis is an experience, it is not in the sense of lived experience (*erlebnis*), but as an experiment, a field artificially formed according to a series of hypotheses. It might be said that psychoanalysis is the assessment and actualization of the reality of the unconscious mind in calculated artificial conditions.[6] In fact, anyone who has participated in psychoanalysis will have noticed that it is an "artificial" situation, both in terms of its governing rules and the placement of the bodies involved.

The statement "psychoanalysis is a theory," is, in turn, not so easily assimilated.[7] This is a surprising fact if we take into account the amount of strictly theoretical psychoanalytic texts connected to other primarily theoretical fields, such as linguistics, mathematics, physics, logic, philosophy, and others, written by masters we commonly reference to sustain this unbridgeable gap. We will not solve this problem by saying that psychoanalysis is a *praxis*. At present it is necessary to tackle the bothersome distinction between theory and experience, understood as independent domains. Only in this way will we be able to think what praxis means.

So, those who analyze "without theory" ignore many things regarding the knowledge that governs them. "Clinical experience" may mean learning mediated by theoretical and practical revision of daily tasks, or the endless repetition of personal prejudice. Eclecticism may be understood as a curious disposition towards other forms of knowledge, an openness to interdisciplinary dialogue, the expression of conceptual vagueness, or naïve relativism. Knowledge always participates in our thoughts, feelings, and actions, whether we know it or not. This is one of the main insights of psychoanalysis. Analysts analyze "with their unconscious" when they do not know what they are doing. They would do better, then, to theorize and conjecture with knowledge—a more precise instrument.

No theory is devoid of practical consequences. Reading, research, writing, and transmission are among the most common, and beyond these lie the incalculable effects of theory on people's behavior. It is difficult to imagine someone "shaking off" theoretical abstractions in order to analyze, as if they were not part of the apparatus in which they participate, let alone aspects of the analyst's subjectivity. Theories make bodies.

What is the purpose of experience? To test theory, to pose important questions, and to discard unimportant ones. And of theory? To find useful, substantiated answers which can then be carried into experience. Is it not the case that theory refines experience, while experience tests theory? This is why, in psychoanalysis, the ethical and the technical are intertwined such that they are not easily differentiated. Technique is the realization of ethics. It cannot be any other way.[8]

Psychoanalytic *praxis* does not coincide with either theory or experience; it is a Möbius strip. It appears to have two sides—on the outside, theory, and, on the inside, experience—when it actually has only one. Likewise, there is no clear cut between the inside and outside of *a single* analysis. It is not easy to say what the limits of a case are, which voices create it. What is seemingly "outside" interferes all the time in the conversation between analyst and analysand. Supervision as an inherent aspect in the production of the text and its textuality is one example. The writing of the analytic text is a *counter psychological* process of a multiplication of voices and of questioning the figure of the author. As the text is being written, its origin fades, and its limits are dissolved.

What is praxis, then? It is the transformation of the real through the symbolic,[9] or, as Farrán said, the "transmutation of matter through specific means and instruments, within defined legal, political, and ideological relationships producing certain objects."[10] Our matter is the subject; our means are words; our specific instruments are concepts (not only technical ones such as free association, evenly suspended attention, transference management, and interpretation, but also "theoretical" concepts such as unconscious, drive, symptom, signifier, and fantasy); our objects are the subject of the unconscious and the object *a*, cause of desire, and surplus-jouissance. Finally, our habitat: the multiple crossed devices of knowledge and power where subjectivities live—a dimension that cannot be forgotten if we wish to avoid becoming functional parts of the devices in which suffering is reproduced.

At Least Two

The clinical consequences of the division between theory and experience appear clearly every time the following phrase by Lacan is referenced: "[i]t is essential that the analyst be at least two. The analyst who produces effects and the analyst who theorizes these effects."[11] On this point, there is widespread agreement: clinical psychology is the *redoubling* of experience through concepts. First, there are effects; then, these effects are theorized. But how can an effect be achieved without any possible calculation to achieve it? Is this capability obtained through analysis itself? Is it the unconscious that leads the cure, or is it a complete surrender to chance?

I agree with Schejtman when he says that sitting behind the couch does not in itself improve the analyst's abilities. One can spend decades listening to patients without being able to grasp the logic of a case. Neither the fox nor the devil gains wisdom from old age alone, he says, exactly, "clinical work is not a question of instinct but of conceptualization, of formalization [...] *it is a superimposition over experience*, and it is not obvious."[12] This is how he distinguishes "what analytic experience is from the clinic that *results* from it."[13] Schejtman highlights the importance of conceptualization and formalization for any psychoanalytic cure, but considers these secondary to experience. This idea is widespread in Lacanian psychoanalysis. That experience is already a "product" of more-or-less-rigorous conceptualization is typically ignored. For example, Freud implemented the method of free association for therapeutic purposes based on a hypothesis. The question he asked himself was how to access the unconscious once hypnosis was no longer a reliable method. Here we have a question, a hypothesis, and an original experience.

I might be accused of highlighting trivialities, since conceptual duplication would imply a return to experience mediated by clinical work. In the end, after some periphrasis, we might say that experience is always accompanied by conjectures. However, the radical separation of the two realms and their corresponding tasks is firmly defended. In psychoanalytic experience, the analyst analyzes; in the psychoanalytic clinic, the clinician (not the analyst, *nota bene*) theorizes its effects. The analyst, therefore, does not think; only the clinician does. Boxaca and Lutereau say it like this:

> When [analysts] think of their practice, they can never be the same as when they produced the effects with the device [...] there is an *immeasurable separation* between the truth of praxis and the knowledge which intends to highlight *this act* which, in the best of cases, surprises the analyst, as well.[14]

Setting aside the philosophical difficulties entailed by the reference to the sameness of the analyst in her two functions, I am interested in pointing out that what Boxaca and Lutereau highlight is knowledge that can be extracted only after the act, completely forgetting that the act could only happen in relation to some theoretical knowledge—concepts—and some clinical knowledge—conjectures—pertaining to a particular case. The analyst's surprise is an atypical response to the impossibility of conjecturally anticipating the reasons for the effectiveness of *a particular act*, but is more likely an effect of the impossibility of foreseeing when and how this conjecture will be inscribed in the text. If the analyst could not anticipate, even by approximation, the possible effects of his words, it would no longer be clear who was directing the cure. It is worth recovering Lacan's idea here:

[a]s an interpreter of what is presented to me in words or deeds, I am my own oracle and articulate it as I please, sole master of my ship after God; and while, of course, I am far from able to weigh the whole effect of my words, I am well aware of the fact and strive to attend to it.[15]

What does it mean that, at the time of the act, the analyst does not think? And, if this is the case, what are the criteria for intervention? There may be some confusion between the analytic act and the analyst's intervention. In this case, it would be wise to talk not about *that* specific act, but about the analytic act.

Now I want to go back to the phrase that, to my understanding, is decisive in the readings above. Rodríguez Ponte's Spanish version states: "[i]t is essential that the analyst is at least two. The analyst, to have any effect, is the analyst who, to these effects, theorizes them."[16] In this translation, which is more interesting to me than the published English translation, the analyst who has any effect *is* the analyst who, to these effects, theorizes them.[17] To have effects, the analyst must theorize them and, at the same time, he must theorize these effects. It is impossible to know where to start. It is not about the theoretical duplication of experience or the incommensurability between the two instances. There is *reciprocity* and *conjecturability*. That is how Lacan puts it: "theory is neither, as our use of the word implies, the abstraction of praxis, nor its general reference, nor the model of its application. Right from its very first appearance, theory is praxis itself."[18] In other words, "This concept directs the way in which patients are treated. Conversely, the way in which they are treated governs the concept."[19] It is equally naïve to believe that theoretical knowledge is extracted from experience as to think that experience is determined by theory. Between both there is what happens and what does not happen, the blind spots, the unthinkable, the problems. This space is not a chasm or a bridge, but an opaque threshold.

Lombardi, following the colleagues above, believes that there is an opposition between therapeutic efficacy and clinical elucidation. An unbridgeable gap between "the previous conditions" of intervention and the causes of its efficacy.[20] In order to assert this, he cites Lacan: "practice does not need to be clarified so as to operate."[21] I do not understand why Lombardi takes this statement as irrevocable attribute (and a positive one at that) of psychoanalysis. It is indisputable that practice does not need to be clarified so as to operate, but it does not follow that non-clarified practice is more effective.

The quandary seems to be this: the analyst either thinks without acting and transmits or acts without thinking and remains silent. The problem is that such "thinking" before acting is hastily linked to theoretical prejudice that would prevent a singular reading of the case. What is omitted is the possibility of carrying out such a reading of *that particular* analytic text, a conjecture for the analyst to think *from*, as opposed to relying on "university" knowledge. At the same time, the concepts that allow for a reading of the case are derived from theory (unconscious, drive, transference, repetition, jouissance, and fantasy, for example) and from the case itself.

For these reasons, I consider it necessary to divide what is classically called interpretation into two distinct functions: *reading* and *writing*. Reading allows for the establishment of a conjecture of the case based on the text itself. Reading must dispense with any external keys that precede the material. It presupposes knowledge *of* the text, not knowledge *about* the text. This is why reading implies thinking. Writing, on the other hand, does not; at least not in the classical sense of the term. What I call writing is the incorporation of conjecture into the text.[22] The way this conjecture is presented, and how it is incorporated, depends on multiple techno-aesthetic variables, including the analyst's sense of style and sense of timing (the how and the when). In order to write, it is not necessary to "think"; rather, writing is faithful to intuition, which is another kind of thinking.

The Analyst's Own Analysis

Another reason why it is crucial to revise the idea of clinical work as an "interrogation outside and following experience" is that the issues concerning the formation of an analyst usually revolve around the experience of her own analysis.[23] The analyst *is made of* experience, and the teacher is made of theory; thus, we analyze from experience and we *clinicize* with theory. Both the analyst's analytic work and his formation are ruled, then, by experience.

Agreement on this subject is widespread, and any nuances that might be incorporated are repressed as shyly as they might be presented. The resistance arising when interrogation is attempted reveals the question's inherent value. Lombardi states it clearly: "the decisive experience for psychoanalytic clinical work is the analysis itself, the most important one […] it is a necessary condition."[24] But, of course! Who would doubt that the analysis itself is paramount for the analyst? The question we must ask ourselves is why this would be *the decisive* experience, the most important one. Is it not just as necessary that the analyst knows about psychoanalytic theory (and so many other things)? How important is reading and writing in each case? The analysis is a necessary condition. Are the others also necessary? Might some necessary conditions be more important than others? What is certain is that what is necessary cannot be missed. However, the need for theoretical formation and the reading and writing of a case is almost never emphasized. This is a symptom which must be interpreted.

Another quote frequently used to support this idea is found at the beginning of Lacan's summary of the seminar on the psychoanalytic act:

> The psychoanalytic act, neither seen nor heard of before me, namely, never mapped out, much less put in question, we suppose here to be something belonging to the elective moment when analysand passes to psychoanalyst.
>
> This is the most commonly admitted recourse as regards what is necessary for this passage, all other conditions remaining contingent as compared to it.[25]

López uses this quote to state that, from the three pillars of the analyst's formation (study, supervision, and personal analysis), "the most relevant one is the transformation of the analysand into the analyst at the end of the analysis, *being any other condition contingent in comparison*."[26] I have a different reading: it is not that the transformation from analysand to analyst is the only necessary condition to perform an analytic act, but that the analytic act is a necessary condition for the transformation from analysand to analyst.

When asserting the need for personal analysis as a requirement for the analyst's formation, we find ourselves with a false problem simply because, across the psychoanalytic world, there is no movement, school, or author that argues otherwise.[27] If there is one thing we analysts do, it is analyze ourselves. In fact, even today, people come to our consulting rooms demanding to be made into analysts. This is a symptom, as I said, for psychoanalysis, though not necessarily for the person consulting. Even if we do not have an explanation for these prevailing ideas, we can at least remark on a certain correlativity: the elevation of personal analysis in an analyst's formation brings with it the devaluation of theory, knowledge, texts, thought, and anything else that is considered an abstraction.

But theory is body! Why do we lighten it? Prieto poses that "nobody becomes an analyst by *only* reading books, [one] becomes an analyst by going through their own analysis, *only* this way may we be in a position to avoid imprinting on the analysand our own prejudices."[28] My opinion is that undergoing analysis does not in itself guarantee that the analyst will not interpret according to her prejudices. In general, prejudices are cured in the streets and at the desk, and symptoms are cured on the couch. The prejudice from which the analyst must be cured is that of the subject supposed to know. But how does this occur? Solely through personal analysis? I consider it a clinical error to assume analysts are safe from making interventions based on their prejudices simply because they have been analyzed. If this were the case, second-generation analysts, who had surely been on the couch, would not have imprinted on their patients the heteronormative prejudices and so many other expressions of normality that they did. We might say that they were not truly analyzed, but then we would have to recognize that the psychoanalytic clinic at the time was intimately connected to the wrong theories they upheld. I suppose that no Lacanian psychoanalyst believes that the ego psychological approach is able to transform someone into an analyst. Determining the analytic experience adequate for the formation of the analyst already necessitates consideration of the theoretical basis that makes it possible, and how this would differ from other types of experience—for example, an analysis based on normative ideas.

It is undeniable that, in the experiential definition of the analyst's work and formation, there is an implicit underlying theory. As sophisticated as it may appear, this epistemological model is merely an update of classic Freudian empiricism: first, experience; then, theorization of what was experienced; lastly, the return to experience, accompanied by hypotheses.[29] But, as Bleger stated in 1969:

in no way can we currently accept the naïve scheme assuming [...] that facts are there and that, by keeping to their observation and study, we can form a hypothesis and then theories, which may be either proven or disputed on the basis of those facts.[30]

"How can we locate that impossible to bear in another subject, if we have not gone through the experience of it first?" wonders Lombardi.[31] This question would not be as odd if it were held as an epistemological position which assumes that, in order to treat suffering, we need to have experienced it. But this is not the case. No one is suggesting the establishment of a Psychoanalysts Anonymous. What is said is that we need to have *that* particular experience and not others, an experience of a Lacanian analysis, with its theoretical basis, its concepts, and its specific means and ends. Epistemological empathy with the real, then, would be valid only for Lacanians. "Feeling is believing," whisper the unconvinced, but we need not pray to the unconscious; rather, we need to put it in motion. It is surprising that this topic does not spark discussions in any psychoanalytic school. "I am not saying—even if it is not impossible—that the psychoanalytic community is a church,"[32] said Lacan, who had studied *Verneinung* closely. Dogma is the order of the day. That may be the most essential.

Rodríguez Ponte says: "[t]he analyst is made through analysis. This is, to me, the most crucial point [...] it is the number one element, and far away from number two [theoretical formation]."[33] The cause, in all the Aristotelian senses, of the analyst is experience. If this hypothesis is followed closely, it is possible to conclude that anyone who is well analyzed—even a tradesman, a lawyer, or an engineer—is a potential psychoanalyst.[34] I wonder how one could analyze without any knowledge of psychoanalytic theory, how one could carry out the practice without those crucial instruments: concepts.[35]

Later, Rodríguez Ponte clarifies that the analyst cannot be confused with the person exercising that role. It is a position that can be occupied only at a definite moment in the course of the analysis. In order to reach that position, which the author calls the "analyst's desire," it is necessary to be analyzed. We are again presented with this unavoidable split between analyst and clinician: the analyst is made through analyzing, and the clinician through studying. I want to eliminate any ambiguity: it is clear that there is a difference between both positions, that analyzing and theorizing are not equivalent, but the distinction does not amount to a "structural divorce."[36] It is more like a couple with an intimate and complex relationship. Does an analyst not read a case in the same way he reads a "theoretical" text? Did Lacan not read Freud using the same critical method Freud himself developed to read cases?

The lack of solid arguments to support that personal analysis is *necessary* to reach the true analytic position is swiftly exposed: "I am not saying that it is impossible without analysis," clarifies Rodríguez Ponte, "it may not be wrong to have some nuance, but it is very difficult to do it without having been analyzed."[37] The transformation from impossibility to difficulty evinces the fragility of the theory on the analyst's formation. He then concludes:

> What we need to understand is that the analysis started with someone who had not been analyzed himself. This needs to be our starting point: Freud was not analyzed, the so-called self-analysis is not analysis [...] we are forced to maintain that there can be analysts who have not been analyzed. That is, we must accept a mysterious moment at the beginning of psychoanalytic history or find a way to sustain a paradox.[38]

It is neither a mystery nor a paradox. It is a contradiction.[39] Unless we admit that Freud is the *at least one who refuses the couch*—a statement which is part of a neurotic logic par excellence (on the masculine side)—we are *forced* to state that it is not *necessary* to have been analyzed to become an analyst and, at the same time, admit that it is not necessary to complete analysis in order to produce psychoanalytic ideas. For instance, it would be absurd to believe that Lacan is the only human being who could draft a powerful theory of the end of analysis (the obliteration of the subject supposed to know) without having ended his own. How did he do it, then? It might come as a disappointment, but there is only one answer: through researching, arguing, and analyzing (himself). In the end, the analyst's formation cannot hinge on his personal analysis. In my opinion, it is crucial that the person analyzing has been analyzed (and also analyzes himself), but not because this is the exclusive path to becoming an analyst.

Nonsense. Go Right Ahead

The issue of the analyst's formation is far from resolved. Even today, the famous Freudian triad—personal analysis, supervision, and theoretical study—which dispenses with both capricious hierarchies and mysteries, seems most consistently accepted, however poorly argued it may be. Here, personal analysis is less an initiation rite than a requirement with a specific goal: treating unconscious conflicts that could hinder not only the life but also the work of the analyst. In this sense, it would be appropriate to return to analysis every few years, not to believe oneself to be an analysand-analyst at all. Conversely, it seems that the experience of the pass was not created with the goal of authorizing analysts, but rather in order to account for psychoanalytic practice. I understand Lacan's proposal in this way: if analysts do not provide reasons for the manner in which they conduct themselves in the Freudian field, analysands and passands might.

There are progressively fewer analysts interested in giving testimony of their own experience as analysands as part of the Pass. Passands, juries, cartels, titles (AS, AMS), and so on are all part of the bureaucratic paraphernalia and seem to serve more as imaginary acknowledgement than as true transmission of our practice. And speaking of imaginary acknowledgement, who wants, in this day and age, to search for it in the Lacanian school? Psychoanalytic institutions—with their hierarchical relationships, endogamous affiliations, conservative practices, weak theories, and repetitious transmission—do not attract new generations of psychoanalysts. Social media has encouraged the development of informal relationships and dynamic connections between analysts (and people generally interested in psychoanalysis) from different cities, countries, schools, and universities. What holds us together is affinity, not identity. Schools are no longer necessary to escape the loneliness of the office. Though we may be in need of offices to escape the institutional logic of the school.

Moreover, many working analysts have not yet completed their analysis, owing not to insufficient time on the couch but to a lack of common criteria regarding what exactly constitutes a completed analysis. There is no common ground regarding what the end of analysis is, in any sense of the term.[40] And we can hardly end an analysis if we do not have a clear and distinct sense of what that end might be. I wonder about the opinion of those who believe that completing one's own analysis is a necessary condition for analyzing others, given the number of professionals who practice without having done so. Would they advise their supervisees to terminate their analyses in order to improve their cases? The end of analysis, in terms of both its goals and termination, is a subject we will resume later.

As regards the analyst's formation, Freud's position still seems preferable to me. When a young practitioner tells me she is not sure whether she should start seeing patients because she is still lacking in her own analysis or studies, I tell her the same thing Freud told Bernfeld:

> In 1922 I discussed with Freud my intention of establishing myself in Vienna as a practicing analyst. I had been told that our Berlin group encouraged psychoanalysts, especially beginners, to have a didactic analysis before starting their practice, and I asked Freud whether he thought this preparation was desirable for me. His answer was, "Nonsense. Go right ahead. You certainly will have difficulties. When you get into trouble, we will see what we can do about it." Only a week later he sent me my first didactic case.[41]

"The analyst is authorized only by himself," said Lacan, and I would like to read it in the immediate sense.[42] No school, institution, or university guarantees that there will be an analyst, nor does studying, nor does personal analysis. Nothing guarantees it, in fact. This does not mean that we should not ask ourselves how to locate, with increasing clarity, how and where to position ourselves in order to act as analysts. Meanwhile—an unending while—we must analyze, be analyzed, supervise, and research.

What Is Said

I would like to end this discussion on the relationship between experience and theory in analytic practice with the words Lacan used in "The Inauguration of the Clinical Program:" "[w]hat is the psychoanalytic clinic? It is not complicated. It has a foundation: *it is what is said during a psychoanalysis.*"[43] The clinic, then, is not what is thought outside and after the analytic experience. It is what is said during the analysis.

As usually happens, there are many readings of this statement, particularly of the phrase, "what is said." What is its value in this context? Who says what is said? What does it mean that what is said is the foundation? A first reading would indicate that what is said is what is spoken during an analysis, that which could be recorded with a tape recorder. But is this the extent of it? Schejtman specifies that what is said during psychoanalysis "comes from the analysand's mouth," and, therefore, the one who is doing the clinical work *in* the analytic experience is not the analyst but the analysand. In fact, analytic experience is not a didactic experience for the analyst.[44] There are formations of the unconscious, he says, following Lacan, but there is no formation of the analyst. Schejtman is consistent, and I agree with him: an analyst does not necessarily learn from experience. "The only one that develops through psychoanalysis is the analysand," he concludes, supporting the radical autonomy of the analyst, who exists fleetingly at the moment of the act, and the clinician, who learns something from experience and conceptualizes it.[45]

Boxaca and Lutereau have a different reading. Basically, they highlight that "what is said" is not the clinic in itself but its foundation, and that, therefore, this is the "conceptual redoubling of experience."[46] Experience is the foundation, and clinic is what is built upon it. Even though it is not a given that the foundation for something should be a different thing from that something, let us follow the authors' argument. They note with precision that "what is said" does not necessarily mean the sentences actually uttered. "In any case, the analyst cares less about what is said than the position from where it is said."[47] Right, but does the position from where it is said not require a reading? Is it not already a "redoubling of experience"? They also note that Lacan does not specify who does the saying of "what is said." In this respect, they disagree with Schejtman, because, although they consider that the analysand is tasked with speaking, the analyst, too, needs to say his piece. In fact, the analyst must pay with his words as long as these can be elevated to the status of interpretation. This means that, if there is interpretation, the words no longer belong to the analyst. To whom do they belong, then? This question is pivotal and will allow us to read Lacan's quote differently.

The question, in my opinion, revolves around Lacan's use of the impersonal "*is said*," which leaves the identity of the interlocutors indeterminate. "What does it matter who speaks?" someone asked. That is what psychoanalytic clinic is about, particularly in the beginning: the transition from "I speak" (whether analyst or analysand) to "it speaks." I agree with Boxaca and Lutereau that the phrase "is said" refers to saying as such and not the words spoken, to what is forgotten in what is heard or understood. It is about a reading and writing effect on what was said, which opens the possibility of a "it is said that ...."

There is no experience that is not *always already* mediated by the clinic, now understood as the more or less calculated intervention of the analyst based on texts, concepts, and his prejudices. The very experience of speaking in analysis, the way it manifests what is "actually said," is already the result of a unique device for the production of the text: free association and evenly suspended attention.

Notes

1   I owe this concept to my friend, the philosopher and psychoanalyst Nicolás Garrera-Tolbert.
2   Cf. Lacan, 1951.
3   Miller, 2008–2009: 170.
4   Ibid.
5   "The whole point is that experience is constituted as such only if we start out by asking the right question. We call that a hypothesis. [...] begins to take a *de facto* form, and a fact [*fait*] always made up of [*fait de*] discourse" (Lacan, 1967: 72).
6   "What is the cure? It is an experimental situation that is in many respects comparable to the experimental set-ups and montages of the well-known experimental sciences. At the same time, however, it is a practical situation that precipitates transformations in its object thanks to instruments of a particular kind used to produce such effects" (Althusser, 1975–1976/2017: 148).
7   "My idea, when I try to spread psychoanalysis—that is, taking it beyond the dialogue with colleagues without it losing its accuracy—is to show others that, in a way, they already know what I am trying to get through [...] In my view, psychoanalysis is not a theory, but a way to experience which is proven in daily life" (Lutereau, 2018).
8   I agree with Miller when he states, "there is no technical point in analysis which is not connected to the ethical question, and it is for our discourse comfort that we differentiate ethics from technique. In the analysis, technical questions are always ethical questions, and this has quite a precise reason: because we are addressing the subject" (1987/2007: 13).
9   Cf. Lacan, 1964/1981.
10   Farrán, 2020: 51.
11   Lacan, as cited by Schejtman, 2013: 28.
12   Ibid.: 25. All italics in the quotes are mine.
13   Ibid.: 24.
14   Boxaca and Lutereau, 2013: 16.
15   Lacan, 1958: 491.
16   Lacan, n.d.: lecture on December 10, 1974. [Translator's note: this is a translation into English of the Spanish translator's interpretation. A published version of this fragment by C. Gallagher is "It is nevertheless indispensable that the analyst should be at least two, the analyst to produce effects, and the analyst who theorizes these effects."]
17   We will never know for certain whether Lacan said "and" (*et*) or "is" (*est*). The first version seems more grammatically correct; the second, as I understand it, is more in line with other instances of Lacan's ideas on the subject. Be that as it may, aside from what Lacan might have actually said, the dispute refers to two different epistemological and clinical positions within Lacanian theory.
18   Lacan, 1960–1961: 79.
19   Lacan, 1964/1981: 124. The same idea, centered on the concept of transference, may be found in "The direction of the treatment and the principles of its power": "For this handling of the transference is at one with the notion, and however little

elaborated this notion is in practice, it cannot do otherwise than range itself with the partialities of the theory" (Lacan, 1958: 184).

20 Cf. Lombardi, 2018: 21.
21 Lacan, as cited by Lombardi, 2018: 21.
22 "The role of writing is building, with all that reading has constituted, a body" (Foucault, 1983: 943).
23 Lombardi, 2018: 27.
24 Ibid.: 29.
25 Lacan, 1967–1968: 198.
26 López, 2020: 73.
27 In several instances, Alfredo Eidelsztein has questioned the exclusive importance given to experience of personal analysis to the detriment of case research and discussion. However, as far as I know, he has never said that one should not be analyzed in order to be an analyst. Even though we can question *the need* (in a formal sense) for personal analysis, it is unwise to say that it is better not to undergo analysis than to do so.
28 Prieto, 2016: 25.
29 Cf. Freud, 1933 (1932).
30 Bleger, 1969.
31 Lombardi, 2018: 27.
32 Lacan, 1964/1981: 12.
33 Rodríguez Ponte, 2005: 26.
34 Cf. Suarez, 2005.
35 Lacan says it in these terms: "[w]hat holds good in the art of the expert cook, who knows how to joint a bird, to disjoint it with as little resistance as possible, is also true for psychoanalysis. We know that there is a method of conceptualization proper to each structure. [...] One has to realize that we do our dissecting with concepts, not with a knife" (1953–1954/1991: 12).
36 Zaffore, 2012: 159.
37 Rodríguez Ponte, 2005: 26.
38 Ibid.: 26–27.
39 This is how Morales Montiel expressed it very clearly: "1. To become a psychoanalyst, it is necessary to have had the experience of being analyzed by an analyst. 2. Freud was the first psychoanalyst. 3. [...] To become a psychoanalyst, it is necessary for Freud to have had the experience of being analyzed by an analyst. 4. This implies that there was at least one psychoanalyst before Freud. 5. (2) and (4) are contradictory" (2017).
40 Tomás Pal usually says that the end of analysis is achieved when the insurance benefits end. It is a definition quite grounded in reality.
41 Roazen, 1995: 119.
42 Lacan, 1973/2012: 327.
43 Lacan, 1977: 4.
44 Schejtman, 2013: 30.
45 Ibid.: 35.
46 Boxaca and Lutereau, 2013: 14.
47 Ibid.

References

Althusser, L. (2017). *Philosophy for Non-Philosophers*. Trans. G.M. Goshgarian. New York: Bloomsbury. (Original work published 1975–1976)

Bleger, J. (1969). Teoría y práctica en psicoanálisis. La praxis psicoanalítica. *Revista uruguaya de psicoanálisis*. Retrieved from www.apuruguay.org/apurevista/1960/16887247196911030405.pdf

Boxaca, L., and Lutereau, L. (2013). *Introducción a la clínica psicoanalítica: Asociación libre, Interpretación, Transferencia, Síntoma, Duelo*. Buenos Aires: Letra Viva.

Farrán, R. (2020). *Leer, meditar, escribir. La práctica de la filosofía en pandemia*. Buenos Aires: La cebra.

Foucault, M. (1983). La escritura de sí. In *Obras esenciales, Vol. III*. Barcelona: Paidós.

Freud, S. (1933 [1932]). *The Standard Edition of the Complete Psychological Works of Sigmund Freud, Volume XXII: New Introductory Lectures on Psycho-Analysis and Other Works*. Eds. A. Freud, A. Strachey, and A. Tyson. Trans. J. Strachey. London: The Hogarth Press.

Lacan, J. (n.d.). *The Seminar of Jacques Lacan, Book XXII: R.S.I. (1974–1975)*. Ed. C. Gallagher. Retrieved from http://hdl.handle.net/10788/179

Lacan, J. (1951). Intervention on Transference. In C. Bernheimer and C. Kahane (Eds.), *In Dora's Case Freud-Hysteria-Feminism*, pp. 92–104. Chichester, NY: Columbia University Press.

Lacan, J. (1958). The Direction of the Treatment and the Principles of its Power. In J. Lacan, *Écrits. The First Complete Edition in English*. Trans. B. Fink, pp. 489–542. New York and London: W.W. Norton.

Lacan, J. (1960–1961). *The Seminar of Jacques Lacan. Book VIII: Transference*. Ed. J.-A. Miller. Trans. B. Fink. Cambridge: Polity Press.

Lacan, J. (1967). The Place, Origin and End of My Teaching. In J. Lacan, *My Teaching*. Trans. D. Macey, pp. 1–56. London and New York: Verso.

Lacan, J. (1967–1968). *The Seminar of Jacques Lacan, Book XV: The Psychoanalytic Act 1967–1968*. Trans. C. Gallagher. Retrieved from www.lacaninireland.com: http://hdl.handle.net/10788/164

Lacan, J. (1977). *Apertura de la sección clínica*. Retrieved from http://ecole-lacanienne.net/wp-content/uploads/2016/04/ouverture_de_la_section_clinique.pdf

Lacan, J. (1981). *The Seminar of Jacques Lacan: Book XI: The Four Fundamental Concepts of Psychoanalysis*. Ed. J.-A. Miller. Trans. A. Sheridan. New York and London: W.W. Norton. (Original work published 1964)

Lacan, J. (1991). *The Seminar of Jacques Lacan. Book I: Freud's Papers on Technique*. Ed. J.-A. Miller. Trans. J. Forrester. New York and London: W.W. Norton. (Original work published 1953–1954)

Lacan, J. (2012). Nota italiana. In *Otros escritos*. Buenos Aires: Paidós. (Original work published 1973)

Lombardi, G. (2018). *El método clínico en la perspectiva psicoanalítica*. Buenos Aires: Paidós.

López, M. (2020). *El inconsciente del analista*. Buenos Aires: Letra Viva.

Lutereau, L. (2018, June 3). El psicoanálisis no es una teoría, sino un modo de experiencia. *El Litoral*, E. Giménez Corte, interviewer. Retrieved from www.ellitoral.com/index.php/id_um/171955-el-psicoanalisis-no-es-una-teoria-sino-un-modo-de-experiencia-entrevista-a-luciano-lutereau-opinion.html

Miller, J.-A. (2006). *Introducción al método psicoanalítico*. Buenos Aires: Paidós. (Original work published 1987)

Miller, J.-A. (2008–2009). *Sutilezas analíticas. Los cursos psicoanalíticos de Jacques Alain Miller*. Buenos Aires: Paidós.

Morales Montiel, F. (2017, August 30). Una contradicción del psicoanálisis contemporáneo. Facebook. Retrieved from www.facebook.com/notes/699651224236335/

Prieto, L. (2016). El analista en el banquillo. In L. Prieto, *El analista en el banquillo. La dirección de la cura en psicoanálisis*. Buenos Aires: Letra Viva.

Roazen, P. (1995). *How Freud Worked. First-Hand Accounts of Patients*. Northvale, NJ and London: Jason Aronson.

Rodríguez Ponte, R. (2005, December). Acheronta 22: Formación del analista. M. Sauval, interviewer. Retrieved from www.acheronta.org/pdf/acheronta21.pdf

Schejtman, F. (2013). Clínica psicoanalítica: Verba, Scripta, Lectio. In F. Schejtman, *Psicopatología: clínica y ética. De la psiquiatría al psicoanálisis*. Buenos Aires: Grama.

Suárez, J.C. (2005, December). Acheronta 22: Formación del analista. M. Sauval, interviewer. Retrieved from www.acheronta.org/pdf/acheronta22.pdf

Zaffore, C. (2012). *Desde dónde responder en el dispositivo de control. Eterità 10: "Che cosa risponde lo psicoanalista? Etica e clinica"*. Rivista di Psicoanalisi. Atti del VII Incontro Internazionale dei Forum del Campo LacanianoJuly 6–8, 2021,Rio de Janeiro. Retrieved from www.champlacanien.net/public/docu/5/heterite10.pdf

Chapter 3

Opening

Free Association and Evenly Suspended Attention

A Hypothesis and a Method

A psychoanalytic treatment is a conversation between two or more people. In our offices, nothing happens but an "interchange of words."[1] Of course, this is not an ordinary conversation like the ones we have daily. Psychoanalysis proposes a subversion of the act of speaking, a specific way of speaking that enables the emergence of a text that can be read by the analyst and the analysand; a text with properly analytic textuality.

Our goal, a hundred years later, remains the same as Freud's: to restore to the word, within the scientific field, its healing power. "Within the scientific field" is an important turn of phrase. There are many other practices that claim to cure (and that do so) through speech. Let's think, for instance, about religion and magic; the priest and the wizard both use the symbolic efficiency of language. It is not necessary to fetishize science or take validation criteria from Anglo-Saxon epistemology as the ultimate truth. On this, I agree with Foucault: "I cannot have such an elevated idea of science [...] we must not exalt the idea of science to the point of labeling as such anything as important as Marxism or as interesting as psychoanalysis."[2] Before asking ourselves whether or not psychoanalysis is a science, we should specify what type of science it would be, and why it would be important for it to be so.[3] For the time being, it seems crucial that psychoanalysis, as opposed to magic and religion, should be a consistent, rational, and transmissible practice. The problems we deal with arose within a scientific world, and the battle must happen there. Our debate remains that of the Enlightenment.[4] As psychoanalysts, we must explain how our practice works. This explanation should be, at least in its basic form, understandable to anyone interested, both within and outside of psychoanalysis. Nothing could be further from this than Oedipalizing the world, as sometimes happens in psychoanalytic texts written for a general audience.

So, how can we construct the textuality of the analytic text? Or, to put it in a way that is "closer" to experience, how does speech happen in psychoanalysis? How does the psychoanalyst ensure that the patient takes the floor

DOI: 10.4324/9781032696423-3

in such a way that the floor overtakes him? Freud's answer is clear: free association and evenly suspended attention. Two related though not symmetrical positions, which will be the basis for any analytic treatment. Without free association and evenly suspended attention there is no psychoanalysis.

Free association is a technical device related to a hypothesis: there is an unknown knowledge, the unconscious. Its purpose is to open "access routes" to this kind of knowledge. As I said, psychoanalysis is the testing of this hypothesis, which is why it is an experiment, but above all it is a praxis, because it does not only deal with the verification of this hypothesis but also its use as an instrument to modify reality. Freud took the idea of the unconscious—already present in philosophy for centuries—seriously insofar as he considered it "something actual, tangible and subject to experiment," and not just an abstraction.[5] Now, since free association is correlative to the hypothesis of the unconscious, our conceptualization of free association depends on how we understand the status of the unconscious. For instance, if we believe that the unconscious *is already written*, we are likely to think that free association is curative in itself, but the truth is that no one cures their neurosis merely by talking.

In his search for a method to amplify consciousness, Freud found in the imaginations of his patients a satisfactory substitute for hypnosis. Free association allowed involuntary thoughts, thoughts that were ordinarily rejected for several reasons we will see later, to break in on the deliberate train of thought and come to the surface.[6] "*Also* say what you would never say in an ordinary conversation" might be a way to state the fundamental rule.

Who Knows?

Freud begins with the assumption that there is an unknown knowledge and that the patient is somehow in possession of it: "Psycho-analysis follows the technique of getting the people under examination so far as possible themselves to produce the solution of their riddles."[7] This seems like a great scam since patients come to us with the assumption that we possess knowledge of their desire. We are *subjects supposed to know*, and it is true that we have some knowledge, but not that. At the same time, when the analyst tells the patient, "Say whatever comes to mind, it will be marvelous," he institutes the patient as a subject supposed to know.[8] These crossed assumptions produced by the fundamental rule are the basis of the transference. However, there is the underlying assumption of a knowledge that no one possesses but that could be read if certain obstacles are overcome. To that end, the analyst will make the patient talk. The analyst assumes a knowledge without a subject: the unconscious.

What is new here is that, to access such knowledge Freud proposes taking an attitude of full ignorance towards the meaning of what is said. One of his great proposals was to treat any text as if it were a dream—that is, as something illegible from the start. In fact, he arrived at dreams only after he had already treated the symptom as an encrypted language (as a dream!). Freud asked himself: what does that mean? He treated the word as a signifier, as something that has no meaning in itself. Thus, he gave life to the unconscious.[9]

We must not understand too soon, Lacan would say. We should not saturate the text with what it seems to want to say (to us). The conceptual and methodical rigor necessary to *let the text open* must be maintained. We must not anticipate meaning with the power invested in us by our position as listeners. No knowledge we believe we possess before an analysis—about the Oedipus complex, the clinical types, the sexuated positions, and so on—can function on its own as a deciphering key. That means, in Freudian terms, that psychoanalysis functions *per via di levare*:

> it does not seek to add or to introduce anything new, but to take away something, to bring out something; and to this end concerns itself with the genesis of the morbid symptoms and the psychical context of the pathogenic idea.[10]

It operates as a sculptor carving away from a stone what is covering the shape of the statue contained within; unlike suggestion, which works *per via di porre*, like a painter placing colors where before there were none. Those who propose pre-established knowledge practice "psychology." On the other hand, the psychoanalyst oscillates between *acknowledged ignorance* and *provisional conjecture*: between free association and interpretation.

The patient must speak "freely" to be able to communicate to us the knowledge he does not know. But, of course, "we do not require him to tell us straight away the sense."[11] The problem is evident: if we ask the patient to tell us the meaning of a dream, a slip, or a symptom, he will answer that he does not know, because that is actually the case: he does not know. It is very common that, when asked why, analysands answer simply, "I don't know." This is why, even though the underlying question is that of the cause of illness, our interventions must be directed to the appearance of a saying that matters: what does this bring to mind? Where does that come from? What does this other thing mean? We ask patients not to reflect but to observe themselves. We do not ask them to think, because, if the ego "thinks," *it* cannot. Lacan says that the subject must be absent so that the signifier can play.[12] The unconscious is reached indirectly, through detours.

The Analytic Conversation

Carrying out a psychoanalysis "involves some psychological preparation of the patient."[13] One does not freely associate as a matter of course.[14] Logically so, given that people are used to having a different kind of conversation. In regular conversation, people speak face to face, rejecting involuntary thoughts that depart from or contradict the deliberate plot, while selecting (more or less intentionally) the signifiers, meanings, and senses conveyed. In daily life, dialogues develop in an imaginary plot which sustains the illusion of a world populated by egos and objects, where one says what is meant and one hears and understands what the others mean to say about an extra-discursive reality. Things do not really happen this way—we live in a deep misunderstanding. Every time we speak, we say both more and less than we mean; the same happens when we listen.

Preparing patients psychically means accustoming them to letting go of the implicit principles of ordinary conversation to enable a different way of speaking. Many of our patients fail to improve because *there is no case*. An analytic text does not appear spontaneously, does not offer itself to us, nor does it turn its legible face towards us to be deciphered. We neither discover nor invent it. We realize it through a specific practice.

Basically, we need to *enable*: "to make someone or something able or capable of something in particular."[15] The analyst sets in motion the *enabling* function so that, together with the analysand, she will be able to produce a text available for reading and writing: an open, dynamic, and impersonal text with neither beginning nor end, neither center nor limits, neither author nor interpreter; a text where regularities, discontinuities, slips, and ambiguities are apparent. This may be a case: a text lacking an author, a unit, an origin, and a final significance; an incorporeal materiality where writer and reader, confused with each other, promote an unfinished and delayed text, of which they are a part.

What must the analyst ask of the analysand, so that this analytical text is produced? According to Freud, two things. The analysand must be asked:

1   To direct her attention to involuntary thoughts.
2   To suspend the criticism with which she would usually reject those thoughts.

So, there is a positive and a negative direction. In general, the positive direction is presented in the following way: "say everything that comes to mind." I believe that this is a bad way to express the fundamental rule. *Say everything* may be confused with *say anything*, and the latter should not occur during analysis. This is a crucial point since it may be the case that analysands say everything that comes to mind so as not to say nothing. This "so as not to," of course, does not indicate ill intentions. Resistance is independent of any kind of intention. Ferenczi referred to this type of abuse of free association in obsessional neurotic patients: "they are sometimes evasive by recounting only those associations which are meaningless, as if they deliberately misunderstood the doctor's instructions asking them to recount everything, even more so those making no sense."[16] It is worth noting that the way in which the fundamental rule is answered already indicates a diagnosis. This kind of obsessive patient follows "literally" (as if that were possible!) what they take to be the analyst's desire: to say meaningless nonsense, incoherent things, and so on. In doing so, they are not entirely wrong, since many psychoanalysts urge their patients to say anything because they think this is how the unconscious blooms. The botanic metaphor is inaccurate since the unconscious is not something that emerges from the patient's mouth, as a bud from the ground. Free association, together with evenly suspended attention, enables the construction of a text which can be read. The unconscious *is* an effect of reading. If it did emerge from a mouth, that mouth would be the analyst's, but this is not correct either. The important thing is that free association does not give rise to the unconscious by itself. As Eidelsztein said, "free association will only be a resource for the constitution of the subject and not the subject itself or the goal of analysis."[17]

Free association means not that the analysand *necessarily* says valueless things, nonsense, or things that diverge from the plot (this is not a positive premise), but that he *does not omit* ideas that might have these characteristics. I disagree with Miller when he states that, during analysis, "anything not only can but must be said [...] if we do not say just anything, the rule is not respected."[18] This does not reflect the purpose of the fundamental rule. The analyst does not instruct the patient to say nonsense, he only asks that nonsense not be excluded from the discourse. We come to analysis to talk about important matters.[19] This is why Freud's analogy falls short when he states that, during analysis, the patient must behave as they would in a conversation comprised of idle chatter. Again, while the patient must not be compelled to talk about unimportant or irrelevant things as if this were a requirement of the method, she should not omit such things from her speech.[20] Be that as it may, this does not seem to be a typical clinical problem; in general, analysands come to talk to us about their suffering, about matters of the utmost importance. Some take longer than others. Urging them to "say anything" is a contradiction.

Another way in which "saying everything" might be misinterpreted is as a requirement to disclose secrets, as a kind of religious or legal confession.[21] The patient then would come to analysis to say what could not be said in any other place without embarrassment. There is some truth to this, since analysands speak of their most intimate experiences. The patient is asked, according to Freud, for *complete candor*. Again, there is no obligation to disclose secrets, but, if this kind of thought appears, it should not be discarded.

I prefer the version of free association which says that the patient must direct his attention to involuntary thoughts. A simpler way to put it might be, for example, "*say what comes to mind.*" As I said, the aim is not the patient's reflection but his self-observation. Freud carried out a very suggestive phenomenological analysis of this distinction. He said that those who reflect have "tense looks and [a] wrinkled forehead," unlike those who observe themselves, who exhibit a "restful expression." "In both cases attention must be concentrated," but the person reflecting criticizes his thoughts and so cuts most of them short. The person who introspects, on the other hand, has no task but to suppress his critical faculty, "He must adopt a *completely impartial attitude* to what occurs to him."[22] In short, he is asked to do the same as the analyst: not understand.

The second premise, the negative one, is as follows: "give up the criticism from which you discard involuntary thoughts." There are four types of ideas that are typically rejected: those considered unimportant, those that are not part of the plot, those that seem nonsensical, and those that cause shame or embarrassment. The first three criticisms are made "automatically," not deliberately, by the speaker. Typical conversations force us to do away with this kind of information. In principle, there is nothing to gain from being superfluous (expressing trivialities), or stupid (uttering nonsense), or "mad" (saying incoherent things). But, during analysis, we ask patients not to omit any of these discursive remainders. Something of great value may be found there.

The simplest example is obsessional neurosis. As opposed to hysteria, in which the primary defense displaces the representation of affect into a bodily representation, in obsessional neurosis, the "isolated" affect is connected to a trivial representation, resulting in a false bond. It is curious that the original representation lies on the surface of consciousness; it is not strictly repressed. The patient could be speaking calmly about something as if it were completely unimportant, a mere banality, when in truth it is a fundamental issue. Leaving aside the metapsychological explanation, the importance of this example is that the psychoanalyst starts from the assumption that neither she nor the analysand knows where the real value is in what is said; therefore, as the text is being written, it must be covered in a cloak of *evaluative equivalence.*

The fourth criticism, unlike the other three, is usually "conscious," and with good reason. Many analysands have a hard time talking about topics which cause them grief or shame, particularly those related to the connection with the analyst. For that reason, analysands are asked for complete candor. Does the analysis pause while the patient deliberately holds back information? I believe that the analyst must give it some time. The analyst's timing is crucial, as is the precise way they request the "confession." When patients say that they want to tell me something, but they are too embarrassed to say it, I usually tell them they are in the right place to talk about these kinds of things and, though I have no preference for a particular type of content, I do have a preference for the way in which it appears: as something they would prefer not to communicate.[23]

Lacan formalized these Freudian premises about free association based on two complementary laws: the law of non-omission and the law of non-systematization.[24] The first promotes "the everyday and the ordinary, to the status of interesting that is usually reserved for the remarkable."[25] The second values incoherence and grants a presumption of meaning to the dross of mental life, the dregs of the world's phenomena, as Freud would say: lapsus, slips, and so on. We must not require the patient's text to be coherent, rational, or extraordinary in nature, or dramatic, logical, or chronological in its systematization. We must free the text from "the chains of narrative."[26]

The analyst, like the patient, *begins by not choosing* which part of the patient's text is meaningful.

Last but not least, the question we must ask is related to the explicit enunciation of the fundamental rule. Why wouldn't we ask it? What is the point of a game where only one player knows the rules?[27] In my case, I state it at the end of the first interview, together with other methodological and framing clarifications. It is clear that this is only the beginning, and that psychoanalysts must work constantly to sustain this mode of writing, to encourage the production of this type of textuality, remembering the rule when necessary but, above all, firmly maintaining our appropriate place.

The Analyst's Availability

The positions of analysand and analyst, while not symmetrical, are correlated. The patient would not be able to associate freely if the analyst did not maintain evenly suspended attention. Basically, the idea is that neither participant immediately understands or maintains an evaluative equivalence about the text being written. However, it is important to say that it is not the analysand but the analyst who is in charge of sustaining such a conversation.

The amazing technique proposed by Freud "consists simply in not directing one's notice to anything in particular and in maintaining the same 'evenly suspended attention' [...] in the face of all that one hears."[28] Evenly suspended attention is *attention without intention*. The incredible part is that, by definition, all attention is focused on something in particular. Paying attention means deliberately applying mental activity to a definite object or stimulus. But evenly suspended attention posits exactly the opposite: we must pay attention to all of the material simply because we do not know which part of the text is important. If we start selecting from among the material, according to Freud, it is because we are guided by expectations or inclinations. There are two dangers: "never finding but what he [the analyst] already knows"[29] according to theoretical biases, or falsifying the material based on personal biases. Another way of saying this is that the analyst must neither anticipate meaning nor rush over the text, because "the things one hears are for the most part things whose meaning is only recognized later on."[30] We must be patient and suspend expectations of meaning. This is very difficult. In normal analytic conversations, we do nothing but understand, focus our attention on "the most important parts," and anticipate meaning. We do all of this automatically. What I mean to say is that evenly suspended attention implies some disposition, some effort, some deliberate attitude that allows the analyst to step away from the imaginary logic of everyday conversation. The analyst and the analysand are in an alert state. Nothing is further from evenly suspended attention than a dreamlike, distracted, or clinically intuitive state. This precept states that the analyst must lay a cloak of neutrality over what the patient says, in spite of the "weight" the patient might give to some parts of the discourse. This is a rule that forces the analyst to not understand immediately what she hears, to suspend the presumed indelible connections between signifier and signified. It is a question not of switching off one's consciousness in order to listen with the unconscious, but, rather, a question of sharpening concentration, making an effort to omit the associations that analysts, just like anyone else, are spontaneously presented with. That the analyst surrenders to evenly suspended attention means he must avoid "the construction of conscious expectations"[31] so as not to fix in his memory anything in particular from among what was heard. Dispensing with conscious expectations does not imply being irrational or insensible: the goal is to enable the appearance of a different kind of thought, as well as different kinds of attention and memory.

It is common for patients to be surprised by the great recall of their analysts. Freud's idea is that the selection of the material, whether in an "abstract" way or by taking notes during the session, prevents the formation of what we might call *transference memory*, resulting unintentionally from such attention. The analyst recalls the text because she pays close attention, she walks its winding and twisted path. The analyst does not take anything for granted, does not prefer or underestimate anything; she tries consistently to silence her ideals and affects. This is the only way to evoke signifiers that were not present in the discourse but that resonate in the text in the face of other signifiers. In an analysis, one remembers more than one would in a regular conversation. What is relevant in the material will become evident over time.

Jullien, a philosopher specializing in Eastern thought, proposed the concept of *availability* to revise that of evenly suspended attention.[32] Availability is an *ethical* and *strategic* concept which can only be understood if certain attributes of the modern Western subject are omitted: consciousness, reflexivity, interiority, rationality, and so on. A subject is one who "from the start, assumes and projects, chooses, decides, sets goals and finds the means."[33] To be available, the analyst must renounce his position as subject. If analysts are trained, it is to enable the existence of people who can occasionally renounce their ego.[34]

Availability presupposes renouncing the self and property, any "power of dominion," to the extent that these characteristics are obstacles to other kinds of ethical and epistemic conquests. The detachment that availability enables allows for a conquest that is not oriented, that projects nothing, that has no intention. "Its capture is completely open because it does not expect to capture anything."[35] Those who are available are open, vigilant but not fixated, tough but not rigid, dispersed but not distracted. This is the analyst's attitude. The analyst must not privilege, presume, or project anything: "he needs to hold equal everything he hears so as not to miss any minor indication [...] therefore it is necessary to maintain diffuse and unfocused attention, that is, attention not governed by any intentionality."[36] Jullien points out that the German term *Gleichschwebende*[37] *Aufmerksamkeit*—usually translated as "evenly suspended attention"—might be translated as "evenly suspended

overlying attention." Kripper also highlights this: *schweben* can be understood as "being suspended," and *gleich* as "evenly."[38] We then have three
words connected in a new way: attention, suspension, and equivalence.
Through evenly suspended attention, the analyst suspends her attention in
order to glide over the text from a sustained, consistent height. In the same
vein, it is diffuse attention because it focuses on everything at once. The
available analyst does not expect, suppose, or anticipate; she glides over the
text without focusing on anything in particular—not even details—observing
the entire picture. Availability is an ethical and strategic *opening*. This is a
characteristic that distinguishes Eastern from Western thought: "no longer
separating the ethical and theoretical from strategic [...] the wisdom of effectiveness."[39] Ethics and technique are indistinguishable.

Freudian Confusion

I want to make a side note here to refer to an aspect of the Freudian theory
of evenly suspended attention that I find problematic. Freud summarizes
this precept in the following way: the analyst "must turn his own unconscious like a receptive organ towards the transmitting unconscious of the
patient. He must adjust himself to the patient as a telephone receiver is
adjusted to the transmitting microphone."[40] This way, analysis would be a
communication between unconscious minds. Does this formula respond to
all the characteristics we have mentioned about evenly suspended attention?
The way Freud continues this analogy will allow us to visualize the problem.
Just as, in telephonic communication, sound waves transform into electric
oscillations and then back into sound waves, during analysis, the patient's
unconscious is codified into concrete discourse and then must be decoded in
the analyst's unconscious. In order to use the unconscious as a receiving
organ, the analyst must carry out a "psychoanalytic purification"[41] of her
own unconscious complexes.

Two questions arise here. The first is whether it is possible for the analyst to
detach himself (and in what way) from his own unconscious complexes—that
is, his ideals, his ego, his symptoms, and his fantasies. It is likely that the
analyst is aware of all that, but can the unconscious be purified? What is the
goal of purifying the analyst? To approach this question, it is necessary to
bring in a series of concepts, including neutrality, transference, countertransference, the analyst's fantasy, and the analyst's desire. This debate is
much more suggestive than it seems. The question pertains, broadly, to the
role of the analyst's subjectivity in an analysis. I will leave this for later.

The second question concerns the problem of "reading" during analysis.
Freud holds that, if purified, the analyst's unconscious can decode the
patient's discourse. Here, the analyst's unconscious, and not the analyst herself, interprets the material. In fact, Freud says any resistance that results in
an objection to a discovery made by the analyst's unconscious must not be

allowed. I want to highlight that, in this analogy, there is a great leap from listening to reading. Here is the issue: evenly suspended attention, as a method correlated to free association, is premised upon the analyst's ability to listen without selecting any part of the material a priori according to his own interests. The analyst must pay attention to all of the material equally. It is a question precisely of not understanding. The same happens on the part of the analysand, with the crucial difference that, while she associates freely—that is, speaks—the analyst enables through listening. Now, the idea of unconscious-to-unconscious communication supposes a *selection* of the material by the analyst's unconscious. The analyst's unconscious interprets the patient's text; the analyst must not select anything, so that his unconscious may do this for him.

Up to this point, I have avoided a crucial question: when Freud replaced hypnosis with free association, he added the element of interpretation. I mean that the substitute for hypnosis is free association *plus* interpretation.[42] Free association—and evenly suspended attention—as such provides us with access not to the unconscious but rather to material subject to interpretation. According to Freud, "the course of free association produced a plentiful store of ideas which could put one on the track of what the patient had forgotten."[43] Free association does not give us access to the unconscious, but it gives us clues to access it. It does not reveal exactly what has been forgotten, but it does give us "such plain and numerous hints at it that, with the help of a certain amount of supplementing and interpreting, the doctor [is] able to guess (to reconstruct) the forgotten material from it."[44] It is interpretation that allows us to extract from the raw mineral of the patient's associations the precious metal of unconscious thoughts.[45] The pairing of free association and evenly suspended attention is intended to enable the analytic text and its textuality, and interpretation is intended to enable the reading (and writing) of that text. In this sense, interpretation unfolds into reading and writing a living text, an open work.

Freud's idea of communication between unconscious minds confuses two questions that are best presented separately: on the one hand, the function of *enabling*—the extraction of raw material—which provides us with a text that can be analyzed, and, on the other, the functions of *reading* and *writing*—the work that is done to the text. When Freud says that the analyst reads with his unconscious, he means nothing more than that the analyst uses the technique of recollection to select the material. Interpretation becomes an automatic and non-transmissible act (no one can understand why *that* was said in *that* moment), carried out by a pure unconscious. In this way, there is a return to the idea that the analytic act dispenses with thought and that intellectual elaboration comes afterwards. It is peculiar that the apocryphal quote attributed to Lacan, "in the act, the analyst does not think," is repeated nonstop, omitting the "original" reference: "it is by not thinking that [the psychoanalyst] operates."[46] This last idea is very significant, though not in the way it is usually presented: the analyst interprets with her unconscious, she must flesh out her hypothesis after the intervention, she must let herself be led by her own experience of analysis, and so on. I will return to the Lacanian reference to clarify the meaning of this "non-thinking." For the time being, I want to highlight the double character (reading and writing) of interpretation. I insist that the construction of an analytic text is a rational and transmissible process, served by a series of provisional and partial conjectures, resulting from a particular way of approaching a text. Psychoanalysis is a mode of reading texts. There is surely an intuitive aspect in the analyst's acts, but he participates more evidently in writing than in reading the material.

The Couch

Free association and evenly suspended attention are attitudes that do not occur naturally. Far from being a practice where one person rambles on and on and the other dozes off while waiting for truth to be revealed, analysis is "a conversation between two people equally awake."[47] As I mentioned, this requires the analysand's preparation and the creation of an "atmosphere of influence."[48] Psychoanalysis implies, both for the analyst and the analysand, a rational and deliberate willingness to occupy a particular place in a conversation.

There are not many technologies necessary to produce an analytical text, and the pairing of free association and evenly suspended attention is one of them. In fact, in psychoanalysis we do not have many technologies. Another one is the couch. Even though the use of the couch is practically universal, there are not many theoretical or clinical references which explain why we use it. At times, it seems that it is more a futile legacy preserved as an homage to Freud than a device for the production of subjectivity. To me, it is definitely the latter.

Freud had three reasons to use the couch: a historical one, a personal one, and a technical one.[49] Historically, the medical clinic was tied to the bed. Sick people lie down. Freud inherited the custom of treating supine patients in his hypnotic practice and from medical clinics in general.

The second reason refers to Freud's personal difficulties in tolerating the gaze of his patients for eight or ten hours a day. This is very enigmatic: why was he unable to stand the gaze of others, just as bank tellers, teachers, and shop owners do daily? To be precise, the fact is that the second and third reasons are the same. Freud was bothered by his patients' gazes not because he was "being observed" but because he did not want his "gestures to offer the patient material for his interpretations or to influence him in his communications."[50] The motives, then, are technical. Face-to-face conversation may be an obstacle to compliance with a fundamental rule because it tends to produce an interruption of associations. How does this interruption occur? It is simple: in face-to-face analytical conversation, as in any other conversation in everyday life, the face of the listener is an element to be read by the speaker. For instance, if we are saying something we consider very important and the person listening to us closes her eyes for a few seconds, we are likely to interpret that what we are saying seems boring or irrelevant, when perhaps it is nothing more than a way of paying close attention. In the end, face-to-face conversation can make what is said lose relevance in favor of what is heard or understood. Psychoanalysis requires exclusive attention to what is said, comprehension aside. This is why it is better to talk to the ceiling or the walls.

This does not mean that, in face-to-face conversations, the analyst cannot use gestures to make interventions. A gesture can also be a signifier. Moreover, the analysand's ideas about the analyst's gestures may hold great value. The fact is that talking to someone without seeing or being seen by them produces an incredible effect on words. They resonate differently. When we speak, the words return to us from the place of the listener as if they were ours: "that is what you say, this is what I say." In analysis, we must listen with particular attention since words return as if coming from the place of the Other. Where did that come from? Was it I who said it? Who is speaking? Again, what is crucial is the passage from "I speak" to "it speaks." It is curious to observe how some analysands bring in something that was said in analysis but without knowing who said it: "I do not remember if I said this or you did, it does not matter." It was said. Everyday conversations take place in the imaginary wall of language, which goes from me to you and back, as interchangeable positions. The imaginary dimension of dialogue—the axis for comprehension and empty words—omits the truth. Therefore, the imaginary wall fractures when a full, true, unconscious word is uttered.[51] A word spoken from the place of the Other. In Lacan's words, in analysis,

> one lets go of all the moorings of the speaking relationship, one eschews courtesy, respect, and dutifulness towards the other. [...] From then on, the subject finds himself relatively mobile in relation to this universe of language in which we engage him.[52]

The couch is a technology that collaborates in the passage from the imaginary axis to the symbolic axis.

Lacan also stated that thinking in a horizontal position is not the same as thinking in a vertical one, for the simple reason that we do many things lying down, including making love, and love "leads to all kinds of statements. In the lying position, a man has the illusion of saying something that is a saying, that is, something which matters in reality."[53] It is likely that this is a very precise definition of the analytical conversation: arriving at saying something that matters in reality.

Needless to say, the couch is a very useful tool, but in no way is it necessary to achieve an analytic conversation. The crucial part is the position taken by the analyst and the analysand: in an office with a couch, face to face, walking through the park, on the phone, and so on. Many of us have practiced psychoanalysis in hospitals, clinics, and austere offices, where naturally there are no couches. It is most important to follow certain rules, like in soccer. We can play in a professional stadium or on a neighborhood pitch. Obviously, the conditions will be superior in the stadium—the ball will bounce better, areas will be well marked, goals will have nets, the limits of the pitch will be visible, and so on—but, as long as there is a ball, the game can proceed.

No one has ever been cured by simply saying what comes to mind. Free association and evenly suspended attention are a means to an end and not an end in themselves. The unconscious does not "bloom." Free association is not a *direct route* to the unconscious, and evenly suspended attention is not a method for selecting material "unconsciously." If this were the case, as some colleagues maintain, it would be necessary to terminate one's analysis before accessing the position of analyst. The analyst's act would then be determined by what he is—someone who has completed an analysis—rather than by what he says and does. Lacan's idea, conversely, is that the directives of the fundamental rule "convey, even in the very inflections of his statement of them, the doctrine the analyst himself has arrived at."[54] The doctrine—the set of ideas, principles, and teachings—and not analysis itself.

It takes much more than a loose mouth and a tuned ear for an analysis to take place. It is necessary to *enable, desire, read*, and *write*.

Notes

1 Freud, 1916 (1915): 17.
2 Foucault, 1971/2013: 280.
3 Furthermore, what contributions has psychoanalysis, particularly Lacan's work, made to epistemology and scientific thought?
4 Just as Lacan claimed in the original back cover of the *Écrits*: "[i]t is necessary to have read this compilation, and all the way through, to feel that there is a single debate in it, always the same one, and that, even though it seems to be dated thus, it is known for being the Enlightenment debate."
5 Freud, 1924 (1923): 192.
6 Cf. Freud, 1904 (1903).
7 Freud, 1916 (1915–1916): 101.
8 "I have often insisted on the fact that we are not supposed to know very much at all. What analysis establishes is this, which is quite the opposite. The analyst says to whoever is about to begin- 'Away you go, say whatever, it will be marvelous.' He is the one that the analyst institutes as subject supposed to know. This is after all not in such bad faith, because in the present case the analyst cannot put his trust in any other person. And the transference is founded on the fact that there is this character who tells me—me, the poor bastard—to act as if I knew what it was all about. I can say anything whatever, it will always produce something. This doesn't happen to you every day" (Lacan, 1969–1970: 52).
9 It is clear that this is not the only reading that can be made of Freud's work. At the same time that he proposed to maintain the cause of the symptom as a question, he plugged this hole with various theories until he built a hermeneutic machine of totalizing scope. The theory of trauma, the theory of seduction, sexual fantasies, infantile sexuality, and, lastly, the Oedipus complex. It is surprising that all of these theories are linked by a fundamental element: the father. This is evident

in the clinical records. In this sense, free association became a parody: all roads led to the same place. In fact, Freud noticed this issue in his own transferential position, as I will show later.

10 Freud, 1905 (1904): 261.
11 Freud, 1916 (1915–1916): 104.
12 Cf. Lacan 1967–1968: lecture on January 24, 1968.
13 Freud, 1900 (1899)/1953: 101.
14 "The direction of the treatment is something else altogether. It consists, first of all, in getting the subject to apply the fundamental rule of psychoanalysis, that is, the directives whose presence at the heart of what is called 'the analytic situation' cannot be neglected, under the pretext that the subject would best apply them without thinking about it" (Lacan, 1958: 490).
15 To enable is also to allow someone to do something that was forbidden to them before: "speak freely."
16 Ferenczi, 1919/2009: 133.
17 Eidelsztein, 2005.
18 Miller, 1993–1994/2011: 26.
19 "The psychoanalytic clinic encompasses the judgment of things that matter and that will be massive from the moment we become aware of them" (Lacan, 1977: 6). "How is this possible, that there are analysts? This thing is only possible because the analysand gets cognition—we could say—from observing a rule, from not saying more than what they might have to say, than what they have in their hearts, as it is said in French" (Lacan 1975: 46).
20 Another rather confusing Freudian metaphor is the railway one: "[a]ct as though, for instance, you were a traveler sitting next to the window of a railway carriage and describing to someone inside the carriage the changing views which you see outside" (Freud, 1913: 135).
21 Cf. Bonoris, 2015.
22 All quotes in this paragraph come from Freud, 1900 (1899)/1953: 101–102.
23 Cf. Freud, 1926.
24 Cf. Lacan, 1936.
25 Ibid.: 65.
26 Ibid.
27 I was asked this question by Tomás Pal and by Facundo Guzmán, who is not a psychoanalyst but a historian and analysand.
28 Freud, 1912: 111–112.
29 Ibid.: 112.
30 Ibid.
31 Freud, 1923 (1922): 239.
32 Cf. Jullien, 2013.
33 Ibid.: 24.
34 Cf. Lacan, 1954–1955: 246.
35 Jullien, 2013: 25.
36 Ibid.: 26–27.
37 "The term 'free-floating' does not imply fluctuation, but rather evenness of level— this is emphasized by the German term, 'gleichschwebende'" (Lacan, 1956: 394).
38 Personal communication.
39 Jullien, 2013: 31.
40 Freud, 1912: 115–116.
41 Ibid.: 116.
42 "Thus free association together with the art of interpretation performed the same function as had previously been performed by hypnotism" (Freud, 1924 [1923]: 196).

43 Ibid.: 196.
44 Ibid.
45 Cf. Freud, 1900 (1899)/1953.
46 Lacan, 1969: 397.
47 Freud, 1904 (1903): 250.
48 Freud, 1912: 120.
49 Cf. Carrere, 2018.
50 Ibid.
51 Lacan will later abandon the concept of full speech simply because no truth is full or complete. As Lacan himself later stated, truth is half-said, is incomplete. However, the idea that the word may both obstruct and transmit some truth is crucial in our practice.
52 Lacan, 1953–1954: 174–175.
53 Lacan, 1977: 6.
54 Lacan 1958: 490. When they comment on this quote, Boxaca and Lutereau say: "each analyst would enforce the fundamental rule according to *the point in which they have advanced to in their own analysis* and in their interrogations on the technique in their articulation with the ethics of psychoanalysis" (2013: 22).

References

Bonoris, B. (2015). La obligación de decir la verdad sobre sí mismo. De la confessio oris a la asociación libre. *Verba Volant. Revista de Filosofía y Psicoanálisis*, 5(2), 7–42.

Boxaca, L., and Luterau, L. (2013). *Introducción a la clínica psicoanalítica: Asociación libre, Interpretación, Transferencia, Síntoma, Duelo*. Buenos Aires: Letra Viva.

Carrere, P. (2018). ¿Para qué sirve el diván? *De Inconscientes*. Retrieved from https://dein conscientes.com/para-que-sirve-el-divan-pedro-carrere/#:~:text=El%20div%C3%A1n%20contribuir%C3%ADa%20a%20la,se%20abandona%20a%20su%20escucha

Eidelsztein, A. (2005). ¿Qué cura el psicoanálisis y cómo? *Revista Imago Agenda*, (94). Retrieved from https://eidelszteinalfredo.com.ar/que-cura-el-psicoanalisis-y-como/

Ferenczi, S. (2009). Sobre la técnica del psicoanálisis. In S. Ferenczi, *Teoría y técnica del psicoanálisis*. Buenos Aires: Hormé. (Original work published 1919)

Foucault, M. (2013). ¿Qué es la arqueología? In M. Foucault, *¿Qué es usted, profesor Foucault? Sobre la arqueología y su método*. Buenos Aires: Siglo XXI. (Original work published 1971)

Freud, S. (1904 [1903]). Freud's Psycho-Analytic Procedure. In S. Freud, A. Freud, A. Strachey, and A. Tyson (Eds.), *The Standard Edition of the Complete Psychological Works of Sigmund Freud. Volume VII: A Case of Hysteria, Three Essays on Sexuality and Other Works*. Trans. J. Strachey, pp. 249–256. London: The Hogarth Press.

Freud, S. (1905 [1904]). On Psychotherapy. In S. Freud, A. Freud, A. Strachey, and A. Tyson (Eds.), *The Standard Edition of the Complete Psychological Works of Sigmund Freud*. Trans. J. Strachey, pp. 257–270. London: The Hogarth Press.

Freud, S. (1912). Recommendations to Physicians Practicing Psycho-Analysis. In S. Freud, A. Freud, A. Strachey, and A. Tyson (Eds.), *The Standard Edition of the Complete Psychological Works of Sigmund Freud, Volume XII: The Case of Schreber, Papers on Technique and Other Works*. Trans. J. Strachey. London: The Hogarth Press.

Freud, S. (1913). On Beginning the Treatment (Further Recommendations on the Technique of Psycho-Analysis I). In S. Freud, A. Freud, A. Strachey, and A. Tyson (Eds.), *The Standard Edition of the Complete Psychological Works of Sigmund*

Freud, Volume XII: The Case of Schreber, Papers on Technique and Other Works. Trans. J. Strachey, pp. 121–144. London: The Hogarth Press.

Freud, S. (1916 [1915]). Parapraxes. Introduction. In S. Freud, A. Freud, A. Strachey, and A. Tyson (Eds.), *The Standard Edition of the Complete Psychological Works of Sigmund Freud, Volume XV: Introductory Lessons on Psycho-Analysis.* Trans. J. Strachey, pp. 15–24. London: The Hogarth Press.

Freud, S. (1916 [1915–1916]). The Premises and Technique of Interpretation. In S. Freud, A. Freud, A. Strachey, and A. Tyson (Eds.), *The Standard Edition of the Complete Psychological Works of Sigmund Freud, Volume XV: Introductory Lectures on Psycho-Analysis (Parts I and II).* Trans. J. Strachey, pp. 100–112. London: The Hogarth Press.

Freud, S. (1923 [1922]). Two Encyclopedia Articles: "Psycho-Analysis" and "The Libido Theory". In S. Freud, A. Freud, A. Strachey, and A. Tyson (Eds.), *The Standard Edition of the Complete Works of Sigmund Freud, Volume XVIII: Beyond the Pleasure Principle, Group Psychology and Other Works.* Trans. J. Strachey, pp. 235–262. London: The Hogarth Press.

Freud, S. (1924 [1923]). A Short Account of Psycho-Analysis. In S. Freud, A. Freud, A. Strachey, and A. Tyson (Eds.), *The Standard Edition of the Complete Psychological Works of Sigmund Freud, Vol. XIX.* Trans. J. Strachey, pp. 191–212. London: The Hogarth Press.

Freud, S. (1926). The Question of Lay Analysis: Conversations with an Impartial Person. In S. Freud, A. Freud, A. Strachey, and A. Tyson (Eds.), *The Standard Edition of the Complete Psychological Works of Sigmund Freud. Book XX: An Autobiographical Study; Inhibitions, Symptoms and Anxiety; The Question of Lay Analysis; and Other Works.* Trans. J. Strachey, pp. 183–250. London: The Hogarth Press.

Freud, S. (1953). *The Standard Edition of the Complete Psychological Works of Sigmund Freud, Volume IV: The Interpretation of Dreams (First Part).* Eds. A. Freud, A. Strachey, and A. Tyson. Trans. J. Strachey. London: The Hogarth Press. (Original work published 1900 [1899])

Jullien, F. (2013). *Cinco conceptos propuestos al psicoanálisis.* Buenos Aires: El cuenco de plata. (Original work published in French in 2012)

Lacan, J. (1936). Beyond the "Reality Principle". In J. Lacan, *Écrits: The First Complete Edition in English.* Trans. B. Fink, pp. 58–74. New York: W. W. Norton.

Lacan, J. (1953–1954). *The Seminar of Jacques Lacan, Book I: Freud's Papers on Technique, 1953–1954.* Ed. J.-A. Miller. Trans. J. Forrester. New York and London: W.W. Norton.

Lacan, J. (1954–1955). *The Seminar of Jacques Lacan, Book II: The Ego in Freud's Theory and in the Technique of Psychoanalysis.* Ed. J.-A. Miller. Trans. S. Tomaselli. New York and London: W.W. Norton.

Lacan, J. (1956). The Situation of Psychoanalysis and the Training of Psychoanalysts in 1956. In J. Lacan, *Écrits: The First Complete Edition in English.* Trans. B. Fink, pp. 384–411. New York and London: W. W. Norton.

Lacan, J. (1958). The Direction of the Treatment and the Principles of its Power. In J. Lacan, *Écrits: The First Complete Edition in English.* Trans. B. Fink, pp. 489–542. New York and London: W.W. Norton.

Lacan, J. (1967–1968). *The Seminar of Jacques Lacan, Book XV: The Psychoanalytic Act 1967–1968.* Ed. C. Gallagher. Retrieved from www.lacaninireland.com: http://hdl.handle.net/10788/164

Lacan, J. (1975). Conferencias y charlas en universidades norteamericanas. Unpublished.

Lacan, J. (1977). Apertura de la sección clínica. Retrieved from http://ecole-lacanienne. net/wp-content/uploads/2016/04/ouverture_de_la_section_clinique.pdf

Lacan, J. (2012). El acto psicoanalítico. Reseña del seminario 1967–1968. In J. Lacan, *Otros escritos*, pp. 395–403. Buenos Aires: Paidós. (Original work published 1969)

Miller, J.-A. (1993–1994). *Donc. La lógica de la cura. Los cursos psicoanalíticos de Jacques Alain Miller*. Buenos Aires: Paidós. (Original work published 2011)

Chapter 4

Othering

Responsibility, Rectification, and Localization

Psi Punitiveness

The question of moral and legal responsibility for an event appears immediately in many of the problems of our age, whether political or social, related to the family or to the individual. "Who is guilty?" is the issue which demands urgent solutions. It seems that finding the author of our misfortunes (even if it is ourselves) would bring some temporary, or even lasting, relief. I do not question the importance of ethical and legal remedies in the face of damages. Moreover, an act of justice may very well be an act of health, and not only for the victim. Difficulties appear when we approach all problems from this perspective. When the "who?" obstructs the questions of how and why.

Psychoanalysis is not exempt from this tendency and is, as a result, rapidly gaining a morally punitive tone. In fact, certain analytic practices have led the way in implementing *psi* punitiveness, which multiplied its effectiveness by masking its moralism in an apparently ethically sophisticated and bold theory.[1] "Neurotics are moral cowards who need to wake up from their soporific complaining!" some analysts say, their mouths full of decided desire. All of this is reminiscent of the marvelous ending to "What Is Psychology?" by Canguilhem:

> A philosopher can also address himself to the psychologist in the form of offering orientation advice (one time does not a habit make!), and say to him: when one leaves the Sorbonne by the street Saint-Jacques, one can ascend or descend; if one ascends, one approaches the Pantheon, the conservatory of great men; but if one descends, one heads directly to the Police Department.[2]

Psychoanalysis was transformed into a *polipsíaca*[3] clinic through one concept: *subjective responsibility*. In short, this clinical orientation holds that, where patients see an unfair destiny, negligent or abusive parents, unloving partners, or cruel bosses, what really are at issue are "the consequences of their own choices [...] of certain ways of enjoyment," and thus they must "take

DOI: 10.4324/9781032696423-4

responsibility for the very thing they complain about."[4] The clinic of subjective responsibility is based on a fundamental premise of psychoanalysis: the symptom, besides being an encrypted message, is a substitute satisfaction. The patient must accept personal responsibility for her suffering insofar as the symptom's persistence depends on the satisfaction it brings. "Where you suffer, *you* enjoy," Miller states.[5] The most important aspect of this approach is that it is not confined to a single specific maneuver at the beginning, but that it becomes a goal of analysis in itself: everyone must assume their own way of enjoyment. There are two ideas in need of discussion. One states that, in order to begin an analysis, we need to take moral responsibility for our own suffering. The other holds that, in order to end an analysis, we need to accept our singular mode of enjoyment, assuming the singular satisfaction underlying the symptom and "knowing how to make do with it." There is solidarity between the clinic of subjective responsibility and the clinic of the sinthome.[6]

It is clear that, for someone to be analyzed, she must believe that part of her suffering is related to her position in life. Madness, in the Lacanian sense, is unanalyzable, at least through typical methods. However, this does not solve the problem. Once stated that it is not tenable to treat the problem of the analysand's relationship with her suffering via subjective responsibility, urging her to "assume what you feel; after all, it is your way of enjoyment" or using any nuanced version of such a statement, the question remains as to how to approach this issue.

The Lacanian Unconscious

In general, the writings of the "clinic of subjective responsibility" are based on two of Lacan's texts, which are heavily referenced. It is curious that both references are misinterpreted. The first is the famous phrase from "Science and Truth:" "[o]ne is always responsible for one's position as a subject."[7] This phrase is often incorrectly quoted. Where it says "a subject" (singular), many say "subjects" (plural).[8] This distinction is crucial because "subjects" refers to each of us as subjects, whereas *the* subject refers to the Lacanian concept of split subject. A psychoanalysis of psychoanalysis should interrogate the reasons for this disciplinary lapsus.[9] In my opinion, this is an unacknowledged ethical predisposition towards individualism, the freedom of self-determination, and moral responsibility on the part of some analysts. The Lacanian unconscious is more liberal than is believed. Moreover, that a plural is added in the place of a singular proves that no act of perception is "pure;" it is, rather, organized according to overrated rationality. The researcher may behave as a child facing the threat of sexual difference: first, he sees something that does not exist—the penis—then he creates a theoretical subterfuge—it is very small, it will grow—and, finally, he draws a false conclusion—she is castrated. This is the most interesting epistemological theory in Freud's work.

If one reads the paragraph preceding Lacan's sentence, it becomes clear that "our position" does not refer to all human beings, not even to analysands. It is a direct interpellation of analysts:

> To say that the subject upon which we operate in psychoanalysis can only be the subject of science may seem paradoxical. It is nevertheless here that a demarcation must be made, failing which everything gets mixed up and a type of dishonesty sets in that is elsewhere called objective; but it is people's lack of audacity and failure to locate the object that backfires. One is always responsible for one's position as a subject.[10]

With the phrase "one's position as a subject," Lacan indicates the subject we operate on in psychoanalysis, not the subject we are. As Eidelsztein pointed out, the French term *position* may best be translated in this context as "positioning" or "positing."[11] Lacanian ethical terrorism exclusively targets the analyst: "to be a psychoanalyst is a responsible position, the most responsible of all."[12]

For Lacan, Freud's discovery is that there exists "a perfectly articulated knowledge for which strictly speaking no subject is responsible."[13] This phrase can be read in at least two different but compatible ways. First, if we define the subject as the fleeting and evanescent effect of the signifying articulation (a signifier represents a subject for another signifier), it is impossible to assign it any kind of responsibility simply because it cannot be assigned any "subjective" attributes: it is neither responsible, nor reflexive, nor volitional, and so on. The same applies to the subject understood as the matter at hand between the analysand and the analyst—that which is dealt with during analysis. Second, if we understand the subject as *parlêtre*, we cannot assign it responsibility either because it is neither the origin nor the author of the unconscious. Only from a metaphysics of substance and on spherical topology can we conclude that the unconscious is an attribute for which we should take responsibility. It is clear, however, that the analysand is deeply interested in the subject because it is the reason for her suffering.

The second reference is from "Intervention on Transference," in connection to Dora's case. Lacan attributes to Freud the following intervention: "look [...] what part you play in the mess you complain about."[14] Let us remember Freud's reading of the case: Dora was right that her father did not want to know anything about her behavior or that of Herr K's, so that his affair with Frau K would not be interrupted. Dora's complaint revealed some truth. However, Freud says, she had been guilty of the same, *she did not want to know anything*, she had become an accomplice in her father's relationship. Now, does Freud tell her she is an accomplice? Does he ask her about her responsibility for what she complains of? Does he tell her it was her choice? Does he interpret a self-reproach behind the reproach of her father? None of that. He supposes it but does not tell her. This is the difference between reading and writing, between conjecture and its incorporation into the material. Of those who claim neurotic illness is the result of intention, Freud says,

> [T]hey overlook the psychological distinction between what is conscious and what is unconscious. ... That is why all [the] asseverations that it is "only a question of willing" and all the encouragements and abuse that are directed to the patient are of no avail.[15]

It is important that Freud does not intend to persuade Dora of her complicity through interventions pointing to her responsibility in the matter she is complaining about, but rather hopes that, by means of analysis, she comes to see that her symptoms are functioning in the libidinal economy of all those involved in the conflict (her father, her mother, Herr K, Frau K, etc.), and not only in her "psychic apparatus." We must also remember that it was Dora's father who decided to bring her to Freud so he could "set her on the right path." Those who come to the analyst of their own volition, except on rare occasions, suppose *from the start* that there is something wrong in their subjective position, even if the problem lies with others. In general, analysands are convinced that they themselves are solely responsible for their misfortunes—they even have the idea that there is some masochistic satisfaction in their suffering. "If I cannot stop doing that which hurts me it must be because I like it," they say, convinced. It takes a lot of work to get rid of this idea. It is not a matter of blaming their misfortunes on others, either. These may be the two parodic faces of psychoanalysis: the blame lies either with the parents or with the patient. The key is to dispense with the logic of innocence or guilt.[16] The emphasis must be on how and not on who; on the text and not on the author; on the subject and not on the ego. It is a question of examining the symptom in its dimension as knowledge: why did Dora change her attitude after the scene at the lake? What happened there so that, from that moment on, she turns from collusion to complaint?

Who Gains from the Symptom?

When Dora states that her complaint comes from reality and not from herself, that things are as she says, and that nothing can be done about it, Freud does not try to persuade her that her complaint is "subjective" or psychological ("it is only your interpretation of reality, it is the lens through which you see the world," etc.). Instead, he includes it in reality and counts it as an interested party in it. Freud's goal was for her to notice her participation in a mechanism which brought her no benefit, not for her to stop complaining about others in order to take responsibility for her enjoyment. She herself served as a cog keeping the machine working. She was adapted enough to reality to contribute to its realization.[17]

If there was satisfaction, it was not Ida Bauer's. Now, if the symptom implies some benefit: who wins? Who should be held accountable for such a gain? Let us remember that, in Freud's opinion, all symptoms are a compromise formation. In this sense, illness avoids the task of solving a conflict within "objective reality." Neurosis is a solution—not a very good one—to a conflict; a solution that satisfies conflictual elements. Think, for example, of "the Rat Man," who replies to a marriage proposal with inhibiting doubt. It is in this sense that neurosis is a false act. From an economic perspective, illness implies satisfaction. In this way, Freud encounters resistance to the cure; somehow, the patient does not want to heal. But how can someone who asks for help regarding her ailment not want to be healed? Freud's words are enlightening:

> The patient wants to be cured—but he also wants not to be. His ego has lost its unity, and for that reason his will has no unity either. If that were not so, he would be no neurotic. [...] The derivatives of what is repressed have broken into his ego and established themselves there; and the ego has as little control over trends from that source as it has over what is actually repressed, and as a rule it knows nothing about them. These patients, indeed, are of a peculiar nature and raise difficulties with which we are not accustomed to reckoning. All our social institutions are framed for people with a united and normal ego, which one can classify as good or bad, which either fulfills its function or is altogether eliminated by an overpowering influence. Hence the juridical alternative: responsible or irresponsible. *None of these distinctions apply to neurotics.*[18]

Freud's answer is clear. The categories of responsibility and irresponsibility are not applicable to neurosis because of the very paradox of its constitution. Analysands want and do not want to be cured, know and do not know their ailment; thus, "there would be no sense in reproaching them for this contradiction."[19] Telling them they are responsible for their symptoms because they enjoy them can only produce two possible results: the message either falls on deaf ears or it is experienced as a guilt-inducing, neuroticizing intervention. The reasons for this are evident: either the ego does not recognize itself in that satisfaction or it does so with honest surprise. To say that the analysand is responsible for her own symptom because she profits from it is false. It is not the individual who gains from it. Let us continue with Freud:

> Indeed, there are cases in which even the physician must admit that for a conflict to end in neurosis is the most harmless and socially tolerable solution. [...] and he learns that a sacrifice of this kind made by a single person can prevent immeasurable unhappiness for many others. If we may say, then, that whenever a neurotic is faced by a conflict he takes flight into illness, yet we must allow that in some cases that flight is fully justified.[20]

It is not certain that gain belongs exclusively to the analysand. It might be that the individual sacrifices herself through neurosis so that others can benefit from the symptom. There may be no gain, but enjoyment. Neurosis is sometimes the most tolerable answer from a social point of view; it has a tendency towards general homeostasis. It allows things to proceed without asking too many questions. In short, it has a "social justification: the 'gain from illness' [it] provides is not always a purely subjective one."[21]

At this point, it is necessary to pause and review the idea that the symptom implies drive satisfaction. Despite being one of the fundamental concepts in psychoanalysis, the drive has always kept a dark profile, being hard to specify. Though Freud said that the drive is not strictly organic but "a concept on the frontier between the mental and the somatic," he also characterized it as a constant energy coming from within the organism, "the demand made upon the mind for work" by the body.[22] The Freudian drive originates in the body. Furthermore, its satisfaction implies a "gain." As Laplanche and Pontalis maintain, "the Freudian theory of neurosis is inseparable from the notion that illness is brought on and maintained by virtue of the satisfaction it affords the subject."[23] Now, why would the symptom imply a gain for the individual if the ego experiences it as grief and distress? It is simple: because the satisfaction is unconscious and it is thus not perceived by the ego as satisfaction. But, then, why would we saddle the individual with a satisfaction she does not know and which she finds unsatisfactory? When we say the drive is a stimulus coming from within the organism, it becomes difficult to think that it is not part of that individual. Additionally, the id, the source of the drives according to the second topology, forms a "biological unit" with the ego.[24] Therefore, it would be incoherent to hold that this satisfaction does not belong to that "organism." If the drive comes from within the body and forms a biological unit with the ego, who is morally responsible for the satisfaction and the gain resulting from the symptom if not the individual who becomes a patient? This is the conclusion Freud draws in "Moral Responsibility for the Content of Dreams" based on the ontological and topological arguments throughout the text. It is not surprising that these contradictions appear in his work. As Deleuze said: "the wonderful thing about Freud is that beautiful things and horrific things are on the same page."[25]

A sensible intervention, if we believe the analysand is the one finding satisfaction from his symptom, would be to help him recognize his enjoyment in the very thing he is complaining about. This is what the clinic of subjective responsibility is about: a nuanced (but equally neuroticizing) alternative to the "personal responsibility" imperative typical of the liberal ethics in our time. The one who enjoys, the one who is satisfied, the one who benefits from the symptom is the patient.

Lacan said something far more interesting. According to his theory, it is contradictory to state that it is the analysand who enjoys. This idea appears, for instance, in Seminar XI:

[Analysands] satisfy something that no doubt runs counter to that with which they might be satisfied, or rather, perhaps, they give satisfaction to something. They are not content with their state, but all the same, being in a state that gives so little content, they are content.[26]

The crux of the matter lies in this question: *what* is it that is content with the symptom? In general, analysands suspect that they derive paradoxical pleasure that is hidden in the most intimate part of their being and whose origin and reasons they do not know. The question is whether we will confirm this hypothesis. The question is whether we will attribute to the ego something that belongs to the unconscious.

What is that something that is satisfied? To address this question, we must start from the Lacanian idea that speaking beings are constituted by language. Broadly speaking, this means that, though we believe that we use language as an instrument (to learn, to communicate, etc.), in truth, "language employs us, and that is how it enjoys."[27] The deception lies precisely in believing that the drive is a stimulus originating in the body. We feel that "the body asks us for something," when, in fact, it is a text requiring something from our body—in other words, *a text that becomes a body.* The drives *"are the echo* in the body of a fact of saying."[28] The illusion is that what seems to come from the body in truth comes from a saying.

Just as Foucault stated that power in its positive aspect does not repressively force subjects to behave in a certain way, but induces people to behave of their own volition, Lacan held that knowledge is not something possessed, something to be had; rather, it is something applied. At the end of Seminar XX, commonly known as the seminar on enjoyment, he said, "the crux of or key to what I put forward this year concerns the status of knowledge, and I stressed that the use (*exercice*) of knowledge could but imply (*representer*) a jouissance."[29] Enjoyment, then, could be partially defined as the embodied exercise of the *limits* of unconscious knowledge.

According to Lacan, the Freudian discovery puts on the table that human beings can be knee-deep in knowledge without knowing it. The clinical problem with respect to enjoyment lies in the fact that we apply knowledge while thinking we are applying different knowledge; or worse, without knowing we are applying knowledge at all, believing that the application of knowledge is actually "each one's way of being," natural and immutable. In this way, we can understand how gaining knowledge entails a loss of enjoyment. The analysand does not benefit from the symptom. The question lies in revealing how discourses make use of bodies, of their inclinations, feelings, and actions.

With regard to the exercise of unconscious knowledge, there are no responsible parties. In analysis, we do not try, as might be believed, to reveal and judge the behavior of abusive or negligent parents. We do not urge the person talking to us to convince himself that he is the cause of his suffering. The analysand is not the author of this text; rather, he is the protagonist.

Although we cannot make the analysand responsible for the invention of a certain "argument," we can reveal and observe that his life is at stake in the work. Psychoanalysis proves that psychological suffering is not a lack of adaptation to reality, but an excess of it. A passion for getting things to work, no matter the personal cost.

Responsibility and Rectification

How is it that subjective responsibility acquired such relevance? My hypothesis is that this clinic emerged from a subtle theoretical shift Miller made in his course "Cause and Consent"—in 1987 and 1988—and in some conferences he gave in Brazil around the same time. In the latter he said:

> That which Lacan called subjective rectification is going from complaining about others to complaining about oneself. We always have reasons to complain about others [...] it is a mistake to think, during analysis, that the unconscious is responsible for the things someone suffers from. If this were so, we would strip the subject from its responsibility [...] Lacan called it subjective rectification when, during analysis, the subject also discovers his essential responsibility in what is happening. The paradox is that the place of the subject's responsibility is the same as that of the unconscious.[30]

Where Miller sees a paradox, I find a contradiction. From what I have presented, I can state that it is absurd to hold the analysand—which he calls, in a very ambiguous way in this context, "subject"—responsible for the unconscious. The goal of psychoanalysis is not that the analysand become more responsible, because psychoanalysis does not have moral intentions, and responsibility, as Freud said, is a legal and moral category. I agree with Gerez Ambertín when she holds that psychoanalysis does not intend to unburden analysands from their responsibility, but—and here is where we disagree—analysis is not about assuming responsibility either.[31] Psychoanalysis neither waives nor assigns responsibility to the analysand because, understood in this way, it is not an appropriate concept for its field of intervention.[32]

Moreover, it is not a rule that people come to complain about others. I am under the impression that we complain rather too little. We are too well adapted. We are disciplined and obedient. Complaint can be the first step in the direction of truth.

It is necessary to study the Lacanian concept of subjective rectification to assess its clinical scope, and so we can distinguish it from the problematic concept of subjective responsibility. "The Direction of the Treatment" is the only text where Lacan uses this phrase, although the idea that runs through it is presented on different occasions.

Subjective rectification, or rectification of the subject's relations with reality, is a concept Lacan used to contrast his clinical hypotheses to those of "post-Freudianism." His diagnosis is that psychoanalysis after Freud became a normalizing practice whose goal was to disabuse patients of their neurotic illusion—including (in) the transference—and adapt them to "reality." Of course, reality, in this case, was nothing but the analysts' ego! They offered themselves as the criterion of reality. In these terms, psychoanalysis was nothing more than a device of normalizing power: a practice of emotional reeducation aimed at producing mature, genital subjects who were well adapted (without complaints) to the ideals of the time.

Post-Freudian psychoanalysts "lost their way" because they inverted the order of the direction of treatment, locating the rectification of the subject's relations with the real at the very end of analysis. For Lacan, conversely, the direction of treatment is ordered "in accordance with a process that begins with rectification of the subject's relation with reality [*réel*], and proceeds to development of the transference and then to interpretation."[33] Psychoanalysis starts "by introducing the patient to an initial situating of his position in reality [*réel*], even if this situating leads to [...] a systematization—of the symptoms."[34]

It is clear that Lacanian and post-Freudian forms of subjective rectification are opposed, not only owing to their position in the treatment—at the beginning versus at the *end*—but also owing to their meaning. The post-Freudian aim was openly adaptive. For post-Freudians, analysis was a passage from illusion to reality, from past to present, from there to the here and now, from childhood to maturity. We analysts find ourselves quite tempted to be the true ambassadors of reality. The wise ones in sex, love, hate, friendship, childhood, adolescence, maturity ... We should never trust a psychoanalyst who *already* knows; they could be at best an excellent *coach*. But one goes to analysis not to get life advice but to find true knowledge that allows one to distance oneself from symptomatic enjoyment and recover the lost ways of desire.

What, then, is subjective rectification according to Lacan, that first movement necessary for the continuation of analysis? In "The Direction of the Treatment," he mentions two examples he does not develop: Dora and the Rat Man. I have already presented the main ideas of the first case. It is worth highlighting that, in this text, Lacan omits the confusing question of Dora's role in her own suffering to focus on the fact that Freud never induced Dora to adapt to reality; rather, he demonstrated that she is too well adapted to it, since she assists in its very fabrication.[35]

The case of the Rat Man is more suggestive because it is clear that he does not come to Freud with a complaint. In fact, he is convinced that he is a criminal. If Dora was innocent, the Rat Man was guilty. In both cases, it is necessary to dispose of this logic. Subjective rectification, then, cannot be an analytic move based exclusively on the complaint. Where is rectification in the case of the Rat Man? In order to respond, it is necessary to go through the case. Let us remember that "the direct occasion" for Paul to consult Freud began with the scene where the cruel captain tells him of the horrifying punishment with rats. At that point, Paul thought that such torture could be inflicted on the two people he loved the most: his father (who was dead!) and "his lady." That day, before the cruel captain described the torture, Paul had lost his glasses and telegraphed his optician to send him a new pair in the mail. The issue is that, the next day, the same captain brought him the mailed package and told him that he should return the money to Lieutenant A., who had paid for the glasses. At that precise moment, two contradictory commands are imposed on him: "do not return the money to lieutenant A., or the dreaded torture will be inflicted on my lady and my father" and "give the money back to lieutenant A." From there, a delirious sequence takes place where the Rat Man is compelled to carry out a series of difficult though unsuccessful tasks (sleepless nights, meaningless railway trips, etc.) to comply with the obsessive commands, which were impossible to accomplish. So much so that he thought of asking Freud to issue a medical certificate saying that he needed to give Lieutenant A. his money back in order to recover his health. The "delusion" temporarily ended when a friend calmed him down and accompanied him to the post office to return the money. This is the part of the story where subjective rectification occurs.[36] Freud says:

> It was this last statement which provided me with a starting point from which I could begin straightening out the various distortions involved in his story. After his friend had brought him to his senses, he had dispatched the small sum of money in question neither to Lieutenant A. nor to Lieutenant B., but directly to the post office. *He must therefore have known that he owed the amount of the charges due upon the packet to no one but the official at the post office, and he must have known this before he started on his journey.* It turned out that in fact he had known it before the captain made his request and before he himself made his vow; for he now remembered that a few hours before meeting the cruel captain he had had occasion to introduce himself to another captain, who had told him how matters actually stood. [...] The cruel captain had made a mistake when, as he handed him over the packet, he had asked him to pay back the 3.80 *kronen* to A., and the patient *must have known it was a mistake.* In spite of this he had made a vow founded upon this mistake, a vow that was bound to be a torment to him. In so doing he had suppressed to himself, just as in telling the story he had suppressed to me, the episode of the other captain and the existence of the trusting young lady at the post office. I must admit that when this *correction* has been made his behavior becomes even *more senseless and unintelligible than before.*[37]

In the next session, after Freud opened the interview asking him how he would continue, the Rat Man spontaneously began to tell his father's story, which will later be found crucial to the constitution of his neurosis, specifically the issue with the debt. Rectification, then, refers to the revealing of an "error" and to the opening of some concern regarding the symptom in its dimension as knowledge. Freud pointed out that the Rat Man knew there was a mistake. He both knew and did not know. He knew but, owing to unknown reasons, he did not want to know anything about it.

Subjective rectification implies "a change in attitude" in the relationship between the analysand and his suffering.[38] It is the passage from "the ostrich-like policy"—where the symptom is perceived as something senseless to get rid of, some shameful and hateful external thing—to the *othering* of suffering, that is, to the opening of concern about the sense of the symptom in its dimension as knowledge: "I do not know, I want to know, do you know?" It entails transforming suffering into a symptom, into s(A): meaning of the Other. "This new attitude towards the illness intensifies the conflicts and brings to the fore symptoms which till then had been indistinct."[39] As Lacan also stated, from there, symptoms systematize and precipitate. It could not be so in any other way: "one cannot overcome an enemy who is absent or not within range."[40] The psychoanalyst must not hold the analysand responsible for anything. It is not about getting the patient to stop complaining of others in order to complain about themselves, but about instantiating the subject supposed to know, of transference, "demonstrating [to the analysand] that what is at stake is something altogether different than relations between the ego and the world."[41] Those who rectify shift the symptom from reference to knowledge. This is how the formal entry into analysis occurs: "[f]rom then on he no longer addressed the person who was in his proximity, which is why he refused to work face to face with him."[42] The symptom is otherized and passes to the couch (or to the phone call).

This primordial maneuver already implies a process of reading and writing (production and inscription of the conjecture) as long as rectification "*takes off from the subject's own words in order to come back to them*, which means that an interpretation can be exact only by being … an interpretation."[43] There is no pretension to objectivity, understood as the adaptation of the enunciations of the ego to the things of the world, but an intention of "inter-subjective" truth arising from reading and writing. In the case of the Rat Man, Freud's questioning of Paul's account might be formulated as follows: why did you return the money to the woman in the post office if you did not owe her? Faced with this question, the Rat Man has no other option but to "confess" that he knew whom he owed. So, what does it mean to "not pay the debt"? The path to the story of the father's debt had been opened.

Bachelard, the French epistemologist, proposed the concept of "subjective rectification" only a few years before "The Direction of Treatment." In the last chapter of *The Formation of the Scientific Mind*, titled "Scientific Objectivity and Psychoanalysis," he holds that there can be no truth from a psychological point of view without the rectification of a mistake. A psychology of objective, scientific attitude is a history of personal mistakes. To reach objective knowledge, it is necessary to radically break with the idea of sensory knowledge, *immediate* knowledge arising from lived experience. "Normal tendencies of sensory knowledge, with all their immediate pragmatism and realism, only lead to a false start and to a wrong direction being taken."[44] Moreover, Bachelard continues, those who know are too attached to the known object because it comes to them as a possession, it is "used like a value [...] it is inward satisfaction; not rational evidence." Only a "failure," such as a symptom, can call into question the pure value of the object.

How might rational knowledge be obtained? Bachelard's proposal is based on the socialization of knowledge. To access the objective form of a phenomenon, one must "choose the other's eye." It is also necessary to be able to make a distinction between mistakes for which it is convenient to look for a cause and "gratuitous affirmations, made without any effort of thought." This is why it is crucial to notice and socialize mistakes. This job cannot be done on our own: "it is every bit as difficult to begin this process as it is to psychoanalyze oneself."

In the end, says Bachelard, researchers must give up their own ideas, intuitions, and images:

> We must constantly strive towards *desubjectification* if we are to live and relive the instant of objectivity, if we are to remain forever in the nascent state of objectification. The mind that psychoanalysis has freed from the twofold slavery of subject and object can savor the heady delight of oscillating between extraversion and introversion. An objective discovery is at once a subjective rectification. If the object teaches me, then it modifies me. I ask that the chief benefit the object brings should be an intellectual modification. Once pragmatism has been successfully psychoanalyzed, I wish to know for the sake of knowing, never for the sake of using.

This magnificent paragraph is key to understanding Lacan's idea. Subjective rectification, far from being a subjectification (adjudication) of moral responsibility, is a desubjectification which spiritually changes those who know, insofar as their relationship to knowledge and truth changes. The subject must modify her subjectivity in order to access true knowledge, and, in turn, that true knowledge transforms her into a subject. *Le souci de soi!* Subjective rectification is a "discursive rectification," which is produced from a personal, intellectual, and emotional renunciation. We pass from immediate, personal, and erroneous knowledge to mediated, otherized, and true knowledge.

The Demand for Analysis

An idea very close to subjective rectification is that of the demand for analysis, more specifically, "the formation of the demand." Both concepts address the problem of entering into analysis, the initial maneuvers to open the question of the dimension of knowledge of the symptom and to install transference as an enactment of the reality of the unconscious.

In the "Geneva Lecture on the Symptom," Lacan holds that, before a patient "lies down," he must become an analysand, and, to that end, it is necessary that the demand be articulated.[45] The analysand, then, is he who demands an analysis, even if that demand does not come from his lips. This note on the couch is important because both subjective rectification and shaping of demand are hypotheses about entering into analysis.

But what does it mean to articulate the demand for analysis? In principle, the demand for analysis is not something "given;" a maneuver in the text is required for it to appear. The demand for analysis is not to be confused with the motive for consultation. It is unconscious and must be read as such: "demand is not explicit [...] it is hidden from the subject as if it had to be interpreted."[46] However, for the demand to be articulated, some analysis of the motive for consultation is needed. This must occur not only via the classic question—what brings you to analysis?—but also through an inquiry into the moment of consultation—why now?—and the choice of interlocutor—why me, an analyst?[47] Sometimes, patients come to analysis with long-standing issues, in which case the motive for consultation is more enigmatic. It is necessary to "consider how suffering is articulated through the consultation with an analyst."[48] The case of the Rat Man is in that sense very valuable. The motive for consultation does not constitute the demand, but it can reveal something about it.

Eidelsztein defines the demand for analysis as the way the patient relates to what she says.[49] The motive for consultation is a statement: "I come to see you because of x," but the analyst must also consider the position of the patient with respect to this statement—that is, the enunciation.

> The subject appears when there is an opening between what he says and the position he assumes with respect to what he says [...] the subject adapts to his demand, not because of what he says, but because of the position he assumes with respect to what he says.[50]

The position one assumes regarding what one says, in contrast to what is explicitly said, requires an Other who enables it, who allows an opening between what is said and the saying. That it is said is forgotten behind what is said in what is heard and understood, according to Lacan. "Let it be said" is the demand. Miller, in the same conference quoted above, names this maneuver at the beginning of analysis "subjective localization" and says it is "questioning the position the person speaking assumes in relation to their own speech. What is essential is, based on the speech, to locate the subject's saying [...] the enunciation."[51] Redundancy is useful to demonstrate the general agreement on this topic. The term "subjective localization" is quite appropriate, even if it may be better to say "localization of the subject." Entry into analysis requires rectification and localization, not localization and responsibility. This clarifies that demand is not what the patient says, and desire is beyond what is said. There are three dimensions: what is explicitly said, the patient's position with respect to what he says, and what lies beyond the demand: desire. These three dimensions form the body. Desire is not subject to articulation, but it is articulated, "suspended in articulations arising elsewhere at the level of the demand."[52]

For desire to appear, it is first necessary to locate the subject of the demand, the position the patient assumes with respect to what he says. The Rat Man will once again be a useful model. After subjective rectification linked to the paying of the debt to the woman at the post office, Paul spontaneously begins to tell his father's story. Also elucidated is his self-reproach for having been absent at the time of his father's death and his self-perception as a "criminal," concentrated in the obsessive idea which has haunted him since his childhood: "my beloved would show me affection if some misfortune were to befall me: like the death of my father." He *vigorously rejects* this idea and defends against the possibility that this thought might be a desire by discounting it as a mere "connection of thoughts."

> By way of objection I asked him why, if it had not been a wish, he had repudiated it.—Merely, he replied, on account of the content of the idea, the notion that his father might die.—I remarked that he was treating the phrase as though it were one that involved *lèse-majesté*; it was well known, of course, that it was equally punishable to say "The Emperor is an ass" or to disguise the forbidden words by saying "If any one says, etc. ... then he will have me to reckon with." I added that I could easily insert the idea which he had so energetically repudiated into a context which would exclude the possibility of any such repudiation.[53]

Paul's position with respect to his own speech and Freud's maneuver to situate it are clear. After this maneuver, the analysis continues with the history of paternal debt, the opposition of father and desire, the quarrel between love and hate, and, correlatively, the constitution of a prohibiting, sadistic Other to whom Paul addresses his speech and which is revealed "along the painful road of transference."[54] This is an Other who is conceived of as faultless and "complete."

In psychoanalysis, there is a displacement of facts to speech—rectification—and of speech to saying—localization. These maneuvers enable the opening of the question of suffering in terms of knowledge, of the unconscious as unknown knowledge, and they also put into play the deceptive, though inescapable, function of the subject supposed to know. The fact that Miller orders the series differently—appraisal, localization, and rectification (understood as responsibility)—accounts for the conceptual and clinical difference from my proposal. For Miller, rectification comes after subjective localization because the patient must take responsibility for her position with respect to what is said. My position is that it is unnecessary to identify any moral responsibility for the complaint. It is about rectifying the discourse, *de-egoing* the analytic conversation through the return to the patient of his own sayings and locating the subject of demand by means of the inscription of a conjecture extracted from the text itself.

Before concluding, I would like to focus for a moment on the concept of "clinical appraisal." Miller holds that preliminary interviews are, among other things, an opportunity for the analyst to question whether she will authorize the demand for analysis, on her own terms. That is, whether she will accept the patient as an analysand. In this view, the patient "is a candidate and the analyst, in some way, a jury,"[55] though Miller situates the primary issue of appraisal on diagnosis, especially on the possibility of consulting with a "pre-psychotic" patient—in which case the analyst should either refuse the demand or "be extremely careful not to trigger it."[56] It is important to highlight the presence of another concept which, owing to its lack of conceptual rigor, produced great clinical errors: decided desire.[57] "[If] there is no decided desire in the subject, it is better not to accept them in the analytic experience," holds Miller.[58] This concept would not be so problematic if it were not understood and applied in its more banal sense, as if it referred to a strong conviction in wanting to be analyzed, and with the considerable caveat that the analyst is the one who evaluates whether or not this conviction is present. Lombardi, for instance, holds that decided desire is necessary in the patient for the symptom to develop in the sense of love for knowledge and search for a solution through desire: "proposing analysis to someone who has no decided desire […] frequently leads to failure of the proposal […] which discredits psychoanalysis."[59] What exactly constitutes decided desire, no one says.

I do not believe "decided desire" is necessary in order to begin an analysis. Nor do I think it is a necessary precondition for the symptom to develop in the sense of love of knowledge. The opening of interrogation of the symptom in its dimension as knowledge depends above all on the analytic maneuvers made. Of course, there are people who are not interested in experiencing an analytic process, in opening questions about their existence, but I see no reason to deduce from this a lack of "decided desire," as if this lack were an inherent trait. In fact, using such an important concept to convey such a vague idea results in an absolute degradation of the concept of desire (which is not decided; if anything, it is "produced"). The discrediting of psychoanalysis can be attributed to many reasons; proposing analysis to those who lack decided desire is not chief among them. For my part, I find only two necessary conditions for accepting someone as a patient: that there is suffering, and that I believe I am in a position to analyze it.

More precisely, Eidelsztein states that it is a contradiction to establish a decided desire at the beginning of analysis since this, "would imply the postulation of an existing desire in order to remove obstacles to the exercise of desire."[60] Desire is something one arrives at through analysis, not something one starts from. This is why we speak of demand for analysis and not desire for analysis. For there to be demand for analysis, the work of both the analyst and the analysand is required. There is no desire to be an analysand. "A demand is analytic if it has the virtue of positioning the unconscious as the discourse of the Other and establishing that there is no subject without the Other."[61]

Psychoanalysis exists only in the inmixing of the subject and the Other.

Notes

1 Cf. Exposto and Rodríguez Varela, 2020: 61–102.
2 Canguilhem, 1956/2016: 212–213.
3 Translator's note: in Spanish, "*polipsíaca*" is a neologism used by the author, combining psi and "*policíaca*" (related to the police).
4 Berenguer, 2007.
5 Miller, 2008–2009/2018: 76.
6 Cf. Miller, 2008–2009/2018.
7 Lacan, 1966: 729.
8 Cf. Eidelsztein, 2015.
9 As I was able to gather, the "original lapsus" was made by Miller in his Lacanian orientation course of 1987–1988, "Cause and Consent." Here he says, quoting Lacan "verbatim," the following: "[w]e are always responsible for our position as subjects." Months later, Miller gave some conferences in Brazil, which were published in Spanish under the title *Introducción al método psicoanalítico* (Introduction to the psycho-analytic method). Both in his course and at the conferences in Brazil, Miller worked on his idea of subjective responsibility. He had such scope in this lapsus that, even today, one is more likely to encounter Miller's formulation than Lacan's.
10 Lacan, 1966: 729.
11 Eidelsztein, 2015.
12 Lacan, 1964–1965: lecture on May 5, 1965.
13 Lacan, 1969–1970: 77.
14 Lacan, 1951: 213.
15 Freud, 1905 (1901): 45.
16 Damián Selci (2020) has worked on this problem very precisely, from a political perspective, in his book *La organización permanente* (The permanent organization).
17 Cf. Lacan, 1953.
18 Freud, 1926: 221.
19 Ibid.: 222.
20 Freud, 1917 (1916–1917): 382.
21 Freud, 1910: 150.
22 Freud, 1915: 121–122.
23 Laplanche and Pontalis, 1967: 182.
24 Freud, 1925: 133.
25 Deleuze, 1971–1972/2005: 133.
26 Lacan, 1964/1981: 166.
27 Lacan, 1969–1970: 66.
28 Lacan, 1975–1976: 9.
29 Lacan, 1972–1973: 125.
30 Miller, 1987/2006: 70.
31 Cf. Gerez Ambertín, 2010.
32 The goal of this chapter is to think of the clinical differences opening the concepts of subjective rectification and subjective responsibility. I do not disregard the

possibility of recovering the term "responsibility" to think of ethical problems linked to psychoanalysis. Pablo Muñoz (2020) has done considerable research on this topic in his book *Freedom and Responsibility in the Practice of Psychoanalysis*.

33 Lacan, 1958: 500.
34 Ibid.: 498.
35 Cf. ibid.
36 I thank Agustín Kripper for this reference.
37 Freud, 1909: 172–173.
38 "First and foremost, the initiation of the treatment in itself brings about a change in the patient's conscious attitude to his illness. He has usually been content with lamenting it, despising it as nonsensical and under-estimating its importance; for the rest, he has extended to its manifestations the ostrich-like policy of repression which he adopted towards its origins. Thus, it can happen that he does not properly know under what conditions his phobia breaks out or does not listen to the precise wording of his obsessional ideas or does not grasp the actual purpose of his obsessional impulse" (Freud, 1914: 152).
39 Ibid.
40 Freud, 1914: 152.
41 Lacan, 1958: 499.
42 Ibid.
43 Ibid.: 502.
44 Bachelard, 2002: 238. All following quotes, until indicated, come from the same text (238–246).
45 Cf. Lacan, 1975.
46 Lacan, 1960–1961: 197.
47 Cf. Eidelsztein, 2003a and 2003b.
48 Eidelsztein, 2003a: n.p.
49 Cf. 2003a and 2003b.
50 Eidelsztein, 2003b: n.p.
51 Miller, 1987/2006: 39.
52 Lacan, as cited by Eidelsztein, 2003b.
53 Freud, 1909: 178–179.
54 Ibid.: 209.
55 Miller, 1987/2006: 34.
56 Ibid.: 21. This idea only caused inhibition for young psychoanalysts who, faced with the possibility of saying something that would trigger a psychosis—as if it were that simple—decided to remain silent. It is good to be careful, but we cannot analyze if we are scared of hurting our patients. Moreover, for something to happen in an analysis, the analyst must speak.
57 Even though the phrase "decided desire" does not appear in Lacan's work, the "idea" is present in "Television": "Psychoanalysis would allow you, of course, the hope of refining and clarifying the unconscious of which you're the subject. But everyone knows that I don't encourage anyone into it, anyone whose desire is not resolute. Furthermore—and I am sorry to refer to some ill-bred you's—I think the analytic discourse should be withheld from the rabble" (1973: 43). It seems clear that Lacan uses the word desire, in this context, in a trivial sense. Moreover, not encouraging anyone who has no strong conviction to get psychoanalyzed is not equivalent to rejecting their request. Refusal, according to Lacan, is reserved for scoundrels.
58 Miller, 1987/2006: 71.
59 Lombardi, 1990/2007: 48.
60 Eidelsztein, 2003b: n.p.
61 Ibid.: n.p.

References

Bachelard, G. (2002). *The Formation of the Scientific Mind. A Contribution to a Psychoanalysis of Objective Knowledge.* Trans. M. McAllester Jones. Manchester: Clinamen. (Original work published 1948)

Berenguer, E. (2007, March 22). ¿Yo, responsable de mi queja? *Página 12. Psicología.* Retrieved from www.pagina12.com.ar/diario/psicologia/9-82091-2007-03-22.html

Canguilhem, G. (2016). What Is Psychology? Ed. and Trans. D.M. Peña-Guzmán. *Foucault Studies, Counter-Conduct,* (21): 200–213. doi:10.22439/fs.v0i0.5019. (Original work published 1956)

Deleuze, G. (2005). *Derrames. Entre el capitalismo y ezquizofrenia.* Buenos Aires: Cactus. (Original work published 1971–1972)

Eidelsztein, A. (2003a). Finales de análisis. *Revista Imago Agenda,* (68). Retrieved from www.eidelszteinalfredo.com.ar/que-cura-el-psicoanalisis-y-como/

Eidelsztein, A. (2003b). Demanda de análisis. Unpublished.

Eidelsztein, A. (2015). La "responsabilidad subjetiva" en psicoanálisis. *El rey está denudo,* (8): 124–138.

Exposto, E., and Rodríguez Varela, G. (2020). *Manifiestos para un análisis militante del inconsciente.* Buenos Aires: Red Editorial.

Freud, S. (1905 [1901]). Fragment of an Analysis of a Case of Hysteria. In S. Freud, A. Freud, A. Strachey, and A. Tyson (Eds.), *The Standard Edition of the Complete Psychological Works of Sigmund Freud. Volume VII: A Case of Hysteria, Three Essays on Sexuality and Other Works.* Trans. J. Strachey, pp. 15–124. London: The Hogarth Press.

Freud, S. (1909). Notes upon a Case of Obsessional Neurosis. In S. Freud, A. Freud, A. Strachey, and A. Tyson (Eds.), *The Standard Edition of the Complete Psychological Works of Sigmund Freud, Volume X: Two Case Histories ("Little Hans" and the "Rat Man").* Trans. J. Strachey, pp. 153–318. London: The Hogarth Press.

Freud, S. (1910). The Future Prospects of Psycho-Analytic Therapy. In S. Freud, A. Freud, A. Strachey, and A. Tyson (Eds.), *The Standard Edition of the Complete Psychological Works of Sigmund Freud, Book XI: Five Lectures on Psycho-Analysis; Leonardo Da Vinci; and Other Works.* Trans. J. Strachey, pp. 139–152. London: The Hogarth Press.

Freud, S. (1914). Remembering, Repeating and Working-Through (Further Recommendations on the Technique of Psycho-Analysis II). In S. Freud, A. Freud, A. Strachey, and A. Tyson (Eds.), *The Standard Edition of the Complete Psychological Works of Sigmund Freud. Volume XII: The Case of Schreber, Papers on Technique and Other Work.* Trans. J. Strachey, pp. 145–156. London: The Hogarth Press.

Freud, S. (1915). Instincts and their Vicissitudes. In S. Freud, A. Freud, A. Strachey, and A. Tyson (Eds.), *The Standard Edition of the Complete Psychological Works of Sigmund Freud, Book XIV: On the History of the Psycho-Analytic Movement; Papers on Metapsychology and Other Works.* Trans. J. Strachey, pp. 109–140. London: The Hogarth Press.

Freud, S. (1917 [1916–1917]). The Common Neurotic State. In S. Freud, A. Freud, A. Strachey, and A. Tyson (Eds.), *The Standard Edition of the Psychological Works of Sigmund Freud, Book XVI: Introductory Lectures on Psycho-Analysis (Part III).* Trans. J. Strachey, pp. 378–391. London: The Hogarth Press.

Freud, S. (1925). Some Additional Notes on Dream-Interpretation as a Whole. Part B: Moral Responsibility for the Content of Dreams. In S. Freud, A. Freud, A. Strachey, and A. Tyson (Eds.), *The Standard Edition of the Complete Psychological Works of Sigmund Freud, Book XIX: The Ego and the Id and Other Works*. Trans. J. Strachey, pp. 131–134. London: The Hogarth Press.

Freud, S. (1926). The Question of Lay Analysis: Conversations with an Impartial Person. In S. Freud, A. Freud, A. Strachey, and A. Tyson (Eds.), *The Standard Edition of the Complete Psychological Works of Sigmund Freud, Book XX: An Autobiographical Study; Inhibitions, Symptoms and Anxiety; The Question of Lay Analysis; and Other Works*. Trans. J. Strachey, pp. 183–250. London: The Hogarth Press.

Gerez Ambertín, M. (2010, November). Intimidación y registros de la culpa. *Psicoanálisis y el Hospital. No. 38: Responsabilidad e imputabilidad*.

Lacan, J. (1951). Intervention on Transference. In C. Bernheimer and C. Kahane (Eds.), *In Dora's Case Freud-Hysteria-Feminism*, pp. 92–104. New York and Chichester, UK: Columbia University Press.

Lacan, J. (1953). The Function and Field of Speech and Language in Psychoanalysis. In J. Lacan, *Écrits: The First Complete Edition in English*. Trans. B. Fink, pp. 197–268. New York and London: W.W. Norton.

Lacan, J. (1958). The Direction of the Treatment and the Principles of its Power. In J. Lacan, *Écrits: The First Complete Edition in English*. Trans. B. Fink, pp. 489–542. New York and London: W.W. Norton.

Lacan, J. (1960–1961). *The Seminar of Jacques Lacan. Book VIII: Transference*. Ed. J.-A. Miller. Trans. B. Fink. Cambridge: Polity Press.

Lacan, J. (1964–1965). *The Seminar of Jacques Lacan, Book XII: Crucial Problems for Psychoanalysis (1964–1965)*. Trans. C. Gallagher. Cormac. Retrieved from http://esource.dbs.ie/handle/10788/161

Lacan, J. (1966). Science and Truth. In J. Lacan, *Écrits: The First Complete Edition in English*. Trans. B. Fink, pp. 726–745. New York and London: W.W. Norton.

Lacan, J. (1969–1970). *The Seminar of Jacques Lacan. Book XVII: The Other Side of Psychoanalysis*. Ed. J.-A. Miller. Trans. R. Grigg. New York and London: W.W. Norton.

Lacan, J. (1972–1973). *The Seminar of Jacques Lacan. Book XX: On Feminine Sexuality. The Limits of Love and Knowledge*. Ed. J.-A. Miller. Trans. B. Fink. New York and London: W.W. Norton.

Lacan, J. (1973). *Television. A Challenge to the Psychoanalytic Establishment*. Ed. J. Copjec. Trans. D. Hollier, R. Krauss, and A. Michaelson. New York and London: W.W. Norton.

Lacan, J. (1975). Geneva lecture on the symptom. *Analysis*, (1), 7–26. Trans. R. Grigg. Retrieved from chrome-extension://efaidnbmnnnibpcajpcglclefindmkaj/https://lacanianworksexchange.net/wp-content/uploads/2023/07/19751004GenevaLectureontheSymptomJacquesLacan.pdf

Lacan, J. (1975–1976). *The Seminar of Jacques Lacan: Book XXIII: The Sinthome*. Ed. J.-A. Miller. Trans. A.R. Price. New York: Polity Press.

Lacan, J. (1981). *The Seminar of Jacques Lacan: Book XI: The Four Fundamental Concepts of Psychoanalysis*. Ed. J.-A. Miller. Trans. A. Sheridan. New York and London: W.W. Norton. (Original work published 1964)

Laplanche, J., and Pontalis, J.-B. (1967). *The Language of Psychoanalysis*. Trans. D. Nicholson-Smith. London: Karnac Books.

Lombardi, G. (2007). *La clínica del psicoanálisis. Ética y técnica*. Buenos Aires: Paidós. (Original work published 1990)

Miller, J.-A. (2006). *Introducción al método psicoanalítico*. Buenos Aires: Paidós. (Original work published 1987)

Miller, J.-A. (2018). *Sutilezas analíticas. Los cursos psicoanalíticos de Jacques Alain Miller*. Buenos Aires: Paidós. (Original work published 2008–2009)

Muñoz, P. (2020). *Libertad y responsabilidad en la práctica del psicoanálisis*. Buenos Aires: Letra Viva.

Selci, D. (2020). *La organización permanente*. Buenos Aires: Cuarenta Ríos.

Chapter 5

Loving
Introduction to the Problem of Transference

You Can't Live off Love[1]

That psychoanalysis is an experience of love is, like any truth, only half true. Love of truth, the truth of love, true love—isn't this what analysis is about? As Lacan says, in the beginning was love. But what about the middle and the end? To what extent is psychoanalysis a treatment *by* and *for* love? Can the matter be settled in this court? In calling the place of love into question, we are not underestimating it but revising its place within psychoanalytic theory and practice.

We all remember Kristeva's famous phrase: "being a psychoanalyst is knowing that all tales are, in the end, about love."[2] Who would dare deny it? My goal is not to deny but simply to point out the inevitable partiality of such statements. This is not a question of taking up a position of disillusionment or indifference, or of arriving at an epistemic rationality that excludes the emotional dimension. What interests me is a consideration of the scope of love, without falling into eloquent sentimentality or theoretical coldness. Love runs throughout the story of any analytic cure, but not all of the cure is a love story.

The question of love in psychoanalysis circles around one concept: transference, which is something quite similar to love. Despite theoretical efforts, transference became the most inspiring way to refer to trust, harmony, rapport, empathy, admiration, and the like. But when we speak of transference love, the concept seems to collapse. This is why it is so common to hear phrases such as "transference to work" or "transference to school." The important thing is not that these are imprecise uses of the word, but that the most important aspect of the concept may be forgotten. In the clinical setting, we speak of transference to refer very generally to the relationship between analyst and analysand, or to indicate when the analyst is the object of the analysand's discourse (in dreams, for instance, or in the here-and-now of the analytic relationship)—that is, when the analytic bond becomes a topic of conversation, as if this were a good in and of itself. The problem is that the establishment of transference, which is necessary for entry into analysis, is confused with a metalanguage of intimacy. It is hastily concluded that, if the patient speaks about the analyst, she is ready to move to the couch.

DOI: 10.4324/9781032696423-5

Lacan diagnosed the imprecision with which the concept of transference was being used as early as the sixties:

> The transference is usually represented as an affect. A rather vague distinction is then made between a positive and a negative transference. It is generally assumed, not without some foundation, that the positive transference is love—though it must be said that, in the way it is used here, this term is employed in a very approximate way. [...] In the case of the negative transference, commentators are more prudent, more restrained, in the way they refer to it, and it is never identified with hate. They usually employ the term ambivalence [...] It would be truer to say that the positive transference is when you have a soft spot for the individual concerned, the analyst in this instance, and the negative transference is when you have to keep your eye on him. There is another use of the term transference that is worth pointing out, as when one says that it structures all the particular relations with that other who is the analyst, and that the value of all the thoughts that gravitate around this relation must be connoted by a sign of particular reserve. Hence the expression—which is always added as a kind of after-thought or parenthesis, as if to convey some kind of suspicion, when used about the behavior of a subject—*he is in full transference*. This presupposes that his entire mode of apperception has been restructured around the dominant center of the transference.[3]

Things do not seem to have changed much since then. Still today, transference is understood as the analysand's feelings towards the analyst on a scale between two poles, a negative one—hate or ambivalence—and a positive one—love. Additionally, direct reference by the patient to the bond with the analyst is granted a special value. Transference has lost conceptual and, therefore, clinical strength. My sense is that the practical importance of transference in conceptualizing cases remains unclear. This is likely owing to an ambiguity in its relation to other concepts such as love, knowledge, desire, and drive as well as the crystallization of its common uses, including in the academic field.

Obstacle and Engine

What, then, is transference? In a very broad sense, it is a concept that refers to the unique relationship between analyst and analysand and the way in which this relationship determines the direction for treatment. Transference explains obstacles in the treatment that present themselves through the arrest of free association and reveals the very possibility of treatment based on the unique value that speech and knowledge acquire in the analytic conversation. Transference is the greatest obstacle to, and, at the same time, the condition of possibility for, the treatment. Now, the meaning of transference as an obstacle and a precondition for analytic treatment is not at all obvious.

At the beginning of his practice, Freud discovered some obstacles to associative work. The greatest was the fact that, at some point in the treatment, the patient begins to develop a particular interest in the figure of the analyst, such that, "[e]verything connected with the doctor seems to be more important to him than his own affairs and to be diverting him from his illness."[4] Patients fell in love. The reciprocal trust, attachment, and tenderness necessary for the intimacy of the analytic conversation gave way to loving passion: an urgent, thick, and penetrating feeling. The bond between analyst and patient had been spoiled; there was nothing else to say. Free association had stopped.

It is worth noting that Freud never believed the emergence of erotism in the treatment had anything to do with his personal gifts, although he did not truly consider whether this could be an effect of the analytic device itself or his own position within it. According to Freud, the cause of this strange infatuation was neurosis. Ferenczi went so far as to suggest that neurosis be defined as a passion for transference.[5] This means that the psychic mechanisms of infatuation with the analyst match those of the symptom. The analyst is, in some ways, also a formation of the unconscious. The relation becomes damaged when the analyst is an object of a "false bond" between affect stemming from a repressed representation of desire and the representation of the analyst. This is a transference of affect, a displacement of value.

It is worth noting that this infatuation is not always conscious. For Freud, it was possible for a patient to desire him, even if she did not know it. In fact, this was the case "most of the time,"[6] and only as sessions progressed, and with the analyst's interpretations, could this desire become conscious.

The following definition by Freud is very accurate:

> What are transferences? They are new editions or facsimiles of the impulses and phantasies which are aroused and made conscious during the progress of the analysis; but they have this peculiarity, which is characteristic for their species, that they replace some earlier person by the person of the physician.[7]

Logically, neurosis does not abandon its productions once analysis begins. Transference is the neurotic symptom produced within the analytic experience. Another way of saying this is that *transference is neurosis under experimental conditions*. It is a rule, it is present in all cases of neurosis. This fact is paramount since we already know that all neuroses will produce transference; we need no "concrete" manifestation to assume it and interpret it.

Regarding infatuation, Freud's idea is that all human beings acquire, depending on our innate dispositions and environmental factors, a specific and sustained way of loving and desiring.[8] Each of us has a cliché that repeats in different ways throughout life. It is not difficult to deduce that innate and environmental conditions are reducible to the Oedipus complex. This cliché is the "Oedipal imprint" we stamp on the people we love and desire. The analyst is the substitute for an *original*: the father or the mother. *Transference is the Oedipalization of the relationship with the analyst*. For this reason, infatuation is not the only feeling transferred; the analyst is also an object of ambivalent feelings (connected, of course, to infantile Oedipal rivalry). For many decades, analysis was conceived as the reproduction and rectification of Oedipal conflicts with parents, embodied in the figure of the analyst. "Stop acting like a child" could be the motto of psychoanalysis practiced in this way.

It was not only female patients who fell in love with their analysts; male patients exhibited "the same overvaluation of his qualities, the same absorption in his interests, the same jealousy of everyone close to him in real life."[9] In short, any mortal who lay on the couch fell in love with the analyst. Infatuation proved to be "the unavoidable consequence" of the analytic situation.[10]

Transference passions constitute the most difficult resistance to overcome: "the only really serious difficulties [the analyst] has to meet lie in the management of the transference," Freud states.[11] The insistence on the challenge of handling transference over the years is astounding. It is described variously as "the most troublesome hindrance," the "most difficult" task, the "greatest difficulty," "the most powerful resistance," and so on. Interpretation, translation, and deciphering seem weak in the face of transference passions. Hence, it is not interpreted, it dominates: "As we know, the passions are little affected by sublime speeches."[12] So, what type of intervention is required to tame transference? As regards interpretation, "[i]t is easy to learn how to interpret dreams, to extract from the patient's associations his unconscious thoughts and memories, and to practice similar explanatory arts: for these the patient himself will always provide the text."[13] In contrast, transference must be discovered "without assistance" and with minimal clues.[14] Its interpretation depends on a supposed law. For instance, one indicator of transference is the analysand's silence—the paralysis of free association. When free association is interrupted, "the stoppage can *invariably* be removed by an assurance that he is being dominated at the moment by an association which is concerned with the doctor himself or with something connected with him."[15] With such an interpretation, says Freud, ideas are no longer denied but silenced. The rabbit is in the top hat. The following example from *Studies on Hysteria* is exemplary:

> In one of my patients, for instance, the pressure procedure suddenly failed. I had reason to suppose that there was an unconscious idea [related to transference], and I dealt with it at the first attempt by taking her by surprise. I told her that some obstacle must have arisen to continuing the treatment, but that the pressure procedure had at least the power to *show her what this obstacle was*; I pressed on her head, and she said in astonishment: "*I see you sitting on the chair here*; but that's nonsense. What can it mean?"[16]

Does the text not illustrate that Freud himself was the obstacle? In any case, what remains clear is that transference appears at the moment of greatest resistance, when, during the analytic process, we approach the pathogenic core. It is the mightiest weapon of resistance. At that moment, Freud says, there can only be a struggle between analyst and analysand, between repetition and memory.[17] What do we do in this scenario? To *tame* the transference and transform it into a reason to remember, the analyst needs to "give him time."[18] Transference is to be tolerated; it should be neither prohibited nor gratified, but rather used for the purposes of analysis. We allow the transference to unfold freely so that the analysand "display[s] to us everything in the way of pathogenic instincts that [are] hidden in the patient's mind."[19] In these cases, we encounter the happy coincidence of moral precepts and technical requirements. The analyst refrains from gratifying the patient's amorous demand, allows it to exist as a productive force for the analytic work, and ensures that it is not satisfied by substitutes, since "[w]hat we could offer would never be anything else than a surrogate."[20] It is the *very motive force of the treatment*. The ultimate goal is to redirect it from the present situation with the doctor to its unconscious origins, to transform repetition into remembering.[21] The maneuver on transference could be summarized as follows: at first, it is located based on resistance and then it is redirected to the past.

It is clear that transference is not only an obstacle, but also the most important tool the analyst has, it is "its most powerful ally."[22] Through the work on transference, one acquires "a sense of conviction" in interpretations, because it allows us to catch the neurosis red-handed, *in flagrante delicto*.[23] For this reason, Freud concludes that it is not adequate to speak of transference as such; rather, it is necessary to divide it into positive transference (transference love and erotic transference) and negative transference (characterized by hate). Transference is resistance if it is positive-erotic or negative. When transference is interpreted—that is, when it is redirected to its Oedipal sources—"we are detaching only these two components [erotism and hate] of the emotional act from the person of the doctor; the other component, which is admissible to consciousness and unobjectionable, persists and is the vehicle of success in psychoanalysis."[24] What remains, positive transference love, is the only means we have to influence neurosis. The success of the treatment is determined by the relationship with the doctor and not the intellectual discernment itself. Transference imbues the analyst with "authority and is transformed into belief in his communications and explanations."[25] No argument is valid without such support; "man is only accessible from the intellectual side too, in so far as he is capable of a libidinal cathexis of objects."[26] Psychoanalysis also uses suggestion, understood in a broad sense as the ability to modify texts through transference phenomena—that is, from our hesitant position with respect to knowledge.

Freud maintains that, as the treatment progresses, all symptomatic production "is concentrated upon a single point—his relation to the doctor."[27] Transference gains such importance that the work of remembering is relegated to second place. In this way, psychoanalysis creates a new neurosis which replaces the original one: transference neurosis. Freud puts it as follows: *"All the patient's symptoms* have abandoned their original meaning and have taken on a new sense which lies in a relation to the transference,"[28] and *"all conflicts* need to be solved in the field of transference, in the end."[29] In this new version of neurosis, as analysts, "we are especially well able to find our way about in it since, as its object, we are situated at its very center."[30] Transference neurosis is what is accessible to treatment. The end of analysis coincides with its dismantling. With transference, psychoanalysis creates an artificial illness, an *"intermediate region* between illness and life through which the transition from the one to the other is made."[31] The analyst *gives it time* and, in this way, allows for the development of an illness that he will later treat; the analyst *enables* the emergence of the object of his intervention. In this way, neurosis is brought into a shared terrain, making the symptom available for interpretation. After all, "[i]t is impossible to destroy anyone *in absentia* or *in effigie.*"[32] In the transference neurosis, the analyst finds herself strategically positioned within the symptom and intervenes from this position with the exclusive power transference provides to her speech. The analyst is inside a text she herself produces and intervenes in together with the analysand. The concept of transference is what prevents psychoanalysis from definitively transforming into psychology. A psychoanalyst cannot do psychology, here understood to be the objectification and production of knowledge about "psychic" suffering, because the analyst is part of the symptom. Analysts are much closer to being good readers than experts on mental illnesses or, in an even more general sense, on ways of life.

The analysis does not create transference but enables it. Freud insists that transference is a creation of the neurosis and not of the analytic device or the analyst's position within the device: "Psycho-analytic treatment does not *create* transferences, it merely brings them to light;" they "are justified neither by the doctor's behaviour nor by the situation that has developed during the treatment;" "we do not believe that the situation in the treatment could justify the development of such feelings. We suspect, on the contrary, that the whole readiness for these feelings is derived from elsewhere."[33]

We are in a position to summarize what we have worked on so far and analyze transference in its *multiple dimensions*:

1   In its *phenomenological* dimension, transference is the way the patient emotionally connects—consciously or unconsciously—with the analyst. The bond between them will gain gravitational importance in the development of the treatment.
2   In its *clinical* dimension, it is both the motive force of the treatment and its greatest obstacle. As a treatment progresses, all symptoms and all

conflicts gain transference meaning, giving way to an illness created by psychoanalysis itself: the transference neurosis. This "intermediate realm" between life and illness is what allows the analyst—inside the symptom and as an object of neurosis—to intervene effectively.

3   In its *metapsychological* dimension, transference is the Oedipalization of the bond with the analyst, the substitution of an Oedipal figure with the figure of the analyst. In this way, a relation from the past is lived through as something current, as a mirage of something real.

4   In its *theoretical-causal* dimension, transference is a creation of neurosis. Psychoanalysis does not create it but reveals it and enables its development. In this sense, it is a law, something necessary that occurs in every case.

Issues

It is now time to point out the multiple problems in Freud's conceptualization of transference. The greatest difficulty could be that he presented transference as a unidirectional phenomenon, which begins in the analysand and ends in the analyst. Why didn't he wonder about the analyst's transference? It is difficult to know, although this is likely related to the lack of consideration of the analyst's neurosis (or psychosis or perversion). There is no indication that Freud took into consideration that he or his colleagues could be neurotic. Neurosis and transference were too closely linked to not inquire about one where the other was involved.

This also explains why it took 50 years for analysts, as a community, to pose this question. Freud was not interested in the analyst's affection towards the patient, except for the note on countertransference, made almost in passing. However, as the name suggests, this concept does not deal with the analyst's transference but with her reactions to the patient's transference. This concept still has *a point of origin*: the analysand. Should we add another point of origin? Is it useful to distinguish the analyst's transference from that of the analysand, or is it better to think of them as phenomena originating in the same structure, as a "semiotic co-vibrating"?[34] Freud and many of his followers did not think that the device itself or the analyst's position within it could trigger the observed phenomena.[35] Several decades went by before certain questions were formulated regarding the analyst's transference and, more generally, the influence of the "psychoanalytic environment" (including the fundamental rule and the use of the couch) on the production of transference phenomena. Horney, Macalpine, Alexander, and Nunberg were a few of the psychoanalysts who worked the most on these matters.[36]

Lacan's work allows us to better think what in the apparatus itself feeds transference and what in the analyst's own position turns it into either an advantage or an obstacle. The question, ultimately, is related to how we analysts participate in our analysands' symptoms: the desire of the analyst in question. Though Freud said that transference neurosis took the analyst into the neurosis and turned him into the object of the symptom, he consistently believed that the unconscious is solely the "property" of its author: the patient. The analyst merely receives the analysand's emissions—drive, fantasies, complexes, and so on—and, therefore, participates in the scene with the ability to get out of it, observe it from outside, and interpret it.[37] The discrepancy lies between interpreting transference—outside the text—or interpreting in transference—inside the text. In my research, *desiring* is the analytic function around which questions and problems orbit in relation to the participation by both the analyst and analysand inside the text that is produced, read, and written between them. We cannot "elide ourselves from the text of the experience which interrogates us."[38]

As I mentioned, the presumption that transference is a law precludes the need for any indication in order for the analyst to interpret it: "owing to the characteristics of 'transference' its validity is not susceptible of definite proof."[39] Dora's case is exemplary: without her saying a word about the bond, Freud conjectured that she would like to have a kiss from him. Where there is smoke, there is fire, but who added the wood?

Interpreting transference meant, first, bringing the analytic conversation into the here-and-now of the treatment, exemplified in the bond between the analyst and the analysand (e.g., "you love me" or "you hate me"), and then redirecting it to its true Oedipal origin. The deception is twofold: even if you do not know it, you love me and you hate me; even if you do not know it, in truth that love and that hate are directed to your parents. Strachey posits these two phases very clearly: first, the analyst tries to make the patient aware that an id drive is directed towards the analyst; then, he makes the patient distinguish between the fantasized object—the childhood parents—and the real object—the analyst. "The confrontation between past and present, between fantasy and reality, according to Strachey, is the most important resource for treatment."[40]

With this, it is easier to understand why transference appeared to Freud as combat, an imaginary argument waged around affects. In fact, Freud's conception of "transference neurosis"—not in the nosographic but in the technical sense—stipulated that, throughout the treatment, *all* symptoms must acquire a transference meaning—that is, they needed to be explained in relation to the bond with the analyst. Finally, he believed that the battle was to be fought in the field of the ego, that of the I and the you. What went unthought is that the battle might begin precisely because it was taken into that field. "The mental conflict the patient brings," according to Etchegoyen, "is transformed into a personal conflict, when the analyst intervenes to mobilize it."[41]

Psychoanalysis as combat, as a battle between analyst and analysand, acquired its standing through the "analysis of resistances." The so-called intellectual aspect of analysis—making the unconscious conscious—became secondary to the affective dimension—abolishing resistances. The resistance was, of course, thought to lie on the side of the patient. Reich, for instance, believed positive transference at the beginning of the analysis was either a defense against latent negative transference, against hatred, or a narcissistic desire to be loved, which disillusionment would ultimately transform into hostility.[42] Analysis of resistance meant interpreting negative transference that lay "beneath" the characterological defenses of the ego. Taken by the passionate delirium of Oedipal transference, analysts transformed their offices into boxing rings of mute affects. You and I, hate and love, your resistance and my courage. Why was there a fear of intellectualizing the analysis, but never impassioning it? I think it is best to take Lacan's advice:

> I urge you, each of you, at the heart of your own search for the truth, to renounce quite radically—if only provisionally, to see if one doesn't gain by dispensing with it—the use of an opposition like that of the affective and the intellectual.[43]

The important thing, according to Lacan, is that the subject who goes to an analyst to investigate his truth is in a position of ignorance. This is the true *disposition* for transference. Thus, analysts should dispense with the lackluster distinction between the intellectual and the emotional, where transference is conceived as the passionate aspect of psychoanalysis and interpretation as the intellectual aspect—chimney sweeping, the talking cure, and so on. Rather, what is at stake is the distinction between three concepts—love, desire, and knowledge—articulated in multiple and different ways.

Freud assumed that patients would fall in love with him, and many in fact did so. But this clinical phenomenon is not so evident today. It is not very common for patients to fall in love with their analysts or, for that matter, to hate them. Moreover, interpreting an "unconscious" infatuation seems to be a serious mistake. Why did patients fall in love with their analysts? Is it possible that the Freudian position itself *collaborated* with such passionate phenomena? Is not this displacement of combat to the field of the ego particularly conducive to trigger them? What does it mean to "love" within an analytic treatment? Do we mean the passionate phenomena described by analysts? Why call what happens between analyst and analysand a love relationship?

The idea that transference was the repetition of a past relation, and thus a mirage, led second-generation analysts to conduct treatment based on the divergence between the past and the present, between the illusory and the real. "When you behave rudely and irrationally, you treat me like I am your father, but that is an illusion, our real relationship, in the here and now, has characteristics to which you must adapt."

It was Alexander and the Chicago School who reaffirmed transference as "the neurotic repetition, in the relationship with the analyst, of an *inadequate* stereotypical behavioral model based on the patient's past," a model that adjusted neither to reality nor to the present.[44] In this view, the analyst must, through interpretation, offer the analysand little "doses of reality."[45]

Transference was understood as what was childish and irrational in the behavior of the analysand, and, accordingly, the aim of analysis was for the analysand to behave in a rational, mature way, in analysis and in life. Alexander, for instance, believed that treatment should be centered on "the present and extra-analytic reality" and not on the bond with the analyst (transference neurosis).[46]

To summarize, many analysts believed that they were normal, mature, and realistic enough not only to ignore the question of their own transference, but also to believe that they themselves could offer a model for a "healthy" bond. Here, too, questions arise: which affects will be considered transferential, and which will not? When is affect justified in adult and rational terms? How can the analyst's word be the measure of reality?

Transference of Transference

Lacan's theories on this concept are marked, in my opinion, by two "transferences" that run throughout his work: first, as opposed to the transference belonging solely to the analysand, Lacan understands transference as the analysand's interpellation by the position of the analyst—a clinical distinction. In this view, the analyst too is implicated:

> we realized that the complexity of the topic of transference could in no way be limited to what takes place in the subject known as the patient [...] the question arises of articulating [...] what the analyst's desire must be.[47]

Lacan illuminates the "other side"[48] of transference by stating that we must think seriously about the analyst's desire. Second, instead of an understanding of transference based on love, Lacan theorizes transference based on knowledge and desire—a conceptual distinction. Love is not a necessary accompaniment to transference; it is an affect that might be expected depending on how the analytic device is structured. It is not that love loses importance as a phenomenon, but that Lacan finds a "transphenomenal" dimension that better explains transference difficulties based on two concepts: the analyst's desire and the subject supposed to know.

In "Intervention on Transference," Lacan shows very early on his interest in the role of the analyst in the transference. There, he says that psychoanalysis "preserves a dimension irreducible to all psychology considered as the objectification of certain properties of the individual."[49] Analysts, according to Lacan, convinced themselves that they were external, neutral observers of patients' symptoms, fantasies, and complexes, but, in omitting their participation in the events in which they intervened, they ultimately treated their patients as objects. Psychoanalysis, finally, had created a new man: the *homo psychologicus*.

The fact that psychoanalysis turns into psychology is not so strange; it requires of the analyst only three things: that she omit her participation—theoretical, practical, and subjective—in the phenomenon; that she assist the patient in adaptation; and that she mistake her office for the world. A generalization from such a small sample serves only to celebrate a prejudice.

The objectification of the subject is the reason Lacan began by positing analysis as an intersubjective bond that should not be confused with the egoic relationship between the I and the you. Analysis is not reducible to what occurs between two people. The intersubjective relationship is determined and articulated by the influence of the symbolic, which "transcends" the participants in it and articulates them based on laws subject to formalization. Transference comes neither from the analysand nor from the analyst; rather, both are subjected to an asymmetry.

Another fundamental idea of Lacanian intersubjectivity is that the presence of the analyst is inseparable from the concept of the unconscious. The former is part of the latter and cannot be conceptualized without it. There is no unconscious without an analyst. Regarding dreams, for example, Lacan proposes that the analyst causes and is part of them, and that, in this sense, the unconscious is that which is both of and other than the analysand (because it is also of the analyst!). A formation of the unconscious is an inmixing (*immixtion*) of the subject and the Other.[50] This is an idea Lacan will never abandon, one which will be paramount to understanding the problem of transference defined as "the enactment of the reality of the unconscious."[51]

The analyst is the one who opens the dimension of dialogue merely by being present. A psychoanalysis is not much more than an exchange of words. This seems obvious, but we constantly hear clinical tales that seem either like monologues owing to the analysts' deadly silence or like bad theatrical performances owing to the idealization of the act and the real body, trivially understood. The issue is that, in an analysis, the analyst speaks from a particular position determined by specific modes of listening. A case does not reside in anyone's mouth, which is why analysis does not amount to someone talking and another person listening and objectively interpreting the material. Listening already contaminates the material or, rather, it produces a *necessarily* contaminated material. There is no such thing as given material which can be made available for objective interpretation. The analytic text is made from an ethical-technical function I have called *enabling*. There is no neutrality, and we had best be aware of that. Here, it might be necessary to clarify that *evaluative equivalence* that is established on top of the text does not imply any neutrality or objectivity because it involves a unique mode of textual production with particular characteristics. The analytic text is an imposition on the "regular" discourse based on the hypothesis of the unconscious.

Psychoanalysis is a dialectical experience that carries on according to "the laws of a gravitation peculiar to it, which is called truth."[52] The truth dimension enters the real, between the subject and the Other, through the investments produced by discursive rectification. This is distinguished from accuracy because it intends to be its own basis, to refer to hard data, facts "in themselves." Conversely, truth refers to the way facts inhabit a discursive network that assigns them value. What we psychoanalysts know is that there is no human fact that is completely unaffected by a discursive network and, hence, that is not already being interpreted. We could say that "there are no facts, only interpretations," as long as it does not lead us to an epistemological totalitarianism or naïve relativism wherein we believe that everyone interprets from her own worldview.

In this context, transference will be defined as an "entity *altogether* relative to the countertransference," and countertransference as "the sum total of the prejudices, passions, and difficulties of the analyst, or even of his insufficient information."[53] As resistance, transference indicates mistakes in the position of the analyst, including hoping for the patient's well-being (probably the most common mistake). Therefore, love and hate are products not of neurosis but of the analyst's incorrect position in terms of countertransference. The resistance is that of the analyst. Transference "is nothing real in the subject [...] [it] does not arise from any mysterious property of affectivity [...] this only has meaning as a function of the dialectical moment in which it occurs," that is, when the analyst loses her "purely dialectal" position. In this sense, interpreting transference is nothing but "a ruse to fill in the emptiness of this deadlock."

Transference can also be read from the imaginary and symbolic registers. In Seminar I, Lacan presents them as two discursive modalities, two orders in which the exchange of words takes place. The imaginary register is that of daily conversation, which may appear in different modes, such as "the call, discussion, knowledge, information," or any other exchange involving a referent—that is, an external object about which an agreement is necessary (reality!).[54] In this type of communication, speech functions to mediate between the self, the other, and the external, real, objective world. Resistance is embodied in the system.

Language drags us towards its own referential beyond, which is why conversations tend towards comprehension, not just of what is said but of what is meant by what is said: "you tell me X, but what you want to tell me is Y, when you should be worried about Z." According to Lacan, this is how analysts used to carry out analyses: along the imaginary axis of the ego, of the I and the you, towards comprehension, in the here-and-now, the present and reality.

But there is another dimension of dialogue on which the analytic conversation is based and in which speech acquires another value: the symbolic axis. This is the vector of the subject and the Other, where "another side to speech–revelation" is constituted, which is "the entire realization of the truth of the subject."[55] "Full speech is speech which performs. One of the subjects finds himself, afterwards, other than he was before."[56] To tell the truth—for a truth to *be told*—is to pass a point of no return.[57] The fundamental rule that establishes symbolic transference points to the dissolution of egos and bodies (think of the couch) so there can appear a dimension of "it speaks." Transference indicates a passage from a constitutive truth, from a supposed external reality, to a truth immanent to discourse, inhabiting the text itself and not some "beyond." The word "appear" may seem tricky since it is not something that appears by itself through the mere act of speaking. It is necessary to enable a specific type of text and its subsequent reading and writing. What transference teaches us, in any case, is that both reading and writing are produced within the text. There is no escaping this because there is no outside the text; therefore, there is no outside of transference.

Lacan's idea is that transference appears as an obstacle when there is a "sharp bend, a sudden turn" in the analytic conversation from a symbolic axis to an imaginary axis.[58] Why does this change occur in the dimension of speech? Basically, "resistance stems from the very process of the discourse."[59] As I have stated, discourse tends towards the imaginary axis. The unwitting analyst—or the analyst who orients her practice precisely in that direction—may be carried away by this tendency. Moreover, resistance increases with proximity to the formulation of something "more authentic, more to the point."[60] This idea is quite Freudian: the closer we get to the repressed, the greater the resistance. Lacan states,

> Look at the paradox of the analyst's position from that moment on. It's just at the moment when the speech of the subject is at its fullest that I, the analyst, can intervene. But I would be intervening in what?—in his discourse. Now, the more intimate the discourse is for the subject, the more I focus on this discourse. But the inverse is equally true. The emptier his discourse is, the more I too am led to catch hold of the other, that is to say, led into doing what one does all the time, in this famous analysis of the resistances, led into seeking out the beyond of his discourse— a beyond, you'll be careful to note, which is nowhere.[61]

The sudden turn in the discursive axes results in the analysand's silence and the sudden appearance of the analyst's presence. The analyst is witness to the closing of the unconscious. What is the relationship between this presence and that required for the emergence of the unconscious? The analyst's presence, in this context, is generated by the move from "it speaks" to "I speak," from the process of historization to the *hic et nunc*, where "the subject loses himself in the machinations of the system of language, in the labyrinth of referential systems made."[62] At the beginning, it may seem that the analyst's presence is nothing more than the sudden and violent appearance of her ego and her body. However, Lacan says that it is difficult to define, like "a mystery from which we distance ourselves" to give our world "its consistency, its density, its lived stability."[63] The feeling of presence, he adds, is something we tend to forget. That said, it is clear that the analyst's presence cannot be reduced to its imaginary dimension. What in that presence is real?

Transference as an obstacle revolves around erotic and aggressive tensions on the imaginary axis. The question of passionate transference love is placed "on the plane of the ego and the non-ego, that is to say, on the plane of the narcissistic economy of the subject."[64] Conversely, transference as a condition and driving force of the treatment will be located in the register of the symbolic. The symbolic transference is "the utterance of speech," the fact that speech no longer refers to any reality but to a different speech, arriving at the act of enunciation itself.[65] In symbolic transference "we must analyse speech in stages, to seek in it the multiple meanings between the lines" until we arrive at speech which tells the truth of desire.[66] It is not a question, then, of illusory behavior or a projection of the past onto the present.[67] There is nothing as useless as showing the patient that the feelings they have towards the analyst are deceptive because they are actually directed at his parents. Interpreting the transference is placing two mirrors face-to-face, showcasing their infinite reflections. Moreover, in this way, the analyst does not offer the subject any kind of knowledge—not even of the transference—but rather guides him "to the paths by which access to this knowledge is gained."[68]

When there is symbolic transference, "something takes place which changes the nature of the two beings present."[69] In what way are analyst and analysand transformed? As I said, the establishment of symbolic transference dissolves the participating egos and bodies, although it does not end there. True speech enabled through symbolic transference produces a transmutation in the subject and, hence, in the analysand. And the analyst? Is she not also changed in her subjectivity when a truth is uttered? Is the analyst not also treated as he analyzes?[70]

Symbolic transference is that which gives value to speech in psychoanalysis. It is a clinical fact that, in the consulting room, speech acquires a special value. We frequently hear that analysands are surprised by hearing or saying something they had already heard or said, but that had had no effect until it occurred in analysis. Why here? Why now? Because the analyst occupies the space of the Other, of the symbolic order and of those who embodied it for the analysand. This enables the appearance of the subject and the elevation of the word to the dignity of truth. It is transformed in the time of analysis.

> [P]resent speech, like the old speech, is placed within a parenthesis of time, within a form of time, if I can put it that way. The modulation of time being identical, the speech of the analyst happens to have the same value as the old speech. This value is the value of speech. There is no feeling, no imaginary projection in it.[71]

Transference is not the displacement of Oedipal affects onto the analyst. What is transferred is the value of the Other's speech onto the analytic conversation. It is important to note that symbolic transference is possible thanks to the hypothesis of the unconscious and its related technical proposal of free association. In the game of "free" discourse, pathways open for the convergence of a "fertile mistake through which genuine speech joins up once again with the discourse of error" in the analysand.[72] The truth arises from the error.

Finally, what can be done with imaginary transference other than interpretation? Lacan's answer recalls the Freudian idea: give it time. Lacan says, "you have to wait." We must take the time necessary for the analysand to dismantle his imaginary bond with the analyst, "the appropriate duration of certain repetition-compulsions, which in some way gives them symbolic value."[73] All in all, imaginary transference is not interpreted: it is read in an oblique sense in order to grant it its status as signifier.

Good and Desire

A few years later, in Seminar VIII, Lacan would charge against the reading of the concept of intersubjectivity by "that sort of university person who doesn't know how to extricate himself from his lot except by latching onto terms which seem levitatory to them, because they can't grasp the connection with where they are of service."[74] The concept of intersubjectivity served Lacan in his review of the tendency towards the imaginarization of analysis. Analysts had transformed psychoanalysis into psychology by reducing the subject to its objectifiable characteristics, and they had forgotten the dialectical character of analytic treatment. But, here, Lacan finds a new difficulty: analysis oriented in terms of countertransference. The concept of intersubjectivity was abandoned by Lacan not because of a radical modification in his theory, but owing to a bad reading that had been made of it. An analysis is not an intersubjective relationship as "the university people" understood it because the positions of analyst and analysand are asymmetrical: there is a marked disparity between the two. In analysis, there is only one subject that clearly does not coincide with the analyst, even though (and this may bring more difficulties) it does not strictly match the analysand either. The analytic experience begins when intersubjectivity is suspended.

The clinic of countertransference, on which I will expand in the next chapter, might be summarized as the analyst intervening from his place as a subject, believing that, from his particular sensibility, he might better read the patient's suffering:

> This, at least, explains the shudder that runs through us when trendy remarks are made about countertransference, which contribute, no doubt, to masking its conceptual impropriety: just think of the high-mindedness we display when we show that we ourselves are made of the same clay as those we shape![75]

From the position of subject, the analyst believes he can calculate the configuration of the other based on his own configuration. After all, the patient is a mortal like me! According to Lacan, "the subject is someone to whom we can attribute what? Nothing other than the fact of being, like us, a being."[76] There is no worse mistake for an analyst than believing that, based on his own feelings or ideas, he can understand the patient's suffering, even if he has spent decades on the couch. This is why interpretations from the unconscious must be examined. Those analysts "of countertransference" became convinced that, using their own unconscious, they could capture their patients' unconscious. "We can only know what is equal, we can only know in the other what is our own," Racker claimed.[77]

Analysts: there is no empathy! Do you not feel how tight the other's shoes are? This does not mean that we should be apathetic, silent, and persecuting. We can be welcoming without being empathetic. Our only loyalty must be to the text, reading to a T. This means that we must think *with* the text, go through it, cut it, and write it, enduring its otherness. This issue should not be taken lightly. Nothing is more difficult than welcoming the inevitable foreignness of the Other. We are caught up in machines for the production of meaning, recognition, and identification, and, thus, it is not adequate to think that personal analysis would enable us to use our feelings and spontaneous thoughts as criteria for reading. The machinery must be dismantled every time.

Based on the criticism of intersubjectivity (analysis is based on the subjective asymmetry) and the concept of the analytic situation ("it is the most artificial situation"), Lacan reviews the concept of transference love taking as his reference the Greek model of masculine love in the figures of ἐρώμενος (*erómenos*, or beloved) and ἐραστής (*erastés*, or lover).[78]

In the same vein, Lacan uses Socrates as a model of the analyst's position for several reasons: first, the Socratic experience is a dialectical experience of "putting the imperatorial effects of questioning as such to the test."[79] Suspension of knowledge, assumed ignorance, and questioning as a principle are part of the foundations of the Socratic and the analytic positions. Second, because Socratic science (*episteme*) considers that truth is generated in the exclusive dimension of discourse, within the "internal coherence that is linked, or that he believes to be linked, to the sole, pure, and simple reference to the signifier."[80] As anticipated in the concept of symbolic transference: "a desire for infinite discourses [...] revealed discourse."[81] Lastly, Lacan takes Socrates as a model because of his *atopia* regarding desire, that unclassifiable place the analyst must inhabit.

Psychoanalysis starts from the dimension of ignorance, of "it is not known." The beloved is he who does not know what he has, and the lover is he who does not know what he is missing. What the beloved does not know he has is not what the lover lacks. What one has is not what the other lacks. There is no sexual relationship; between beloved and lover there is inadequacy. What is love, then? It is an effect of signification produced as a result of the substitution of the lover by the beloved. In a metaphor: she who was in the position of the loved object comes to occupy the desiring subject's position. This movement is a displacement from having to not having, from good to desire. A patient begins his analysis searching for something he has but does not know, but "what he discovers is what he is lacking in:"[82]

Desire is not a good [*un bien*] in any sense of the term. It certainly is not a good in the sense of a κτῆσις (*ktésis*) [...] something one could have in some way. An inversion must be detected in the time—"time" defined in both chronological and topological senses—it takes for transference love to blossom, which turns the search for a possession [*un bien*] into the realization of desire.[83]

At the beginning of analysis, the patient introduces herself as worthy of interest and love from the analyst. "The analyst is there for him,"[84] Lacan states. This would be the manifest side of the matter, but there is a "latent" dimension. Once suffering is interrogated in terms of knowledge, it is immediately supposed that the desired object is in the place of the Other, and "as this is the case ... whether [the analysand] knows it or not, he is virtually constituted as *erastés*."[85]

The beloved's question is about what he has, about a good (*un bien*), about the object *of* desire. The lover's question is about what he lacks, about a void, about the desired object. From the place of the beloved, the analysand asks the analyst for a sign of his desire, encouraging the analyst to voice her desire, and what he is as object of desire for the analyst. "State your desire!" analysands say without saying it. Why would the analysand look for a sign of the analyst's desire? Because the analysand assumes the analyst knows, that she has in her the most intimate part of her being: the *ágalma*, the object of desire. Then, the analysand loves the analyst because she is the one who can give him the answer to desire, and, since love essentially means wanting to be loved, the analysand reads the analyst's desire to occupy the place of the lovable object: "*Che Voui?* [...] 'What do you want?' [...] 'Is there any desire that is truly your will?'"[86] The "mainspring of the birth of love" is, then, desire as the desire of the Other. "The whole problem is to perceive the relationship that links the Other to which the demand for love is addressed, to the appearance of desire."[87]

From this perspective, transference is not a characteristic of neurosis but an effect produced in the opening of the question of desire in terms of knowledge. Transference is not exclusive to analytic treatment; however, according to the way it is structured, psychoanalysis uses transference for its own purposes. The analyst serves Eros in order to make use of him.[88] We can then invert the formula and say that it is not a question of transference as neurosis in experimental conditions, but that *neurosis is transference in experimental conditions*.

The scene of the Symposium between Alcibiades and Socrates is exemplary for demonstrating this movement. What arouses Alcibiades's love is that Socrates is the bearer of the *agálmata*. But Socrates—the one who knows that he does not know—knows about matters of desire and knows, therefore, that he possesses nothing. Socrates's position is analytic because he rejects that he is worthy of love and so prevents the metaphor from being fulfilled from his side.

If he presents himself to Alcibiades as not being able to show him signs of his desire, it is insofar as he challenges the idea that he himself is, in any way, an object worthy of Alcibiades' desire, or of anyone else's for that matter.[89]

Alcibiades asks for a sign of desire, and Socrates refuses to provide it, maintaining his *atopia* to the limit regarding desire. He offers instead a void in the center of knowledge. This is the key to the analyst's desire: "where you see something, I am nothing."[90]

Notes

1 Translator's note: this is a reference to the popular song *"No se puede vivir del amor"* by Andrés Calamaro.
2 This famous phrase appears on the original back cover of her book *Histoires d'amour* (Tales of Love) from 1983 (Kristeva, 1983).
3 Lacan, 1964/1981: 123–124.
4 Freud, 1917 (1916–1917): 439.
5 Quoted by Etchegoyen, 1986/2014: 112.
6 Freud, 1905 (1901): 101.
7 Ibid.: 116.
8 Cf. Freud, 1912.
9 Freud, 1917 (1916–1917): 442.
10 Freud, 1915 (1914): 169.
11 Ibid.: 159.
12 Ibid.: 164.
13 Freud, 1905 (1901): 116.
14 Ibid.
15 Freud, 1912: 101.
16 Freud, 1893–1895: 303.
17 "This struggle between the doctor and the patient, between intellect and instinctual life, between understanding and seeking to act, is played out almost exclusively in the phenomena of transference. It is on that field that the victory must be won—the victory whose expression is the permanent cure of the neurosis" (Freud 1912: 108).
18 Freud, 1914: 139.
19 Ibid.: 154.
20 Freud, 1915 (1914): 165.
21 "The doctor tries to compel him to fit these emotional impulses into the nexus of the treatment and of his life-history, to submit them to intellectual consideration and to understand them in the light of their psychical value" (Freud, 1912: 108).
22 Freud, 1905 (1901): 117.
23 Ibid.
24 Freud, 1912: 105.
25 Freud, 1917 (1916–1917): 445.
26 Ibid.: 446.
27 Ibid.: 444.
28 Freud, 1917 (1916–1917): 444.
29 Freud, 1912: 102.
30 Freud, 1917 (1916–1917): 444.
31 Freud, 1914: 154.
32 Freud, 1912: 108.

33 Freud, 1905 (1901): 117; Freud, 1917 (1916–1917): 440–442. Only in "Observations on Transference-Love," does Freud state that transference "is caused by the analytical situation." However, causing is not the same as creating. The conclusion would be that neurosis gives rise to transference, which the analyst then "causes" or "baits."
34 Lacan, 1973–1974: lecture on June 11, 1974.
35 "The doctor does not play any role in its production; even if the patient holds on to real details, the origin of transference is in the neurotic process" (Lagache, 1953/1975: 16). "Regarding nature and identity, then, Freud is clear and definitive and will hold the same opinion throughout his work: transference is the same during analysis and outside of it—it must not be attributed to the doctor but to the illness, the neurosis" (Etchegoyen, 1986/2014: 115).
36 Cf. Lagache, 1953/1975.
37 "It is an error in the method, whose explanation must be searched for in the particular relationship between the patient and their psychotherapist, which is why it is external, extrinsic and *not inherent to the material*" (Etchegoyen, 1986/2014: 106).
38 Lacan, 1962–1963: 50.
39 Freud, 1905 (1901): 74.
40 Cf. Lagache, 1953/1975: 56–58.
41 Etchegoyen, 1986/2014: 125.
42 Cf. ibid.: 52–55.
43 Lacan, 1953–1954/1991: 274.
44 Lagache, 1953/1975: 80.
45 Cf. ibid.: 56–58.
46 Lagache, 1953/1975: 82.
47 Lacan, 1960–1961: 103: lecture on January 11, 1961.
48 Lacan, 1964/1981: 133.
49 Lacan, 1951: 93.
50 Cf. Lacan, 1954–1955: 155–160.
51 Lacan, 1964/1981: 146.
52 Lacan, 1951: 93.
53 Ibid.: 102 (all quotes in this paragraph).
54 Lacan, 1953–1954/1991: 108.
55 Ibid.: 48–50.
56 Ibid.: 107.
57 "Nothing is to be feared more than saying something that might be true. For it would become entirely true if it were said, and Lord knows what happens when something can no longer be cast into doubt because it is true" (Lacan, 1958: 515).
58 Lacan, 1953–1954/1991: 40.
59 Ibid.: 39.
60 Ibid.: 40.
61 Ibid.: 51.
62 Ibid.: 50.
63 Ibid.: 42.
64 Ibid.: 112.
65 Ibid.: 107.
66 Ibid.: 243.
67 Cf. ibid.: 261.
68 Ibid.: 278.
69 Ibid.: 109.
70 This is a question I am always reminded of by Tomás Pal.
71 Ibid.: 243.
72 Ibid.: 282–283.

73 Ibid.: 286.
74 Lacan, 1967.
75 Lacan, 1958: 489.
76 Lacan, 1960–1961: 145.
77 Racker, 1959/1981: 31.
78 Lacan, 1960–1961: lecture on November 16, 1960.
79 Ibid.: lecture on November 23, 1960.
80 Ibid.: lecture on January 11, 1961.
81 Ibid.
82 Ibid.: lecture on December 14, 1960.
83 Ibid.
84 Ibid.: lecture on March 8, 1961.
85 Ibid.
86 Ibid.: lecture on February 1, 1961.
87 Ibid.: lecture on March 1, 1961.
88 Cf. ibid.: lecture on November 16, 1960.
89 Ibid.: lecture on February 8, 1961.
90 Ibid.

References

Etchegoyen, H.R. (2014). *Los fundamentos de la técnica psicoanalítica*. Buenos Aires: Amorrortu. (Original work published 1986)

Freud, S. (1893–1895). The Psychotherapy of Hysteria. In S. Freud, A. Freud, A. Strachey, and A. Tyson (Eds.), *The Standard Edition of the Complete Psychological Works of Sigmund Freud, Volume II: Studies on Hysteria*. Trans. J. Strachey, pp. 253–306. London: The Hogarth Press.

Freud, S. (1905 [1901]). Fragment of an Analysis of a Case of Hysteria. In S. Freud, A. Freud, A. Strachey, and A. Tyson (Eds.), *The Standard Edition of the Complete Psychological Works of Sigmund Freud. Volume VII: A Case of Hysteria, Three Essays on Sexuality and Other Works*. Trans. J. Strachey, pp. 15–124. London: The Hogarth Press.

Freud, S. (1912). The Dynamics of Transference. In S. Freud, A. Freud, A. Strachey, and A. Tyson (Eds.), *The Standard Edition of the Complete Works of Sigmund Freud, Volume XII: The Case of Schreber, Papers on Technique, and Other Works*. Trans. J. Strachey, pp. 109–120. London: The Hogarth Press.

Freud, S. (1914). Remembering, Repeating and Working-Through (Further Recommendations on the Technique of Psycho-Analysis II). In S. Freud, A. Freud, A. Strachey, and A. Tyson (Eds.), *The Standard Edition of the Complete Psychological Works of Sigmund Freud, Volume XII: The Case of Schreber, Papers on Technique and Other Work*. Trans. J. Strachey, pp. 145–156. London: The Hogarth Press.

Freud, S. (1915 [1914]). Observations on Transference-Love (Further Recommendations on the Technique of Psycho-Analysis III). In S. Freud, A. Freud, A. Strachey, and A. Tyson (Eds.), *The Standard Edition of the Complete Works of Sigmund Freud, Volume XII: The Case of Schreber, Papers on Technique, and Other Works*. Trans. J. Strachey, pp. 157–171. London: The Hogarth Press.

Freud, S. (1917 [1916–1917]). Transference. In S. Freud, A. Freud, A. Strachey, and A. Tyson (Eds.), *The Standard Edition of the Complete Psychological Works of*

Sigmund Freud, Volume XVI: Introductory Lectures on Psycho-Analysis (Part III). Trans. J. Strachey, pp. 431–447. London: The Hogarth Press.

Kristeva, J. (1983). *Tales of Love*. Trans. L.S. Roudiez. New York: Columbia University Press.

Lacan, J. (1951). Intervention on Transference. In C. Bernheimer and C. Kahane (Eds.), *In Dora's Case Freud-Hysteria-Feminism*, pp. 92–104. New York and Chichester: Columbia University Press.

Lacan, J. (1954–1955). *The Seminar of Jacques Lacan, Book II: The Ego in Freud's Theory and in the Technique of Psychoanalysis*. Ed. J.-A. Miller. Trans. S. Tomaselli. New York and London: W.W. Norton.

Lacan, J. (1958). The Direction of the Treatment and the Principles of its Power. In J. Lacan, *Écrits: The First Complete Edition in English*. Trans. B. Fink, pp. 489–542. New York and London: W.W. Norton.

Lacan, J. (1960–1961). *The Seminar of Jacques Lacan, Book VIII: Transference*. Ed. J.-A. Miller. Trans. B. Fink. Cambridge: Polity Press.

Lacan, J. (1962–1963). The Seminar of Jacques Lacan, Book X: Anxiety, 1962–1963. Trans. C. Gallagher. Unpublished. Retrieved from http://hdl.handle.net/10788/160

Lacan, J. (1967). Première version de la " Proposition du 9 octobre ". Trans. A. Chadwick. Retrieved February 24, 2024, from www.freud2lacan.com/lacan/:https://freud2lacan.b-cdn.net/PROPOSITION-bilingual.FINAL.pdf

Lacan, J. (1973–1974). The Seminar of Jacques Lacan. Book XXI: Les Non Dupes Errent Part 1: 1973–1974. Trans. C. Gallagher. Unpublished. Retrieved from http://hdl.handle.net/10788/171

Lacan, J. (1981). *The Seminar of Jacques Lacan, Book XI: The Four Fundamental Concepts of Psychoanalysis*. Ed. J.-A. Miller. Trans. A. Sheridan. New York and London: W.W. Norton. (Original work published 1964)

Lacan, J. (1991). *The Seminar of Jacques Lacan, Book I: Freud's Papers on Technique*. Ed. J.-A. Miller. Trans. J. Forrester. New York and London: W.W. Norton. (Original work published 1953–1954)

Lagache, D. (1975). *La teoría de la transferencia*. Buenos Aires: Nueva Visión. (Original work published in French 1953)

Racker, H. (1981). *Estudios sobre técnica psicoanalítica*. Buenos Aires: Paidós. (Original work published 1959)

Chapter 6

Causing
The Analyst's Desire

Neutrality

The question of the role of the analyst's subjectivity in the treatment remained unexplored until the fifties. While it is true that there are some notable exceptions, such as Ferenczi's "active technique" or Reik's "third ear," the question was not completely articulated simply because there was already an answer most agreed on: analysts must be neutral.

Neutrality is one of the few technical recommendations limiting the analyst's attitude; there are not many others. The principle is clear: we must be *neutral* with respect to ethical and aesthetic values when carrying out the treatment. A psychoanalyst must guide the treatment but never the analysand: "[w]e refused most emphatically to turn a patient who puts himself into our hands in search of help into our private property, to decide his fate for him, to force our own ideals upon him."[1] Neutrality mitigates any pedagogical (or therapeutic!) desire on the analyst's part that could get in the way of the treatment. This idea does not usually provoke much controversy—psychoanalysis is not a practice of suggestion or coaching. We do not tell patients how they should act in their lives; we do not even tell them what to talk about during the session. We only ask them to follow the rules of the game. The analyst must follow the model of the surgeon, "who puts aside all his feelings, even his human sympathy, and concentrates his mental forces on the single aim of performing the operation as skillfully as possible."[2] We must silence all emotions, not only because they might compromise our reason or our clinical judgment, but also because they convey ideals, which we must be careful not to impose. Ideals are not merely "thought constructions." For the analyst, they might appear as anger, joy, tenderness, disgust, compassion, powerlessness, or something else.

In a broad sense, neutrality might be summarized as the *analyst having to get rid of any trace of subjectivity in analysis*. But what does this mean? What constitutes the analyst's subjectivity? Her ideals, her gestures, her office, her clothes, her hair, her slips, her dreams? The neutrality principle, like other relevant concepts, has a much wider scope than Freud intended. You never

DOI: 10.4324/9781032696423-6

know how far an idea can go. Etchegoyen, for instance, said in an interview that he refrained from placing a picture of Gardel in his office because he did not want to send an "impertinent message" to his patients.[3] The idea that the analyst might pollute the analysand with her own ideology reached unanticipated limits.

This particular nuance of neutrality is one of the origins of the analyst's silence. We analysts decided that, faced with the possibility of infecting the "object" of our practice with our subjectivity, we should remain silent. So ... shh! Unfortunately, we were the only ones who did not realize that not speaking, laughing, or being alarmed indicated not neutrality but hostility and ignorance. The figure of the silent and unfriendly Lacanian analyst is curious if we consider that Lacan openly said that it was a mistake for analysts to speak very little. In the same vein, Blanton wrote in his diary of analysis that Freud was simple, warm, and highly sensitive in the face of his patients' suffering, without any harsh or exaggerated countenance.[4]

On the other hand, isn't the choice to remain neutral a part of subjectivity? If transference is the enactment of the sexual reality of the unconscious, it can hardly be maintained that we are neutral. The analyst is the one who must apply the "hypothesis of neutrality" to its ultimate consequences; it is he who defends a lost cause.[5]

The difficulties associated with analytic neutrality are deeply rooted in the epistemological foundation that supports this technical indication. Neutrality, let us remember, is a key concept of "classic epistemology," or, as Lacan called it, theory of knowledge. From this perspective, which Freud explicitly maintained—despite the various texts in which he contradicted it—the foundation of science is observation. The only way to know the world is through intellectual elaboration of carefully verified observations. For Freud, science can know reality in the same way all human beings do: by first making unprejudiced observations of empirical facts and then thinking and theorizing about them. From this perspective truth is the correlation between statements of observation and reality.[6] All in all, if I consider that access to reality depends on unprejudiced observation, my position as an agent of knowledge must be neutral. I cannot know reality *as it is* if I pollute it with my ideas, prejudices, and opinions. In the case of psychoanalysis, the reality that must be known, that must not be "infected" with our subjectivity is the patient's unconscious. It is clear that, in order to do that, the analyst must "purify" her own unconscious. Here we see the possible conditions for what would later become the psychologization of psychoanalysis, the objectification of the subject.

Let us take dreaming as an example. According to Freud, dreaming is exclusively proof of the dreamer's unconscious (just like a slip, a joke, or an instance of forgetting), so the idea that one person's dream may indicate something about another person's unconscious was proof of superstition. In contrast, according to Lacan, the unconscious is realized in the place of the Other, and the Other is not within anyone. There is an interesting example in

"The Direction of the Treatment and the Principles of its Power" where Lacan relates the case of a patient who was cured of his symptom of sexual impotence after his wife told him a personal dream. Here, a person's unconscious is realized in another's dream. This means that, among other things, the unconscious is the discourse of the Other. From the Freudian perspective, my unconscious can only manifest itself in a personal act—whether discursive or not—and anything that might occur within another person will be a chance event for me and, at most, an unconscious phenomenon for them. In other words, for Freud, a person's unconscious can only come from his own body.

The clinical consequences of putting this hypothesis into practice are clear. One of them is the curious obsession with fidelity to the word, with what the analysand "actually said." But reading closely is not the same as transcribing. Analytic reading is much closer to editing than transcription. That the analyst pays with his person, with his words, and with the heart of his being means that he participates just as the analysand does in the constitution of the unconscious.[7] That is why it is weak in its ontological dimension. The status of the unconscious is ethical because its realization depends on certain positions being occupied during analysis.[8]

This leads us to question the limits of what can be considered "clinical material." For instance, if an analyst dreams of one of her patients, can this be presented in supervision as part of the clinical material or is best left for the analyst's analysis? Can a slip made by the analyst during supervision be useful material for the case? What if the slip happens in the middle of the session? Unless we conceive of the unconscious as an objective reality existing by itself, external to the analyst and internal to the analysand, all of these occurrences might be considered material for that analysis. The conditional merely reveals that any element of the text is potentially important. It depends on the other elements in the text and on how they are read.

Neutrality loses conceptual strength when analysts admit—as we should— that we are not purified, no matter how much time we have spent on the couch. In each case we carry out, we inevitably put our subjectivities—our ideals, fantasies, symptoms, and so on—into play. Problems arise when we are not aware that this is happening, when we believe ourselves to be purified, free of conflict, outside the transference, out of the picture, beyond all fiction. In any case, we analysts are the ones who must be able to read where the analysis itself (and not the analysand) takes us. An analyst might read that an analysand puts him in the place of his father, and the analysand might hold that it is the analyst who is putting him in the place of the son. The situation is indiscernible. The key question is not who assigns the places, but what places are occupied. Freud was keenly aware of this problem. When he was asked, near the end of his life, what he had been like as an analyst, he answered: "I have a series of handicaps which prevent me from being a great psychoanalyst. Among other things, I am too much of a father."[9] The father of psychoanalysis said he had been too much of a father! Are we not *too much* Freud's children?

Since analysts are not purified, the transformation of the ethical position that enables the appearance of the unconscious must happen every time. Personal analysis does not guarantee it. A person in a "neutral" position could never give rise to the analytic device. It is not a question of neutrality but of desire. The psychoanalyst is characterized by being the practitioner of a science that wonders about the place of his own desire in the field that determines his *praxis*:

> What is it that makes us say at once that, despite the dazzling character of the stories he recounts from ages past, alchemy, when all is said and done, is not a science? Something, in my view, is decisive, namely, that the purity of soul of the operator was, as such, and in a specific way, an essential element in the matter. This remark is not beside the point, as you may realize, since we may be about to raise something similar concerning the presence of the analyst in the analytic Great Work, and to maintain that it is perhaps what our training analysis seeks. I may even seem to have been saying the same thing myself in my teaching recently, when I point straight out, all veils torn aside, and in a quite overt way, towards that central point that I put in question, namely—what is the analyst's desire? What must there be in the analyst's desire for it to operate in a correct way? Can this question be left outside the limits of our field?[10]

Alchemists, unlike chemists, had to undergo spiritual transmutation in order to transform metals. They had to purify themselves, to convert themselves. What kind of transformation must the analyst undergo? Must she purify her unconscious? What is the analyst's desire, and how does it operate? Lacan proposed the analyst's desire as an alternative to both neutrality and the ideal of "purification." It is a direct criticism of epistemological, ethical, and technical objectivity, and of the naïve subjectivism of some psychoanalysts. Moreover, the analyst's desire is not a characteristic that is acquired at the end of analysis; it is not something we have or use. People do not emerge from an analysis with the "desire of the analyst." If that were the case, we wouldn't have had to wait for Lacan—who did not finish his own analysis, if he ever started it—to propose it as the key to the analytic position. It is a function an analyst can perform based on certain theoretical and clinical coordinates regarding the position assumed with respect to desire.

In *The Hermeneutics of the Subject*, Foucault held that modern science and Cartesian *cogito* reinforced a characteristic in the access to the truth that had been slowly gaining ground in Western history: the subject will no longer need to transform itself to access truth. Psychoanalysis, on the other hand, would remain linked to the ancient practices of "care of the self" insofar as both analyst and analysand must transform themselves as a necessary condition for truth's revelation. This very difference characterizes that between alchemy— which can only be practiced after the agent's spiritual transmutation—and chemistry—where access to knowledge does not depend at all on an *ethical* transformation of the subject. This is why science presents itself as "neutral," beyond ethical or ideological criteria. The scientist's subjectivity, her "personal" drama, the truth which marks and determines her are irrelevant to the access to knowledge, which is universal and equal for all.

> [T]o have access to the truth is to have access to being itself, access which is such that the being to which one has access will, at the same time, and as an aftereffect, be the agent of transformation of the one who has access to it [...] it is quite clear that the Cartesian type of knowledge cannot be defined as access to the truth, but is knowledge (*connaissance*) of a domain of objects. So, if you like, the notion of knowledge of the object is substituted for the notion of access to the truth.[11]

The analyst's neutrality and the analyst's desire are two ethical concepts that correspond to different epistemologies. In Foucauldian terms, neutrality corresponds to the problem of knowledge of the object, the analyst's desire to the problem of access to truth. My idea is that in the question of the analyst's desire lies the key to analytic treatment: what must the analyst's ethical position be in order to enable the analysand's unconscious desire?

Countertransference

In the fifties, analytic neutrality entered into crisis for a considerable period until it was rescued, unluckily for Lacanianism. The reasons for this crisis can be explained by a single concept: countertransference. As I said, Freud never inquired about the analyst's transference; he mentioned countertransference in passing as "a result of the patient's influence on [the analyst's] unconscious feelings."[12] The analyst does not transfer, he reacts with his unconscious to the patient's transference. However, this reaction might cloud the analyst's judgment and cause him to dispense with objectivity. Countertransference was understood, then, as an obstacle to the development of the treatment, and so efforts were made "to reduce manifestations of counter-transference as far as possible by means of personal analysis so that the analytic situation may ideally be structured exclusively by the patient's transference."[13] In order to be neutral, to reflect only what was shown to him, the analyst had to rid himself of countertransference.

Everything changed when, following Freud's indication that "everyone possesses in his own unconscious an instrument with which he can interpret the utterances of the unconscious in other people," some analysts posited that countertransference could be a highly valuable tool, crucial for understanding a case.[14] The logic here is clear: if countertransference is a reaction to transference, it is a *creation* not of the analyst but of the patient and so it must be interpreted as any other unconscious formation.

Two figures stand out at this important moment in the history of psychoanalysis: Paula Heimann, in London, and Heinrich Racker, in Buenos Aires. Though they worked at great geographical distance from each other, both psychoanalysts put countertransference at the forefront of international psychoanalytic debate. In "On Counter-Transference," Heimann begins by criticizing a misreading of the Freudian notion of neutrality, recovering the figures of Ferenczi and Balint who had acknowledged, more or less fairly, the analyst's emotions and her participation in the treatment. "My thesis," Heimann states, "is that the analyst's emotional response to his patient within the analytic situation represents one of the most important tools for his work. *The analyst's counter-transference is an instrument of research into the patient's unconscious.*"[15] Heimann's idea is that the feelings roused by free association provide the analyst with "a most valuable means of checking whether he has understood or failed to understand his patient." The analyst's unconscious "understands" the patient's unconscious. When the analyst—that is, his ego—*does not understand* the case, countertransference serves as a compass because the analyst's feelings are "closer" than his intellectual reasoning to the pathogenic nucleus. The analyst's unconscious perception of the patient's unconscious—through feelings—is "more acute and in advance of his conscious conception of the situation"—through reason. The *immediate* emotional response to the patient's associations, as Heimann states, is a significant indicator of the patient's unconscious: "it helps the analyst to focus his attention on the most urgent elements in the patient's associations and serves as a useful criterion for the selection of interpretations from material."

It is worth asking here why feelings would be connected to the unconscious and reason to consciousness. Once again, there appears the idea that the analyst must not think. I do not think that there are obvious reasons to suppose that feelings are closer to truth than reason. There are even fewer reasons to think that my feelings are telling the truth about another person. In fact, as I mentioned above, the analyst's emotions, the type that must be silenced, can be the roaring of personal ideals. On the other hand, assuming we support Heimann's thesis, why would the analyst's feelings grant access to the truth of the patient's unconscious and not the other way around? This is, of course, because the analyst's unconscious is transformed into a machine that reads through feelings. Not surprisingly, what transforms the unconscious is the analyst's didactic analysis:

> when the analyst in his own analysis has worked on his infantile conflicts and anxieties (paranoid and depressive), so that he can easily establish contact with his own unconscious, he will not impute to his patient what belongs to himself.

Lastly and most crucially, Heimann believes that the analyst must not communicate these feelings to the patient: "[i]n my view, such honesty is more in the nature of a confession and a burden to the patient." Feelings, then, are used but not disclosed. This difference is close to the one I draw between reading and writing. The caveat is that something might be said and not written, and something might be written even if it is not explicitly said. For the time being, the crucial thing is that the analyst's feelings, according to Heimann, are *key* elements of reading, just as any other formation of the unconscious.

The thesis is clear: if the analyst works *enough* on his conflicts in his personal analysis, his unconscious will become an instrument that allows him to distinguish which of his *immediate* feelings can be attributed to the patient's transference and which cannot, and, therefore, which can be elements for reading and which cannot. The concern centers on the scope of the analyst's personal analysis.

Racker, whom I mentioned above in connection to empathy, also finds in countertransference "a technical instrument of great importance since it is *mostly* an emotional response to transference and can, as such, indicate to the analyst what is happening to the analysand in their relationship with the analyst."[16] The model is that of the unconscious as a receiving organ and, consequently, as an instrument of interpretation. Racker holds that, in evenly suspended attention, analysts also surrender to free association: "they create an internal situation where they are willing to admit in their consciousness all possible thoughts and feelings." In this way, "thoughts and feelings arising in them will be those which have not appeared in the analysand, that is what is repressed and unconscious." To do this, the analyst must split her ego in two: the irrational and the rational. The irrational ego surrenders to free listening to "receive" the analysand's transference through the associations. The rational ego, meanwhile, observes and analyzes these receptions. And so, suddenly, the analyst's desire appears:

> where [the analyst] *desires*, for instance, that the patient behave in a certain way, *knowing* that the patient should do so, but does not, it is possible to often see that the analyst's knowledge and ambition are, in the end, also the analysand's, but in a repressed or dissociated way, and unconsciously originated and placed in the analyst.[17]

What the analyst desires in connection with what the patient should do, externalized as involuntary thoughts and feeling, seems to originate in the analyst, but in truth it is deposited "from the outside" by the analysand. In this sense, the analyst's desires constitute the most important knowledge of the patient's unconscious complexes. It is not necessary for the analyst to disclose them; the patient "senses" the analyst's desires through her interpretations, voice, attitudes, and even through "telepathic perceptions."[18] To me, this last idea seems important in thinking about the analyst's position.

That countertransference is *mostly* a response to the patient's transference means that part of it comes from a different source. From each countertransferential response we need to "subtract [...] the personal factor."[19] Not all the things the analyst feels or thinks spontaneously are responses to the patient's projections. There is also the analyst's neurosis. Countertransference may "help, hinder or falsify"[20] the interpretation of the analysand's unconscious. The key difference from the analysand, and what allows for the use of the unconscious as an instrument for interpretation, is that the analyst has already been analyzed. In this way, analysts can "open themselves in their sensibility and psychological intuition when faced with the analysand's material; in identifying themselves with the patient, they must turn their unconscious into a resonance body for the patient's unconscious."[21] Analysis allows the analyst to internally split to achieve "true objectivity"— that is, the ability to take oneself (one's own subjectivity or counter-transference) as an object of continuous observation and analysis.[22]

There are two issues worth noting in Racker's hypothesis: first, the criticism of the "myth of the analytic situation."[23] An analysis is not the meeting of a sick person—the analysand—and a healthy one—the analyst. The analyst can induce or inject his own neurosis into the patient. Transference neurosis could be the analyst's neurosis. The analyst's desires come from both the analysand's and the analyst's neuroses. If the analyst is not well enough aware, she might intervene from her own unanalyzed neurotic complexes. Be that as it may, personal analysis can give analysts the ability to read "their own personal disposition towards making specific mistakes coming from their own neurosis."[24] Second, Racker supposes that transference and countertransference are two elements of the same phenomenon that keep each other going and create the analytic interpersonal relationship. Countertransference is the answer to the patient's transference, and, at the same time, the patient's transference is a response to the analyst's countertransference. Overall, transference has "two points of origin," with the crucial difference that one of them is capable of splitting so as to read the situation objectively. Personal analysis is the most decisive. We can surely rebuke Racker for his excessive trust in countertransferential ideas, but we cannot omit his insistence on bringing to the fore two topics which had been generally repressed in the psychoanalytic movement: the analyst's desire and the analyst's neurosis.

Today, the technique proposed by Heimann and Racker might seem somewhat extravagant. Who would dare believe these days that our spontaneous, emotional, or imaginative ideas are any indication of truth? But is it not the case that something very similar is said when it is asserted that, at the moment of the act, the analyst does not think? I am under the impression that, no matter how theoretically strange we find them, these practices are commonplace. It is fairly common to hear in the Lacanian field that a diagnosis of perversion is made based on the anxiety the analyst feels in response to the analysand's associations. This question is difficult to resolve because there is no measure to calculate the appropriate amount of sensitivity to what is heard. There are sensitive analysts who become distressed by stories that colder and more detached analysts would receive like water off a duck's back. We must also say that Lacan's theory of anxiety does not refer to an "emotional state" but to precise clinical coordinates connected to the presence of the desire of the Other. Moreover, the appeal to the analyst's sensitivity as a guiding indicator for diagnosis is not limited to perversion. Some colleagues believe that they can reach a diagnosis in cases of psychosis or borderline personalities based on the feelings their patients provoke in them. "You feel borderline personalities in your gut," I was once told. Those who do not properly chew their ideas might get indigestion!

A Stronger Desire

On March 8, 1961, Lacan taught a memorable class commonly known as "A Critique of Countertransference." It is worth studying it slowly. First, he gives a brief summary of the concept to arrive at this idea: it is very common among psychoanalysts to rely on the communication of the unconscious to obtain "decisive insights."[25] For this reason, unanalyzed complexes, the blind spots of the unconscious, are decisive for the position and actions of the analyst. There is something very contemporary in this basic conjecture. Setting aside some notions that now seem strange to us—communication between unconscious minds, insight, and so on—the idea remains similar. Many analysts affirm that they do not intervene based on their clinical experience, their theoretical knowledge, or their ability to read the cases, but that they do so based on what their own experience as analysands enables: holding a position in which they could *act without thinking*, as if some part of their subjectivity guided the treatment, beyond their ability to reflect.

However, Lacan continues, how far does the purification of the unconscious go in a didactic analysis? What are the limits of this emptying? The goal of analysis evidently does not coincide with the goal of the unconscious. Not everything can be analyzed. In this sense, "to take things as far as they can go, one might theorize a reserve unconscious," which someone shaped by the experience of training analysis could use as "an instrument, like the shell of a violin whose strings he also possesses." This would not be a raw unconscious, but rather "an unconscious plus experience of that unconscious." However, there are two major problems here. First, what is the turning point from which this qualification is gained? What transformation must someone go through so as to be "close" to her unconscious? Second, and most important for my point, how can anyone access their reserve unconscious, no matter how analyzed they are? The unconscious is defined by being inaccessible to the conscious mind. "It is not the case that it is accessible to men of goodwill—it is not," Lacan says, ironically. What led analysts to think that they had the sole ability to access the unconscious? But Freud did it! Did he not reach his unconscious by analyzing his own dreams? Lacan's idea is different:

It is under strictly limited conditions that one can reach it, through a detour, the detour via the Other, and this makes analysis necessary and infrangibly eliminates the possibility of self-analysis. How can we situate the point of transition by which what is thus defined [as inaccessible] can nevertheless be used as a source of information included in a directive praxis? [...] To you who at least have the keys, something immediately makes the point of access recognizable, which is that there is a logical priority in what you hear—namely, that it is first of all in the form of the Other's unconscious that all experience of the unconscious is gained. It was through his patients that Freud first encountered the unconscious. And for each of us, even if this fact is elided, it is first of all as the Other's unconscious that the idea presents itself that such a thing might exist.

The psychoanalyst neither discovers nor creates the unconscious, but rather realizes it by enabling the dimension of the Other. This is what I have been pointing out from the beginning: psychoanalysis is an exchange of words where at least two people occupy previously calculated places in order to give rise to the unconscious. We never know what will be said, or how, or when; the signifiers leading the cases and the value they acquire in each one are enigmas. However, we know *from where* we must speak so that there can be a proper analysis. Analytic listening presupposes the Other as logical priority, and the unconscious is always experienced as the discourse of the Other. As Lacan reminds us, Freud discovered this not in his dream but in his patients' speech.[26] Before the analyst and the analysand—both with their respective "unconscious" and transference—there is the Other establishing the transferential positions and opening the dimension of the unconscious as "transindividual" existence.[27] The origin is neither the analysand nor the analyst, but the Other. In the end, the unconscious is not a more or less empty reservoir of thoughts and feelings, and so we cannot count on it as a source or interpretations. The analyst makes interventions *from* the unconscious and not *with* his unconscious. What needs emptying, then?

Once we recognize the function of the Other, according to Lacan, the true problem for the analyst is not a lack of access to her unconscious but

> the same obstacle we encounter in ourselves in our own analysis when the unconscious is involved. [...] the positive power of misrecognition in the illusions of the ego, in the widest sense of the term—that is, in imaginary capture.

Intervening *with* the unconscious, based on spontaneous feelings as some post-Freudian (and also Lacanian) psychoanalysts understood it, means jumping with both feet into the imaginary dimension of analysis. Let us imagine a situation where the analyst is bored during a session because the analysand is saying uninteresting things. Ferenczi, for instance, explains the numbness he felt with some of his patients "as an unconscious reaction in the face of the vacuity and uselessness of the associations manifested by the retraction of conscious excitement."[28] What a time it was when we could justify taking a nap by "metapsychologically" blaming the patients! In the example of the bored analyst, the analysand could reasonably argue that she said uninteresting things because the analyst did not seem to pay attention, and the analyst might argue back that he was not paying attention because the analysand's associations were not interesting, and so on.

Relationships between peers, with the little others, like our analysands, cannot be fully explained by the efficacy of the unconscious, which is why recognizing the unconscious does not free the analyst from passions. In fact, Lacan said:

> the better the analyst is analyzed, the more it will be possible for him to be frankly in love with—or frankly averse to or repulsed by—his partner, according to the most elementary modes of relations between bodies.

The final result of an analysis is that we know better what we like and what we do not like, what we love and what we hate, what we are attracted to and what repels us. So, it is not strange that we become passionate about our analysands. Analytic *apathy* is explained not by an absence of passions but by the fact that the analyst is "possessed by a stronger desire [...] insofar as a change has occurred in the economy of his desire." That the analyst occupies the place of the dummy (as in the game of bridge) does not imply that the analyst must keep her mouth shut, or have expressions on her face, or have feelings, and so on; it means that, "the analyst must always know which cards were dealt to whom." The analyst is the one who shows her cards so the analysand can play.

If the "point of origin" lies neither in the analyst nor in the analysand, but in the Other, then transference is

> a phenomenon in which subject and psycho-analyst are both included. To divide it in terms of transference and counter-transference—however bold, however confident what is said on this theme may be—is never more than a way of avoiding the essence of the matter.[29]

From this point of view, countertransference is more than "the analyst's necessary involvement in the transferential situation."[30] It is a legitimate effect of any analysis. The analyst is "taken" by the analysis because, depending on the place she occupies, she is the one supposed to have the analysand's object of desire. And where desire is put into play, passions emerge.

The Analyst's Neurosis

In the history of psychoanalysis, it is remarkable how little consideration was given to what the analyst could "transfer" to the patient—in other words, how transference neurosis could be determined by the analyst's neurosis. Curiously, it was through a difficulty of this nature that "Freud sees the entrance into the unconscious."[31] I am referring to the "Viennese soap opera" starring Josef Breuer and Bertha Pappenheim, better known as Anna O. The treatment started in December 1880 and ended in June 1882. Bertha was a 21-year-old woman who presented a series of very diverse symptoms: paralysis and muscle cramps, disturbances in vision and speech, disordered eating, a nervous cough, and a notable split in her personality. Doctor and patient met daily, morning and afternoon, and she told him of her daily dramas while also elaborating the history of each of her ailments. In this way, the symptoms subsided, one by one, with some occasional relapses. In short, everything was on track in the talking cure. The more Bertha "provided signifiers, the more she chattered on, the better it went. [...] There was no trace, in all this, of the least embarrassing thing. Look again. No sexuality, either under the microscope or in the distance."[32] Sexuality eventually came into play, and the treatment was interrupted. The official story, coyly hidden in a footnote in *Studies on Hysteria*, says that "when the treatment had apparently reached a successful end, the patient suddenly made manifest to Breuer the presence of a strong unanalyzed positive transference of an unmistakably sexual nature."[33] Other versions maintain that the young doctor also "developed what we would now call a strong countertransference."[34] Records confirm it: sexuality would have snuck into the healing words Bertha and Breuer exchanged daily. As Jones tells it, after a long period of silence about her jealousy and bad mood, Breuer's wife began expressing her annoyance at the excessive interest her husband showed towards his patient.[35] Faced with a situation that he *did not know how to interpret* and that put his marriage at risk, Breuer decided to end the treatment and go to Venice with his wife the following day. Upon Breuer's announcement of the end of the treatment,

> The patient, who, in his opinion, had presented herself as an asexual being [...] was now feeling the pains of a false hysteric labor (pseudocyesis), the logical end to an imaginary pregnancy which had started and run its course, inadvertently, *in response* to Breuer's medical attention.[36]

What would this psychological pregnancy show? It is evidently one of Bertha's transferential symptoms. Lacan's interpretation is different:

> not without cause, there is a tendency to say quite simply that it was Bertha's fault. But I would beg you to suspend your thoughts on this matter for a moment—why is it that we do not consider Bertha's

pregnancy rather, according to my formula man's desire is the desire of the Other, as the manifestation of Breuer's desire? Why do you not go as far as to think that it was Breuer who had a desire for a child? I will give you the beginning of a proof; namely that Breuer, setting off for Italy with his wife, lost no time in giving her a child, [...] let us observe what Freud says to Breuer—What! The transference is the spontaneity of the said Bertha's unconscious. It's not yours, not your desire, it's the desire of the Other. I think Freud treats Breuer as a hysteric here, since he says to him: your desire is the desire of the Other. This brings us to the question of what Freud's desire decided, in diverting the whole apprehension of the transference in a direction that has now reached its final term of absurdity, to the point at which an analyst may say that the whole theory of the transference is merely a defense of the analyst. I swing this extreme term in another direction. Indeed, I show precisely the opposite side when I say that it is the desire of the analyst.[37]

Bertha interprets Breuer's desire and manifests it through a symptom. This does not mean that Breuer had declared his love for her or anything of the sort. In fact, if the interpretation is correct, and it seems it is, Breuer "did not want to know anything about it." Desire is articulated, but it is not articulable, it is not about what is actually said, but about what appears beyond what is "said without saying it," and that only becomes real through its interpretation. Desire is its interpretation.

To summarize, Lacan shows us the other side of countertransference when he argues that the question is not what the analysand's unconscious causes in the analyst and its consequent use as a clinical indicator, but rather what the analyst could provoke in the analysand through his desire; that is, what appears in the space between what is said and what is manifested beyond what is said. "It is not only a question of what the analyst wants to do with his patient in the matter. It is also a question of what his patient wants to do with him:"[38] the patient may want a stern father, a loving mother, or an understanding sibling, for example. Are these not roles that the analyst could play unwittingly? Could not the patient's symptom be an interpretation of the analyst's desire? The question of the analyst's desire is one that every analysand has: does my analyst want me to get divorced? Does he want me to study this or that at university? Does she want me to find another job? What does my analyst want from me? It is not that they want the analyst to like them; they believe that what the analyst thinks will accord with their desire. This is why it is so easy to fall into the trap: the analyst unknowingly places his own agalmatic object in the analysand. Transference is only the replacement *through some identification* of the fundamental problem of the link between our desire and the desire of the Other.[39] The analyst hides *in* the transference when she cannot read the effect of her desire. Dora's case is a clear example. Freud positions himself as the ideal in presenting to Dora an object worthy of desire (Freud's desire!): Mr. K. In this way, the inventor of psychoanalysis evades the transference by being placed in the role of the father. Then, he sparks the imaginary flame by interpreting a repressed erotic transference: "you do not know it, but you want to kiss me." As Lacan said, "transference neurosis is a neurosis of the analyst."[40]

Lastly, countertransference—the sum of the analyst's prejudices, passions, ignorances, and so on—must be cleared, but not so as to "purify" our unconscious as receivers of the analysand's unconscious, but to enable a place, in no way neutral, that would allow the unconscious to appear in its ethical state. There is no desire of the patient outside the encounter with the desire of the analyst. Desire is the desire of the Other.

The Proper Place

Lacan's canonical formula for desire is "man's desire is the desire of the Other." There are many readings of this statement. From an imaginary perspective, this means that we desire the object the other desires, but transference is not mere child's play. The question we must ask ourselves in order to have a stronger version of this formula concerns the genitive of the phrase. In principle, the question presents no major difficulties: in its subjective dimension, the formula would be "I desire what the Other desires" and, in its objective dimension, "I desire the Other." Which is Lacan's version? Ambiguity reigns on this point. In "The Subversion of the Subject," Lacan affirms that the determination of this formula is subjective, although it should not be understood that we desire what the Other desires, but rather that *we desire as Other*. This definition is key to understanding the notion of unconscious desire. Desiring as Other means that the problem of desire in psychoanalysis refers to the conditions of desire, not to the object of desire, but to the question of how and from where we desire, and to the question of what is desired.[41] What is crucial is that we desire as alterity, that there is nothing like "my own desire." How does the analyst's desire fit into this conceptualization of desire?

> Desire of the Other—this genitive is both subjective and objective. Desire in the place where the Other is [i.e., to desire as if one were the Other] in order to be in the Other's place—desire for some alterity. To fulfill the search for the objective—namely, for what this other [the patient] who seeks us out desires—we must lend ourselves here to the function of the subjective, so that in some way we may be able, for a while, to represent, not what people believe—and it would be derisive, good Lord, admit it, and so terribly simplistic too [to believe] that we could be the object aimed at by this desire—but rather the signifier. Which is both far less, but also far more. We must occupy the empty place where a signifier is summoned that can exist only by canceling out all the others, and that is the signifier Φ whose central position and condition in analytic practice I have been trying to demonstrate for you.[42]

This is a very precise clinical indication: the analyst must not occupy the place of the analysand's object of desire. She must not be the one to point out which this object is, either. She must surrender herself to a desiring function, occupying an empty space. The analysand demands a signifier that signifies him, an ideal that names him, an object to fill him. The analyst, on the other hand, gives back Φ, the sign of the missing signifier, the lack in the Other, the cause of desire.[43]

This is also found in Lacan's lecture of January 11, 1961, where he defines the position of the analyst as,

> the coordinates the analyst must be able to attain simply in order to occupy the place that is his, defined as the place he must offer up as vacant to the patient's desire in order for the latter to be realized as the Other's desire.[44]

In this way, we can understand why the genitive in the phrase "desire is the desire of the Other" is both subjective and objective.[45] The analyst embodies the subjective sense since he is the one who must surrender to the function of the "desire of the Other" in the subjective sense; that is, he is the one who should hold the place of the Other as one who desires in order to enable the subject to locate desire as alterity. On the other hand, for the analysand, the "desire of the Other" is taken, in principle, objectively. Only if the analyst maintains his desire as an empty space can the analysand's desire emerge as alterity.

Transference love is a logical consequence of the structure of the analytic device and not the result of neurotic frustrations. The analysand loves the analyst because the latter represents knowledge related to the analysand's own desire, and "to love is, essentially, to wish to be loved."[46] At the beginning of analysis, the analysand is forced to occupy the place of i(a), offering himself as an object worthy of love to the ideal of the Other, I(A), where the analyst is located. This does not imply that the analysand wants to please or be liked by the analyst. As Miller says, "To really love someone is to believe that by loving them you'll get to a truth about yourself. We love the one that harbors the response, or a response, to our question: 'who am I?'"[47] As I see it, this is the most important question regarding transference love, beyond any affection, sympathy, or admiration that a patient might feel towards the analyst. Now, how does the analyst come to fill that empty space? Lacan puts it as follows:

> through the impact whereby the subject experiences in this interval something that motivates him Other [*Autre chose*] than the meaning effects by which a discourse solicits him [...] he in fact encounters the Other's desire, before he can even call it desire, much less imagine its object.[48]

The analysand encounters the desire of the Other in the intervals of discourse, beyond the effects of meaning. Every communicative act can be divided into three parts: first, what was actually said, the concrete aspect of the communicative act, what we can call in this context the dimension of the signifier; second, what we understand of what is said, the dimension of meaning; lastly, the indelible residue that fills every communication with ambiguity: "I understand what you say, but what do you want to tell me with what you say?"[49]

Lovers are those who best express the anxiety concealed in every communicative act. Infatuation is the negative side of paranoia. Both the lover and the paranoid are fanatical interpreters, never ceasing to read between the lines. However, while the paranoid becomes ill from the persistent encounter with signs, the lover suffers from an endless search for an unambiguous message. The paranoid finds it everywhere; the lover never does. In contrast to paranoia, which never stops stumbling upon unequivocal signs, lovers inhabit the flight of meaning, they are pierced by the question: "what did you mean by that?"

Desire plays a part in love, but it is not directed at the loved object but at something illusory within it, the partial object, the object *a*: "the analysand says to his partner, to the analyst, what amounts to this—I love you, but, because inexplicably I love in you something more than you—the *objet petit a*—I mutilate you."[50] This is one reason why Socrates is, to Lacan, the paradigmatic example of the analyst's position. Alcibiades's demand goes beyond Socrates as an individual—the Silenus—because it points to the enigmatic object of desire that is "within him:" the agalma. It is an object with irreplaceable value, not an object of exchange; "it is outside any dialectic of beauty or any other social ideal."[51]

> By the sole fact of transference, the analyst is situated in the position of he who contains *agalma*, the fundamental object involved in the subject's analysis. [...] This is a legitimate effect of transference. There is no need to bring in countertransference, as if some aspect of the analyst himself were involved, and a faulty aspect to boot. But in order to recognize it, the analyst must know certain things. He must, in particular, know that his occupying the correct position is not contingent on the criterion that he understand or not understand. It is not absolutely essential that he understand. I would even say that, up to a certain point, his lack of comprehension can be preferable to an overly great confidence in his understanding. In other words, he must always call into question what he understands and remind himself that what he is trying to attain is precisely what in theory he does not understand. It is certainly only insofar as he knows what desire is, but does not know what the particular subject with whom he is engaged in the analytic adventure desires, that he is well situated to contain within himself the object of that desire.[52]

To occupy that empty place that allows for the appearance of something beyond the effects of meaning, it is crucial, in principle, that the analyst does not understand. Lacan's position is the inverse of that of the analysts of countertransference. The objective of these analyses was to reach the highest level of comprehension of the patient. Countertransference was the place to turn when misunderstanding dominated the scene, as if feelings were some kind of analytic compass. Lacan, on the other hand, postulates that the analyst must be ready to assume a position of complete incomprehension. This means that the analysand's speech must not be caught in any hermeneutic net, not even an Oedipal one. There is no way to interpret except by the logic of the text itself. This is why the analysis advances further and more smoothly as long as the analyst "does not know" how or what the analysand desires. The greatest difficulty we face is assuming a pendular position between acknowledged ignorance and provisional conjecture, knowing that we are a part of the text we must read. The analyst's double vision consists in that she must know and not know at the same time. The analyst knows a thing or two about desire, love, the unconscious, drive, and so on, but she does not know how these concepts work in each analysis, which signifiers command each case, and how they vary in correlation. In order to know about the case, to establish a conjecture that attempts to modify it, it is necessary to put the analyst's desire to work and give it time. The analyst knows how to conveniently maneuver when he is able to "notice the reach of the words for their analysand, what they undoubtedly ignore."[53] To that end, the analyst must suspend the imaginary effects of signification and maintain a maximum distance between I and *a*: the ideal—the object I want to be or have for the Other—and the cause—the condition of possibility for, and the matrix of, intelligible desire. The analyst must mourn the Good, in the sense that there is no object that, in principle, has more value than another. In other words, it is about embodying the support of a veiled desire: *Che Voui?*[54]

The Analyst's Tits

A good way to exemplify what we have studied up to this point is through "the fable of the Chinese restaurant," narrated by Lacan in Seminar XI. According to this tale, beginning psychoanalysis is like entering a Chinese restaurant for the first time. To begin with, you order from the menu, which is merely "signifiers, since we are concerned with speech only."[55] In analysis, we do nothing but talk; the point is that signifiers, when they are not immediately understood, have an enigmatic character, we do not know their meaning, and so they require an interpreter. We ask the restaurant owner to translate: "imperial pâté, spring rolls, etc. etc." But since it is our first time at a Chinese restaurant, the translation will likely mean nothing to us, so we ask the owner to recommend a dish, to give us advice. We ask, "can you tell me what I want?"

At this point, when you abdicate your choice to some divination of the patronne, whose importance you have exaggerated out of all proportion, would it not be more appropriate, if you felt like it, and if the opportunity presented itself, to tickle her tits a bit? For one goes to a Chinese restaurant not only to eat, but to eat in the dimensions of the exotic. [...] Well! Paradoxical, not to say free and easy, as this little apologue may seem, it is nevertheless precisely what is at issue in the reality of analysis. It is not enough that the analyst should support the function of Tiresias. He must also, as Apollinaire tells us, have breasts. I mean that the operation and manipulation of the transference are to be regulated in a way that maintains a distance between the point at which the subject sees himself as lovable—and that other point where the subject sees himself caused as a lack by a, and where a fills the gap constituted by the inaugural division of the subject.[56]

So, faced with the analysand's question about the object of his desire, the analyst does not respond from the position of the ideal. He shows his tits, he offers his veiled desire in order to reveal the drive object of the symptom. If we have learned anything from psychoanalysis, it is that, when someone "demands something, it is in no way identical to—and, sometimes, in full opposition with—what they desire."[57] An analysand can ask us to relieve her of her suffering, while simultaneously being "completely tied to the idea of keeping it."[58] It is important to remember that the satisfaction implied in the symptom does not mean a gain for the patient. However, the patient might be, as Lacan says, taken with the idea of preserving the illness. This means that the demand is not explicit: it must be interpreted. We need not respond to the demand, we know, but it is not a matter of rejecting it, either! As Eidelsztein says, "we must receive the demand for analysis as if we had what is valuable in ourselves, but putting into play the fact that, for the analyst, the value is somewhere else."[59] If, in hypnosis, the ideal signifier is confused with the object a, psychoanalysis is about obtaining the absolute difference between them. The analyst must produce the inversion from the place she is led to occupy—the ideal—to be at the maximum distance—in the place of a—embodying the hypnotized person before the brilliance of the analysand's words. Speak, everything you say will be interesting! Analytic reading, supported in the function of "the desire of the analyst," will reveal the place of the subject as cause of the Other's desire and the signifiers that secure it as the supposed object of the Other's enjoyment. This is the reason the analyst's desire once again links the demand with the drive, which had been set aside by the transference in its loving aspect.

In conclusion, if "the fundamental mechanism of analytic operation,"[60] driven by the analyst's desire, consists of maintaining the distance between I and a, it is for the following reasons:

1 The analyst must evacuate the place of the ideal where the analysis places him in order to offer himself as an object worthy of love and represent *a*, cause of desire, an empty place enabling the question of the conditions for desire.

2 The analyst does not indicate what the object of desire is but allows the question of the cause to surface. In other words, the analyst does not say what direction to take, but asks how it is desired.

3 The analyst's desire is the ethical position that enables the function of the between, the only possible place for the unconscious, drive, and desire to appear, respectively, as the discourse of the Other, the demand of the Other, and the desire of the Other.

The analyst's desire is a desire to "not desire," but it is not a neutral desire.[61] It is the desire to maintain maximum distance between the ideal—the signifying trap that turns the neurotic into an object of sacrifice for the Other—and the object *a*, cause of desire, what rescues us from symbolic petrification. Psychoanalysis is ethics and, as such, it requires a unique positioning in the history of therapeutic practices, a positioning informed by a technique. Its effectiveness depends on maintaining this desire to the furthest extent. "Only desire can read desire."[62]

Notes

1 Freud, 1919 (1918): 164.
2 Freud, 1912: 115. The idea that the analyst must be like a surgeon has always appealed to me, but not for the reasons stated by Freud. During analysis, we cut, we extract, we close, we fix, and we suture. And blood is spilled! An analyst's office is like an operating room: at the beginning, it is sterile, clean, and orderly but, in the end, there are stains and scars that mark the journey.
3 Cf. Vainer, 2008.
4 Cf. Blanton, 1971.
5 Cf. Lacan, 1964/1981.
6 Cf. Freud, 1933 (1932).
7 Cf. Lacan, 1958.
8 Cf. Lacan, 1964/1981.
9 Freud quoted by Tort (2014).
10 Lacan, 1964/1981: 9.
11 Foucault, 1981–1982: 191.
12 Freud, 1910: 144.
13 Laplanche and Pontalis, 1967: 93.
14 Freud, 1913: 320.
15 Heimann, 1950: n.p. All following quotes are from the same text, until otherwise noted.
16 All of the following quotes, until otherwise noted, are from Racker, 1959/1981: 32–34.
17 Racker, 1959/1981: 48.
18 Ibid.: 184.
19 Ibid.: 47.
20 Ibid.: 183.
21 Ibid.: 187.

22 Ibid.: 231.
23 Ibid.: 230.
24 Ibid.: 218.
25 Lacan, 1960–1961: lecture on March 8, 1961. All quotes in this section, except as otherwise noted, come from this lecture.
26 "My self-analysis is still interrupted; now I see why. I can only analyze myself with all the objectively acquired knowledge. [...] Since I still run into enigmas in my patients, this necessarily gets in the way of my self-analysis. I have gotten only one idea of universal value. In me [as in my patients], I have also found the infatuation with the mother and the jealousy towards the father, and now I consider it a universal event of early childhood" (Freud, as quoted by Gómez, 2018). I recommend this article by Leandro Gómez to study the problem of communication between unconsciouses.
27 Cf. Lacan, 1953.
28 Ferenczi, 1919/2009: 135.
29 Lacan, 1964/1981: 231.
30 Lacan, 1960–1961: lecture on March 15, 1961.
31 Lacan, 1964/1981: 157.
32 Ibid.
33 Freud, 1893–1895: 41.
34 Jones, 1953/1959: 235.
35 "In this story, there is another point we cannot disregard. In researching these years in Freud's life, Ernest Jones quotes an unpublished letter from Martha to Freud [...] after he told her the state of things; that is, he had heard through Breuer that something had happened between him and his patient: Martha immediately talks to Breuer's wife, hoping nothing similar would ever happen to her, *to which Freud answered by criticizing her vanity in assuming that other women could fall in love with 'her' husband. You would need to be Breuer for that, concluded Freud*?" (Maldonado, 2017).
36 Jones, 1953/1959: 235–236.
37 Lacan, 1964/1981: 157–158.
38 Ibid.: 159.
39 Cf. Lacan, 1964–1965: lecture on February 3, 1965.
40 Ibid.: 124
41 "For it is clear here that man's continued nescience of his desire is not so much nescience of what he demands, which may after all be isolated, as nescience of whence he desires" (Lacan, 1960b: 774).
42 Lacan, 1960–1961: lecture on May 3, 1961.
43 Ibid.
44 Lacan, 1960–1961: lecture on January 11, 1961.
45 Sauval, n.d.
46 Lacan, 1964/1981: 253.
47 Miller, 2011.
48 Lacan, 1960a: 715.
49 I took this idea from Eidelsztein.
50 Lacan, 1964/1981: 268.
51 Eidelsztein, 2006: 258.
52 Lacan, 1960–1961: lecture on March 8, 1961.
53 Cf. Lacan, 1977–1978: lecture on November 15, 1977.
54 Cf. Lacan, 1961–1962: lecture on May 9, 1962.
55 Lacan, 1964/1981: 269.
56 Ibid.: 269–270.

57 Lacan, 1966/2006: 91.
58 Ibid.
59 Eidelsztein, 2006: 270.
60 Ibid.: 281.
61 Ibid.: 281.
62 Guattari, 2013: 63.

References

Blanton, S. (1971). *Diary of My Analysis with Sigmund Freud*. New York: Hawthorn Books.

Eidelsztein, A. (2006). *La topología en la clínica psicoanalítica*. Buenos Aires: Letra Viva.

Ferenczi, S. (2009). Sobre la técnica del psicoanálisis. In S. Ferenczi, *Teoría y técnica del psicoanálisis*. Buenos Aires: Hormé. (Original work published 1919)

Foucault, M. (1981–1982). *The Hermeneutics of the Subject. Lectures at the Collège de France*. Eds. A. Fontana, F. Ewald, A.I. Davidson, and F. Gros. Trans. G. Burchell. New York: Palgrave Macmillan.

Freud, S. (1893–1895). The Psychotherapy of Hysteria. In S. Freud, A. Freud, A. Strachey, and A. Tyson (Eds.), *The Standard Edition of the Complete Psychological Works of Sigmund Freud, Volume II: Studies on Hysteria*. Trans. J. Strachey, pp. 253–306. London: The Hogarth Press.

Freud, S. (1910). The Future Prospects of Psycho-Analytic Therapy. In S. Freud, A. Freud, A. Strachey, and A. Tyson (Eds.), *The Standard Edition of the Complete Psychological Works of Sigmund Freud, Book XI: Five Lectures on Psycho-Analysis; Leonardo Da Vinci; and Other Works*. Trans. J. Strachey, pp. 139–152. London: The Hogarth Press.

Freud, S. (1912). Recommendations to Physicians Practising Psycho-Analysis. In S. Freud, A. Freud, A. Strachey, and A. Tyson (Eds.), *The Standard Edition of the Complete Psychological Works of Sigmund Freud, Volume XII: The Case of Schreber, Papers on Technique and Other Works*. Trans. J. Strachey. London: The Hogarth Press.

Freud, S. (1913). The Disposition to Obsessional Neurosis. A Contribution to the Problem of Choice of Neurosis. In S. Freud, A. Freud, A. Strachey, and A. Tyson (Eds.), *The Standard Edition of the Complete Psychological Works of Sigmund Freud, Volume XII: The Case of Schreber, Papers on Technique and Other Works*. Trans. J. Strachey, pp. 311–326. London: The Hogarth Press.

Freud, S. (1919 [1918]). Lines of Advance in Psycho-Analytic Therapy. In S. Freud, A. Freud, A. Strachey, and A. Tyson (Eds.), *The Standard Edition of the Complete Psychological Works of Sigmund Freud, Volume XVII: An Infantile Neurosis and Other Works*. Trans. J. Strachey, pp. 157–168. London: The Hogarth Press.

Freud, S. (1933 [1932]). *The Standard Edition of the Complete Psychological Works of Sigmund Freud, Volume XXII: New Introductory Lectures on Psycho-Analysis and Other Works*. Eds. A. Freud, A. Strachey, and A. Tyson. Trans. J. Strachey. London: The Hogarth Press.

Gómez, L.E. (2018). ¿Comunicación entre inconscientes? (Unconscious communication?). *El rey está desnudo*, (11).

Guattari, F. (2013). *Líneas de Fuga. Por otro mundo de posibles*. Buenos Aires: Cactus.

Heimann, P. (1950). On Counter-Transference. *International Journal of Psycho-Analysis*, 31, 81–84.

Jones, E. (1959). *Vida y obra de Sigmund Freud*. Buenos Aires: Editorial Nova. (Original work published 1953)

Lacan, J. (1953). The Function and Field of Speech and Language in Psychoanalysis. In J. Lacan, *Écrits: The First Complete Edition in English*. Trans. B. Fink, pp. 197–268. New York and London: W.W. Norton.

Lacan, J. (1958). The Direction of the Treatment and the Principles of its Power. In J. Lacan, *Écrits.: The First Complete Edition in English*. Trans. B. Fink, pp. 489–542. New York and London: W.W. Norton.

Lacan, J. (1960a). Position of the Unconscious. In J. Lacan, *Écrits: The First Complete Edition in English*. Trans. B. Fink, pp. 703–721. New York and London: W.W. Norton.

Lacan, J. (1960b). The Subversion of the Subject and the Dialectic of Desire in the Freudian Unconscious. In J. Lacan, *Écrits: The First Complete Edition in English*. Trans. B. Fink, pp. 671–702. New York and London: W.W. Norton.

Lacan, J. (1960–1961). *The Seminar of Jacques Lacan, Book VIII: Transference*. Ed. J.-A. Miller. Trans. B. Fink. Cambridge: Polity Press.

Lacan, J. (1961–1962). The Seminar of Jacques Lacan, Book IX: Identification. Trans. C. Gallagher. Unpublished. Retrieved from http://hdl.handle.net/10788/159

Lacan, J. (1964–1965). *The Seminar of Jacques Lacan, Book XII: Crucial Problems for Psychoanalysis (1964–1965)*. Trans. C. Gallagher. Retrieved from http://esource.dbs.ie/handle/10788/161

Lacan, J. (1977–1978). Seminar XXV: El momento de concluir. Unpublished.

Lacan, J. (1981). *The Seminar of Jacques Lacan, Book XI: The Four Fundamental Concepts of Psychoanalysis*. Ed. J.-A. Miller. Trans. A. Sheridan. New York and London: W.W. Norton. (Original work published 1964)

Lacan, J. (2006). Psicoanálisis y medicina. In J. Lacan, *Intervenciones y textos 1*. Buenos Aires: Manantial. (Original work published 1966)

Laplanche, J., and Pontalis, J.-B. (1967). *The Language of Psychoanalysis*. Trans. D. Nicholson-Smith. London: Karnac Books.

Maldonado, N. (2017). Un amor de transferencia. Retrieved from https://ecole-lacanienne.net/wp-content/uploads/2017/03/Un-amor-de-transferencia.pdf

Miller, J.-A. (2011). On Love. Interviewer H. Waar and Trans. A. Price. Retrieved from https://artandthoughts.fr/2013/12/03/jacques-alain-miller-on-love/

Racker, H. (1981). *Estudios sobre técnica psicoanalítica*. Buenos Aires: Paidós. (Original work published 1959)

Sauval, M. (n.d.). Sentidos del genitivo en "deseo del Otro." Retrieved from www.sauval.com/angustia/s2deseodeA.htm

Tort, M. (2014). La subjetivación patriarcal y la función paterna de rechazo de lo femenino. *Revista Topía*. Retrieved from www.topia.com.ar/articulos/subjetivacion-patriarcal-y-funcion-paterna-rechazo-lo-femenino

Vainer, A. (2008). Neutralidad y Abstinencia. Una introducción. Retrieved from www.topia.com.ar/articulos/

Chapter 7

Pretending to Forget

The Subject Supposed to Know

The Erotics of Knowledge

One of the fundamental ideas of psychoanalysis is that discovering the meaning of symptoms coincides with the cure, and so there is an essential coincidence of "scientific research and therapeutic effort."[1] Psychoanalysts propose to analysands that knowledge can be healing. We believe that there are important things that are ignored and that determine our suffering. We feed both ourselves and the desire to know and we strongly resist the horror it produces.

Psychoanalysis is a cure through investigation (or a therapeutic investigation) because it transforms suffering into a symptom, a question about suffering in terms of knowledge: what kind of knowledge determines suffering? Who has that knowledge? In fact, these two questions are the same. At least in principle, one cannot exist without the other. Logically, if there is knowledge and I do not have it, then someone else must have it, because that knowledge already exists. There is no need to pose the question for the assumption to be active. It is no surprise that the analyst is put in the position of one who has knowledge if we take into account that she offers herself as someone with knowledge of human suffering and as one who suggests to analysands that *there exists* knowledge that determines their suffering. Psychoanalysts should be certain that these two kinds of knowledge do not coincide, but they cannot ask the same of analysands.

Once knowledge is supposed to exist, it is immediately supposed that there exists someone who knows it. Freud presents this problem in the following terms:

> psycho-analysis follows the technique of getting the people under examination so far as possible themselves to produce the solution of their riddles. Thus, too, it is the dreamer himself who should tell us what his dream means. […]
>
> Since he knows nothing and we know nothing and a third person could know even less, there seems to be no prospect of finding out. If you feel inclined, then, give up the attempt! But if you feel otherwise, you can

DOI: 10.4324/9781032696423-7

accompany me further. For I can assure you that it is quite possible, and highly probable indeed, that the dreamer does know what his dream means: *only he does not know that he knows it and for that reason thinks he does not know it.* [...]

The assumption that in a dreamer too some knowledge about his dreams is present, though it is inaccessible to him so that he himself does not believe it, is not something entirely out of the blue.[2]

According to Freud, the analyst's technique induces analysands to articulate the answer to the question of the symptom. This results in two very interesting points. The first is the selection of the pronominal verb. Analysts must *do* something so that patients tell *them*. In other words, there is no solution to the riddle if there is no analyst to make the patient speak. The second is that, even though analysts are put into such positions of knowledge, the ones who truly know are the patients, except they do not know that they do know. The patient is supposed to know. What a curious thing: the patient assumes that the analyst knows, and the analyst supposes the patient knows. Analysis is based on crossed suppositions.

Before moving forward with the problem of knowledge, let us focus on the connection between scientific research and therapeutic practice. The following fragment from Freud's work will allow us to review this connection thoroughly:

One of the claims of psycho-analysis to distinction is, no doubt, that in its execution research and treatment coincide; nevertheless, after a certain point, the technique required for the one opposes that required for the other. It is not a good thing to work on a case scientifically while treatment is still proceeding to piece together its structure, to try to foretell its further progress, and to get a picture from time to time of the current state of affairs, as scientific interest would demand. Cases which are devoted from the first to scientific purposes and are treated accordingly suffer in their outcome; while the most successful cases are those in which one proceeds, as it were, without any purpose in view, allows oneself to be taken by surprise by any new turn in them, and always meets them with an open mind, free from any presuppositions. The correct behavior for an analyst lies in swinging over according to need from the one mental attitude to the other, in avoiding speculation or brooding over cases while they are in analysis, and in submitting the material obtained to a synthetic process of thought only after the analysis is concluded. The distinction between the two attitudes would be meaningless if we already possessed all the knowledge (or at least the essential knowledge) about the psychology of the unconscious and about the structure of the neuroses that we can obtain from psychoanalytic work. At present we are still far from that goal, and we ought not to cut ourselves off from the possibility of testing what we have already learnt and of extending our knowledge further.[3]

There are at least two readings of this passage, depending on how we under-stand that the analyst subjects "the material obtained to a synthetic process of thought only after the analysis is concluded." Both readings are, in my opi-nion, problematic. The first holds that the analyst "does not think" (does not develop the case scientifically, does not construct its edifice, does not attempt to determine its progress, does not establish from time to time conjectures about its present state, for example) while the analysis is underway. In this reading, the clinician and the analyst never meet. This position, which at first seems too extreme, nevertheless has its clinical implementation, as we will see later. The second reading holds that the analyst "thinks" between sessions but not while analyzing. The major problem with this perspective is that it does not explain the connection between what is thought between sessions and what happens during the sessions themselves, or how what is thought relates to the disposition of not thinking. I believe this question remains unasked because of its inherent obstacle: the false opposition Freud presents between psychoanalytic techniques and those of scientific research. What scientific researcher does not believe that the appropriate attitude to maintain is to let oneself be surprised and act freely in connection to one's hypotheses? Is it not possible to determine the structure of the case, to orient it, and also to maintain an unbiased attitude in the face of new developments? Why would "thinking" imply speculating or brooding? Are there not modes of thought that would not necessarily entail useless abstract reflections or neurotic doubts built on certainties?

A third reading of this quote, then, is that the opposition is useless and it is possible to think differently about the analyst's relationship to thinking, both within and outside of analysis, lessening the importance of the distinction between inside and outside. Eventually, the analyst must form a conjecture, and there is no prejudice more evident than the idea that a conjecture is necessarily a prejudice. This can only be stated if one supposes that there is an unavoidable barrier between speculation and experience. It is possible to think between the extremes of protocolization and *laissez-faire*.

The analyst, the only master of his ship after God, directs the treatment, and directing the treatment means—pardon the redundancy—giving it direction. When we supervise, do we not precisely try to develop a case, construct its "logic," and determine its trajectory? Why would this "scientific interest" be detrimental to the treatment? In this sense, Freud has a strong empirical bias. On the contrary, I believe the scientific elaboration of a case is usually very positive for the development of the treatment. There is nothing better than reading, writing, transmitting, and discussing a case for it to be correctly pursued.

As Freud said, we act as if we were not pursuing a particular goal, allowing ourselves to be surprised by the material. And it is true that, at first, we do not have a specific goal, but once a conjecture is added, it is inevitable that an orientation will be established as well.[4] This does not mean that analysts will abandon their predisposition to surprise, or that they will stop revising their conjectures every time they prove to be false or irrelevant. We must be prepared to welcome the unexpected.[5] Our position oscillates from conjecture to ignorance and back.

What is the connection between what analysts think about the case and the way they intervene? As Cosentino states, the analyst cannot access all the knowledge that passes through him at the moment of intervention.[6] There will never be full consciousness of the motives for an act. However, the analytic act can retroactively provide a clue about the unknown knowledge operating in it, beyond the conjecture which provides direction. The fact that the analyst cannot access all knowledge does not mean that there is no knowledge or that there should be none.

Freud's stance on the role of speculation during analysis is a result of the aforementioned confusion between floating attention and interpretation. Freud believed that the unconscious as a receiving organ allowed him to select material without biases, in contrast to voluntary reflection. For this to be possible, the unconscious must be purified, free of "blind spots." My idea is that evenly suspended attention is a method for the production of texts and not for their reading and writing. I will need to return later to this issue that, according to my diagnosis, is one of the most important problems for the psychoanalytic clinic. Many analysts are convinced that their interventions must preclude any reflection because it would falsify the material. When it is said that, "in their acts, analysts do not think," this same model is repeated but with concepts that seem better formalized. What holds true is that something in the "being" of the analyst, simply for having been analyzed, allows her to read the material without thought and then theorize it. Nasio states it clearly: "psychoanalysts treat their patients not just because of what they know, say or do, but *above all* due to what they *are*, even more, to what they *unconsciously are*."[7] In the end, the ability to analyze would be a *condition* some people have acquired upon finishing their analysis.

Freud's hypothesis, taken to the extreme, would make us conclude that a psychoanalysis could be taken to its end without the analyst having formed a single hypothesis about the case; as if free association and evenly suspended attention were therapeutic in themselves; as if the unconscious directed the treatment. It is also clear that Freud did not have this attitude. In all of his cases, he had at the start a hypothesis—sexual trauma, childhood sexual trauma, childhood sexual fantasies, the Oedipus complex—on which he based his interventions, to a greater or lesser extent.

In any case, it is possible to hold that Freud contradicts himself in this regard. While he takes an extreme position regarding the role of speculation—while analyzing, one does not think; it is not convenient to develop the case; evenly suspended attention must determine the material; and so on—he maintains the opposite based on the most speculative speculation: a universal theory of the human psyche he derived from his own clinical experience and self-analysis. Again, it is better to state here that the analyst must submit neither to theory—a group of related hypotheses which would explain most or all cases—nor to pure experience; rather, he must submit to *a* text he enables, reads, and writes together with the analysand, based on some theoretical coordinates that can be established and transmitted. The following quote may clarify further:

> Analytic therapy, on the other hand, does not seek to add or to introduce anything new, but to take away something, to bring out something; and to this end concerns itself with the genesis of the morbid symptoms and the psychical context of the pathogenic idea which it seeks to remove. It is by the use of this *mode of investigation* that analytic therapy has increased our knowledge so notably.[8]

The production and incorporation of a conjecture imply introducing not necessarily anything "from the outside" but something *new* which *must have been* in the material produced. In this sense, investigation refers to a way of approaching the analytic text that is not based on any prior speculation external to the text. Analytic functions allow us to think that, during analysis, a specific text is produced, conjectures are made, they are incorporated, and everything is carried out in a position of textual immanence. From this point of view, psychoanalysis could be defined as the *erotics of knowledge*, a practice of research within a text saturated with desire.

Another noteworthy point in Freud's theory is that the attitude he proposes for the analyst, as opposed to that of the scientist, is based on a lack of knowledge regarding the psychology of the unconscious and the structure of neurosis. We do not know *yet*, but we will someday. This has resulted in many misunderstandings. The "most knowledgeable" analyst is the most functional to the mechanisms of power.

When asked about research, Lacan paraphrased Picasso: "I do not seek, I find." There are at least two types of research: one that finds what it looks for; and one that finds a difference with respect to its question, which implies a gain of knowledge. The first kind, where one knows what to look for, can be called religious or hermeneutic; the second kind can be called scientific or even psychoanalytic (why not?). It is well known that many scientific discoveries were made by chance. However, this does not mean that such discoveries were not a consequence of exposure to conditions of possibility. The starting point is always a basic idea that might be confirmed, modified, or directly refuted. Conversely, an invention only finds us if we are willing to be found. Unconscious knowledge exists, but it must be found by asking good questions. For the time being, let us open with the following questions: how is psychoanalysis an investigation? What knowledge must the analyst suspend in order to analyze? What is the place of the analyst with respect to knowledge? What place should the analyst occupy? What does it mean that the analyst should not reflect or speculate?

Later, depending on what finds us, we will be able to assess if these questions are good ones or not.

The Deceived Deceiver

In Lacan's work, knowledge is an operational concept. This means that it is incorporated into other concepts elliptically related to it. "Knowledge, then, is placed in the center, in the dock, by psychoanalytic experience," Lacan states.[9] The word *center* seems inappropriate because, in a strict sense, psychoanalysis has no central concept. The very concept of structure calls into question ideas such as center, origin, and end. Be that as it may, knowledge is a very relevant concept. Let us think of these definitions: the unconscious is an unknown knowledge, drive is a knowledge without knowledge, jouissance is the exercise of knowledge, the subject is what is missing from knowledge, the symptom is a question about knowledge, and interpretation is knowledge applied as truth.

However, the concept most affected by the incorporation of the problem of knowledge was transference. These quotes prove my point:

- "As soon as the subject who is supposed to know exists somewhere [...] there is transference."[10]
- "We know that the subject of the analytic act can know nothing about what is learnt in the analytic experience, unless there operates in it what is called transference. The transference that I restored in a complete fashion, by relating it to the subject supposed to know."[11]
- "Naturally, if one does not introduce into it the subject supposed to know, transference maintains all its opaqueness."[12]
- "[T]he fact that in what she refers herself to she implies the subject supposed to know [...] has made the neurotic naturally a psychoanalysand because here and now constituting in herself, and before any analysis, the transference."[13]
- "[T]ransference is essentially founded on the fact that for the one who enters into analysis, the analyst is the subject who is supposed to know."[14]
- "This transference [...] can only be organized by being referred to this truly fundamental function that is always present in everything that is involved in any progress of knowledge."[15]

These quotes simply confirm the displacement of the concept of transference in Lacan's work, from love to desire and knowledge. I agree with Miller's statement that, if the phenomenon of transference centered on love exists in psychoanalysis, Lacan's subject supposed to know "is placed as the transphenomenologic basis of transference."[16] The subject supposed to know and the analyst's desire are constitutive of transference, while love is its constituted effect.[17] Le Gaufey also says it clearly: transference love stops "being at the forefront of the scene so naturally since it acquires the place of effect from the start."[18] Transference love is an imaginary effect of the symbolic and real dimensions: the subject supposed to know and the analyst's desire. The closing of the unconscious is explained, among other things, by the transference deception through which the analysand presents himself as an object worthy of love to the one who is *supposed* to possess the object of desire: the analyst. In this way, "he tries to induce the Other into a mirage relation in which he convinces him of being worthy of love."[19] We know how to fall straight into this speculative relationship: interpreting the transference. In fact, every time the analyst takes things personally ("it seems you feel x about me," "I did not say that, what I meant is...," etc.), she fully enters the dimension of deceit.

> [T]he transference is not, of its nature, the shadow of something that was once alive. On the contrary, the subject, in so far as he is subjected to the desire of the analyst, desires to betray him for this subjection, by making the analyst love him, by offering of himself that essential duplicity that is love. The transference effect is that effect of deception in so far as it is repeated in the present here and now.
> [...] It is not a shadow of the former deceptions of love. It is isolation in the actuality of its pure functioning as deception.[20]

To be more precise, the closing of the unconscious is not explained solely by transference deception because, if all goes well, where the analysand searches for the kind image in the ideal of the Other she encounters the analyst's desire, her real presence. The *a*, then, stops the "radical" closure of the unconscious, following the model of the causation of the subject (alienation-separation). What rescues the subject from alienation to signifiers, from petrification before the ideal, or from fading infinitely into metonymic signification is his condition as the object of the Other's desire. This is how the analysand "detaches." It is worth remembering that the unconscious is not a closed bag full of signifiers that it expels from time to time. The border topology of the unconscious circumscribes it to its signifying articulation, so it opens at its closing—that is, when there is articulation between signifiers with the consequent loss this implies: the *a*. This is why the cause of the unconscious is always a lost cause.

The analyst's presence does not mean her "real" body, her physical presence, but her desire, which can be realized from a distance. The distance the analysand takes from the presence of desire is not physical. In this way, we can understand the mysterious presence Lacan points out in his first seminar.

When transference closes the doors of the unconscious, the analyst can fill that void with another deception—for instance, by interpreting transference—or she can intervene according to the analyst's desire, since that is the moment when "interpretation becomes decisive."[21] Therefore, though the analyst's presence triggers a closing of the unconscious, "we [analysts] are linked together in awaiting this transference effect in order to be able to interpret," where the deceptive dimension of love carries a question about the desire of the Other: *Che vuoi?*[22]

What is the dimension of deception where love is put into play? Psychoanalysis is not a practice where two people try to agree on some referential knowledge, where the analysand deceives himself, and the analyst attempts to disabuse the analysand of this deceit. Analysis develops in the dimension of deception because the analysand tries to persuade the analyst that the latter has what could complete him and, in this way, the analysand continues to ignore what he lacks. It is also likely that analysts often feel they do have the knowledge which could complete the analysand. The transference bond around the object *of* desire is in itself a deception. This happens only because the analysand supposes that the analyst has knowledge about desire, the science of the intimate.[23] Lacan says, however, that experience proves this does not happen from the start. In the initial phase, the analysand does not grant the analyst this place. The danger is that the one deceived is the Other, the analyst.

> [T]he patient may think that the analyst may be misled if he gives him certain facts. He holds back certain facts so that the analyst may not go too quickly. [...] Should not he who may be misled (*être trompé*) be *a fortiori* under suspicion of being capable, quite simply, of being mistaken (*se tromper*)?[24]

The analyst is neither evil genius nor God. It is clear that an analyst does not know everything. Everyone knows that, except for some analysts. Though the analysand supposes that the analyst has enough knowledge to warrant requesting an appointment, the analysand thinks that the analyst can be deceived. Therefore, the analysand takes care not to provide false clues that could lead to incorrect conclusions about the truth of her desire. But what could be a false clue in the analytic text? Not wanting to deceive the analyst means stepping away from the rules of the game and also deceiving oneself regarding the object of desire. In the same way, according to Lacan, "even the psycho-analyst put in question is credited at some point with a certain infallibility"; the analysand may even attribute certain intentions to random gestures.[25] You made that face for a reason! In the end, the analyst, like any other speaking being, cannot not desire and cannot not assume some intention in what he says: why did you say what you said? "It is at this point of meeting that the analyst is awaited. As far as the analyst is supposed to know, he is also supposed to set out in search of unconscious desire."[26]

The Most Radical Bias

Is the analyst the subject supposed to know or not? The answer cannot be decided in these terms. In order to posit all of its aspects, we must better study the place of this concept in Lacan's theory.

The subject supposed to know appears in Seminar IX where Lacan tries to give conceptual substance to the subject based on his theory of the signifier. In fact, it is in this seminar that he comes to his definitive thesis: a signifier represents a subject for another signifier. On November 15, 1961, in the opening lecture, he presented for the first time the subject supposed to know. No doubt both "subjects" are in solidarity in that they are constituted around knowledge.

In this lecture, Lacan pointed out that psychoanalysts are called to subvert the most radical bias, "the true support of this whole development of philosophy [...] the limit beyond which there commences the possibility of the unconscious."[27] The unconscious appears beyond the limit marked by the most fundamental modern bias: the subject supposed to know. What is this bias? It is based on three main ideas:

1   All knowledge implies a subject.
2   There is progress towards absolute knowledge (the diachronic perspective).
3   Knowledge already exists (the synchronic perspective).

The psychoanalyst does not assume any subject supposed to know because her basic assumption is that knowledge has no subject. The subject of the unconscious is the other side of the subject supposed to know. The subject supposed to know is the source and support of the totality of signifiers. Conversely, the subject of the unconscious is what is yet to be known.[28] There is no harmony, no completeness, and no determination of the subject we are interested in. As psychoanalysts, we do not suppose any subjects of knowledge because,

> Knowledge is intersubjective, which does not mean that it is the knowledge of all, nor that it is the knowledge of the Other—with a capital O— and the Other we have posed. It is essential to maintain it as such: the Other is not a subject, it is a locus to which one strives, says Aristotle, to transfer the knowledge of the subject.[29]

That the Other holds the knowledge does not mean that the Other knows. The Other does not know precisely because he is not a subject. The subjective powers transferred to the Other are reflectivity, will, freedom, intention, and so on. But the Other as such neither knows nor wants. It is a pure signifying automaton.

The function of the subject supposed to know is inherent in any question regarding knowledge, and, as I said, psychoanalysis is exactly that: "[i]t is that immanent to the very start of the movement of analytic research, there is this subject supposed to know."[30] The analysand is articulated around "I did not know," and the analyst "is summoned, in the situation, as being the subject who is supposed to know."[31] According to Lacan, a symptom can be defined as knowledge the analysand knows concerns him but that he does not know anything about. The analyst "supports the status of the symptom,"[32] inserting herself as subject supposed to know. This means that the analyst maintains the most radical bias while, at the same time, going in the opposite direction, abandoning *part of her knowledge*, and letting herself be carried away by the game of the signifier, *applying another knowledge* that allows her to participate in the game. Again, the position of the analyst is pendular. In order to analyze, knowledge is required that cannot be gained through personal analysis or through theory but that is extracted from the signifying automaton. However, in order to read this knowledge, it is necessary to have (theoretical) knowledge different from that articulated in the analytic text. It is even necessary to have knowledge to enable the appearance of that text.

Analysands do not grant analysts the position of subject supposed to know. It is the device itself that puts them there. This does not mean that it is obvious. Analysts know by experience that, most times, significant work is required to introduce the question of the symptom in terms of knowledge. Patients do not necessarily arrive at analysis asking questions about the symptom and they do not need to. Often, the demand is for the elimination of the symptom without any accompanying question. I would even say that the so-called "current clinic" must be thought of from an epistemological perspective rather than an ontological one. The rejection of the unconscious is not inherent in contemporary symptomatology but a sign of a position subjects take regarding their suffering: absolute horror in the face of knowing what constitutes it. This says much less about the "moral cowardice" of the patients than it does about the way power works, hiding its *moteriality* and eliminating the possibility of establishing any basis from which to call it into question. The so-called "end of theory" and the "flood of data" are correlated to the rejection of the unconscious. This is another reason why the unconscious is political. Therefore, the analyst must *otherize* the symptom, so that the subject supposed to know is formally installed. This is the order of the treatment that Lacan proposed: the rectification of the relationship between the subject and reality, transference, and interpretation.

The installation of the subject supposed to know can happen with relative ease or it can be an arduous process. Analysis cannot be carried out without the analyst embodying this function to some extent. If it is already embodied in another person—for example, in another highly prestigious analyst, a self-help guru, or God—some difficulties will arise for whoever is in charge of the analysis. In the end, "in order that the analysis may be engaged in and sustained, the analyst assuredly is supposed to know."[33] However, psychoanalysis knows that nobody can be the subject supposed to know, because knowledge exists without any subject who knows.

I cannot agree with Miller and so many other analysts when they hold that the unconscious is the subject supposed to know.[34] On the contrary, the unconscious refutes it as an illusion that must be eliminated to conclude the analysis. The fall of the subject supposed to know is the fall of psychic determinism. This, in turn, means that the unconscious is not an instance of determination. In Lacanian terms, Freud confused the unconscious with the subject supposed to know. Apparently, this confusion is not completely dispelled.

It can only be said that the unconscious is the subject supposed to know if the whole Other is confused with the barred Other. Lacan's idea is that there is no Other of the Other, there is no metalanguage—that is, there is no whole Other. This can appear in different ways: nothing and no one can guarantee the truth, there is no absolute knowledge, there is no ultimate meaning. In any case, the fact that there are no guarantees when it comes to truth does not mean that there are no truths that are more meaningful than others; the fact that there is no absolute knowledge does not mean that there is no knowledge more relevant or powerful than others; the fact that there is no ultimate meaning does not mean that all meanings are desirable or appropriate. It can be inferred that this problem directs us towards the question of interpretation. It is clear that the Lacanian Other is not Descartes's God. The unconscious does not guarantee any truth, but it tells many. The barred Other exists; it is the incomplete and inconsistent Other that offers a contingent and partial truth. In short, the subject supposed to know is the non-existent whole Other, and the unconscious is the barred Other that exists.

If we believe that the Other (without distinguishing between whole and barred) does not exist, we can logically conclude that the unconscious, as the discourse of the Other, does not exist either. From this perspective, the unconscious is an illusion the analyst establishes in order to momentarily elaborate meaning about the symptom with the ultimate goal of realizing that this meaning could have been any other. In Miller's words, since the Other does not exist, the analysand must notice that, "they need to count on themselves more [...] know how to hold themselves without apologies, excuses, explanations or complaints."[35] It is no surprise that in this way Miller finds that, "something cynical appears at the end of the analysis, a cynical solitude that arises from the fact that the Other is semblance. [...] an affect of depression accompanies it." Miller then claims that the pass comes to fix the place of the Other, "because without that Other, analysts go mad and they can even have a tendency to believe that they are the Other." Indeed, the conviction that the Other does not exist is the Lacanian definition of madness. I wonder what happens to people who end a Millerian analysis and do not carry out the pass. The world is full of mad psychoanalyzed people!

I must insist: the unconscious is not a subject supposed to know but knowledge with no "subject." As Eidelsztein expressed it, "the unconscious revokes the postulate of the subject supposed to know."[36] It is true that the analyst *goes along* with the illusion of the subject supposed to know where several "biases" are at play regarding knowledge: that it already exists, that someone possesses it, and that it is whole. At the end of analysis, what is verified as an illusion is the subject supposed to know and not the unconscious. If, upon termination, analysis proved the non-existence of the unconscious it would mean the end of the psychoanalyst! It is actually the opposite: the analysis ends when we observe the effectiveness of the unconscious and, consequently, the non-existence of the Other of the Other. If the most radical bias of modern thinking is the subject supposed to know, the most radical bias of contemporary psychoanalysis is that the unconscious is the subject of knowledge. Lacan states it clearly:

> I did not say that the Other does not know, it is those who say that who do not know very much, despite all my efforts to teach it to them! I said that the Other, as is obvious since it is the place of the unconscious, knows; only it is not a subject. The negation "there is no subject supposed to know," if in fact I ever said it in that negative form, it concerns the subject, not the knowledge. It is moreover easy to grasp provided one has an experience of the unconscious. It is distinguished precisely by the fact that in it one does not know who it is that knows.[37]

Saying that "the Other knows" may be confusing because, as Lacan himself says, the Other is not a subject but a position. In the Other, *there is knowledge* that no one knows. I am interested in pointing out that the "there is no" of the subject supposed to know refers to the subject and not to knowledge. To summarize, the subject supposed to know is put to work every time a question arises regarding the progress of knowledge and acquires value in analysis "precisely from the fact that the existence of the unconscious puts it in question."[38]

The unconscious exists!

A Roll of the Dice

While it is hard to accept the existence of knowledge without a subject, it is harder to accept that such knowledge is not *already in existence* waiting to be discovered. In fact, it is not possible to accept one of these biases without accepting all of the others. Only superficially could one admit the existence of knowledge without a subject without questioning, at the same time, that knowledge is already all there. This is why, for Freud, the unconscious was the subject supposed to know, an instance of determination.

Where was that knowledge before it was "known"? According to Lacan, no one thought to ask this question because it was taken for granted that the subject supposed to know already existed. Even "the statements of science, in principle the most atheistic, [are] firmly theist on this point."[39] The issue, then, is exclusive not to psychoanalysis but to science in general or, rather, to any questioning of knowledge. For example, one might wonder if the theory of gravity was true before Newton formulated it or, in other words, if this theory was already in existence waiting for the physicist to discover it.

I will happily put my cards on the table by saying that it seems to me to be very unlikely to say that Newtonian knowledge was true before it was constituted by Newton for the good reason that now and in the first place it no longer is so. It is no longer completely so.

In the very necessity of knowledge, of signifying articulation, there is this contingency of being only a signifying articulation, an assembled lock.[40]

Lacan is clear: the theory of gravity was not true before Newton "discovered" it—and this is the bottom line—for the simple fact that it is not true anymore. This means, among other things, that there was no need for things to have been presented in this way. Scientific knowledge is a contingent body of signifiers, a roll of the dice. There is no need for signifiers to be articulated in a certain way or, at least, there is no original need or purpose. It is worth clarifying that just because it is a roll of the dice does not mean that anything can happen.

In Ancient Greece, it was believed that mathematics expressed an unchanging order. Numbers and geometric figures were ideal, intelligible, eternal, and immutable entities. Greek mathematics, in its ontological status, was necessary and eternal and could not be anything other than what it was. Conversely, the letter, understood as the unit of formal writing in modern science, has no original reason for being the way it is. It could have been different; it is contingent and historical. However, once the letter is fixed, "only necessity remains, which imposes the forgetting of the contingency that authorized [it]."[41] Writing becomes transcription, and creation becomes discovery. Once the dice fall, a new order of possibilities, impossibilities, needs, and contingencies is established.

Newton's theory of gravity is perhaps the most paradigmatic example of the functioning of the subject supposed to know. The famous phrase "*Hypotheses non fingo*," which he presented in the second edition of the *Principia*, did not logically refer to the fact that his theory was not made up of hypotheses in a general sense but, rather, indicated that it omitted any kind of hypothesis regarding the causes of gravity. His problem was with "metaphysical" hypotheses. Newton explained how gravity worked but he never said what it was or why it worked the way it did. This movement is fundamental to thinking about interpretation. The question Newton discarded was: how can a planet or any object know how far it is from another planet so it can enter into gravitational interaction? For Lacan,

there is in effect no doubt the fact that this presupposes in itself a subject who maintains the action of the law. [...] the operation of gravity does not appear to him to be able to be supported except by this pure and supreme subject, this sort of acme of the ideal subject that the Newtonian God represents.[42]

For Newton, physics; for God, metaphysics. The important thing is that his theory was backed by a God who guaranteed its truth, who allowed him to trust in the existence of an unchanging rationality behind what could be theorized.

> The *subject supposed to know* is God, full stop, nothing else. And one can be a savant of genius […] one can in a word be Einstein, and have recourse in the most articulated way to this God. He has to be already there, supposed to know, since Einstein, arguing against the restructuring of science on the foundations of probability, argues that the knowledge that he articulates in his theory presupposes somewhere, commends itself, by something that is homogenous to what is indeed a supposition concerning this subject. He names him in the traditional terms the good old God, difficult perhaps to penetrate in that he sustains the order of the world, but not a liar. He is fair. He does not change the goalposts during the game.
>
>   And it is on this admission that the rules exist already, that somewhere the rules of the game, the one that presides over this deciphering that is called knowledge, are established simply by the fact that the knowledge already exists in God. It is at this level that one can question what results from a veritable atheism, the only one, as you see, that merits the name, which is the following: is it possible for thinking to sustain the confrontation of the putting in question of the *subject supposed to know*?[43]

Einstein, Newton, and Freud all theorized a deterministic universe, or, in the case of the last, an unconscious. This means that, if we knew all variables of this *absolute knowledge that already exists*, we could perfectly predict the future. In this sense, the illusion is that the accumulation of knowledge would lead to progress towards absolute knowledge: *the* truth.

Modern science has a paradoxical relationship to God. On the one hand, it was established based on his silence. God guarantees the truth but does not say anything about it. Scientific knowledge is nothing more than a signifying body that dispenses with any instance of expression or intentionality. God is a retired engineer. There is no message He wants to communicate to us through the workings of the world; we simply need to discover how his great design works. According to Lacan, scientific knowledge is an *ex nihilo* creation. It is produced from nothing—that is, from pure signifying materiality. This does not mean that a theory is invented "from scratch." All knowledge is preceded by a signifying articulation that serves as an antecedent to new knowledge. There is nothing resembling knowledge that is "already ordered somewhere"; there are possibilities in the signifying articulation that enable certain questions and answers and make it impossible for others to surface. On the other hand, modern science starts from an act of faith; it needs that silent God who guarantees the truth. "Science is not as atheist as it is believed to be."[44] This is because it depends on a God who does not change the structure of reality to lie or deceive.[45] As Miller argued, "this is something against which it is impossible to defend ourselves, from the moment when a significant invention takes shape and develops, we cannot stop thinking that it has always been there."[46] God does not play dice.

What happens to knowledge that takes shape in psychoanalysis? The function of the subject supposed to know makes that shape a knowledge that was *already all there*, waiting to be discovered. The Freudian unconscious is the subject supposed to know, with the notable exception that Freud pointed out what is not subject to interpretation in the unconscious: the navel of the dream. Lacan, on the other hand, posits it as incomplete and inconsistent knowledge without a subject, with a weak ontological status. The Lacanian unconscious exists in that it is not realized. We cannot say that the unconscious was already there, but that it will have been there owing to the presence of the analyst. In the terms in which I am presenting this revision of technical concepts, the function of the subject supposed to know makes the analytic material into a text that is already all written and that should be revealed. However, the analyst knows that the reading of the analytic text is, at the same time, its writing—that is, what is presented as already written is actually a consequence of reading and writing within the material. An analyst is someone who radically assumes the existence of the unconscious: the impersonality and the meaninglessness of knowledge and, therefore, of jouissance; and the partiality, historicity, and contingency of truth. Conversely, the analysand writes a text with her hands tied. That reading and writing are contingent, again, does not mean that they can be anything. The limits of interpretation are imposed by the movement of the text itself. We firmly maintain that there is knowledge, but we cannot say that someone knows it and that it was already there; we know that our presence is essential for its realization.

Between Two Stools

The paradox of the subject supposed to know is that the analyst must sustain it as a condition of possibility for analysis, but with an eye towards its dissolution.

> [The analyst] is between two stools. Between the false position of being the subject supposed to know (which he knows well he is not) and that of having to rectify the effects of this supposition on the part of the subject, and this in the name of the truth. This indeed is why transference is the source of what is called resistance. The fact is, if it is quite true, as I say, that truth in the analytic discourse is placed elsewhere, at the place of the one who is listening to it, in fact the one who is listening can only function as a relay with respect to this place. Namely, that the only thing he knows, is that he himself, as subject, is in the same relation as the one who is speaking to him, to the truth.[47]

As Soler said, the analyst is a pyromaniac firefighter; she sustains a fire that she herself must put out.[48] Analysts are in a divided position: they speak "in the name of truth," knowing that this is a false position. The analyst and the analysand are in the same relationship towards the truth, with the difference that the first knows its partial, contingent, and historical condition and, consequently, knows that nothing and no one can guarantee it. What must be guaranteed for analysis to happen is the subject supposed to know. As Freud believed, the analyst is not opposed to the development of transference, does not feed it or reject it, but "the place from which the psychoanalyst speaks is not the same as the one from which, in the transference, he is supposed to speak,"[49] because, where the sign of desire is expected, the signifier of lack is returned. The analyst *pretends to forget* that he has been able to notice the illusory character of the subject supposed to know and its reduction to the object *a* as cause of desire. He pretends that there is a subject supposed to know, knowing, however, that it is

> nevertheless doomed to *désêtre* and which thus constitutes, as I might say, an act that is out of synch since he is not the subject supposed to know, since he cannot be it. And if there is someone who knows it, it is above all the psychoanalyst.[50]

The analytic act is an act of faith, insofar as it consists of supporting the idea that there is an Other who already knows everything, when the analyst knows that she is the very cause of the process. The analyst's main goal, "because of the existence of the unconscious, consists precisely in eliminating from the map this function of subject supposed to know."[51] This is a way of thinking about the end of analysis: the elimination of the subject supposed to know, the fall of the triple bias with the consequent mutation of the subject's relations with knowledge. Knowledge has no subject, it is not absolute, and it did not exist prior to being found. Finally, the analyst becomes the residue, the waste of the analytic operation, the "remainder of the thing known, which is called [object *a*]."[52]

I will later return to the question of the analytic act and its relationship to the subject supposed to know. Now I am interested in pointing out two issues about the mutation required with respect to knowledge and truth in order for one to occupy the position of the analyst. The first question is whether there is anything like an absolute elimination of the subject supposed to know. If this were the case, analysts would be the only people we could call true atheists. This reminds me of an anecdote a colleague once told me in which a group of armed thieves violently broke into a psychoanalytic institution threatening to kill its members. The curious part is that, while the thieves were collecting their belongings, many prestigious analysts who had already finished their analysis began to pray! You never know...

This little story helps us wonder whether the subject supposed to know falls "all at once," once and for all, the day the analysis ends, or whether it is something that is slowly liquidated with each manifestation of the unconscious, but that never completely disappears. This refers to the very strength of this bias and not to the lack of analysis. Of course, the fact that one has been diagnosed with a bias does not mean that one does not suffer from it. The question is important because what is at stake is whether someone who has finished her analysis is naturally aware of the illusion of the subject supposed to know. I do not believe that this is so. The analytic act, which involves supporting the paradoxical position of the subject supposed to know, requires a reflective and conscientious disposition. It is not something that goes without saying. As Lacan says, an analyst not only is one who has experienced the fall of the subject supposed to know and the realization of subjective division but, especially, is one who *thinks about it*.[53] Furthermore, given that the subject supposed to know is not something that falls once and for all, it becomes harder to know when it is well enough eliminated for one to practice as an analyst. The second question, which has already been mentioned, refers to the paradox that it was Lacan, someone who did not complete his analysis, who formalized this theory. Again, it seems important to highlight that it is not enough for someone to have experienced the unconscious to be an analyst; one must also need to keep in mind the theory that enables the end of analysis, in all its senses. One must think about it and keep it always in mind. The fact that we had to wait for Lacan to conceive of the end of analysis as the fall of the subject supposed to know, with the correlative fall of the analyst, indicates that analysts who ended their analysis before Lacan did not do it correctly, at least based on this theory. Lacan diagnosed that a great number of analyses ended with the identification of the analysand with the analyst as representative of truth—that is, with the identification with the subject supposed to know.

It is not correct to say, then, that the analyst coincides with the subject supposed to know. This is a mistaken assumption. While oscillating between sustaining and reducing the subject supposed to know, the analyst invites the analysand to occupy that position. "The analyst is the one who is given the function of the subject supposed to know."[54] This is what Freud told his patients: "you know, you just do not know that you know." The inventor of psychoanalysis was convinced that it was the patients who had all the knowledge about their suffering, and that this knowledge was already there in the unconscious, waiting to be revealed. Obviously, once Freud began to know what was in the unconscious, he did not need patients to say much in order to propose his Oedipal hypotheses. This also explains the Freudian expectation of achieving a more "complete" knowledge about the unconscious every day. Freud understood the unconscious as a subject supposed to know. It is not entirely accurate to say that, in an analysis, it is the analysand and not the analyst who knows because, strictly speaking, neither of them knows, although the analyst, through the imperative of free association (say what comes to mind), establishes the analysand as subject supposed to know. Speak, everything you say will be important! "I can say anything whatever, it will always produce something. This doesn't happen to you every day. There is a lot there to cause the transference."[55] Through the illusion of the subject supposed to know, the analyst *enables* the appearance of the unconscious.

What then must the analyst know? To begin with, the analyst knows about desire, but does not know the conditions of desire for a particular patient. The learned ignorance of the analyst refers not to the suspension of his theoretical knowledge in general, but rather to that of theoretical knowledge as a standard way to explain cases. The psychoanalyst does not know what the relevant signifiers are and how these covary with each other. This is why the signifier of the transference is *any* signifier that does not coincide with the reserve knowledge constituting the subject supposed to know. This is what both Freud and Lacan mean when they recommend approaching each new case as if we had no knowledge acquired from previous cases. This is why, "[t]his in no way authorises the psychoanalyst to be satisfied in the knowledge that he knows nothing, for what is *at issue is what he has to come to know*."[56] Analysts must know how to use their concepts to position themselves in the right way, in order to read and write the particularity of the analytic text. The four analytic functions of enabling, desiring, reading, and writing require rigorous conceptualization in order to be put into play. The analyst is not the subject supposed to know, but she must know what she is doing. In fact, every time she hits the target with her intervention, she paradoxically calls into question the subject supposed to know. With each writing, it becomes less important. The ultimate gesture of the analyst is that of her own erasure.

Notes

1   Freud, 1923 (1922): 236.
2   Freud, 1916 (1915–1916): 101–104.
3   Freud, 1912: 114–115.
4   In truth, this is also relative. Analysts have a conception—perhaps a weak one—of the end of analysis, with its respective coordinates, and we head towards it even if we do not know which path will take us there.
5   Lacan, 1964–1965: lecture on May 19, 1965.
6   Maximiliano Cosentino was one of the readers of the first draft of this book in Spanish. I took this paragraph almost verbatim from one of his comments. I thank him for this and other points he made which were paramount in the final draft of this text.
7   Nasio, 2017: 22.
8   Freud, 1905 (1904): 261.
9   Lacan, 1969–1970: 30.
10   Lacan, 1964/1981: 240.
11   Lacan, 1967–1968: lecture on January 10, 1968.
12   Ibid.: lecture on February 21, 1968.
13   Lacan, 1968–1969: XXIV 17.

14 Lacan, 1965–1966/1989: lecture on December 22, 1965.
15 Lacan, 1967–1968: lecture on November 29, 1967.
16 Miller, 1981/2006b: 79.
17 A few years before formally introducing the concept of subject supposed to know, Lacan had already anticipated it: "[The subject], of course, does not have to answer for this subjective error which, whether it is avowed or not in his discourse, is immanent in the fact that he entered analysis and concluded the original pact involved in it. And we can still less neglect the subjectivity of this moment because it reveals the reason for what may be called the constitutive effects of transference, insofar as they are distinguished by an indication of reality from the constituted effects that follow them" (1953: 254).
18 Le Gaufey, 1998/2001: 70.
19 Lacan, 1964/1981: 268.
20 Ibid.: 254.
21 Ibid.: 131.
22 Ibid.: 253.
23 Cf. Lacan, 1960–1961: lecture on December 14, 1960.
24 Lacan, 1964/1981: 234.
25 Ibid.
26 Ibid.: 235.
27 Lacan, 1961–1962: lecture on November 15, 1961.
28 Cf. Lacan, 1964–1965: lecture on May 12, 1965.
29 Lacan, 1961–1962: lecture on November 15, 1961.
30 Lacan, 1967–1968: lecture on November 29, 1967.
31 Lacan, 1964–1965: lecture on May 5, 1965.
32 Ibid.
33 Lacan, 1964–1965: lecture on May 12, 1965.
34 Cf. Miller, 1993–1994/2011.
35 This and the following quotes come from Miller, 1993–1994/2011: 462.
36 Eidelsztein, 2020: n.p.
37 Lacan, 1968–1969: lecture on June 11, 1969.
38 Lacan, 1967–1968: January 17, 1968.
39 Ibid.: lecture on February 21, 1968.
40 Lacan, 1964–1965: lecture on May 5, 1965.
41 Milner, 1995: 41.
42 Lacan, 1964–1965: lecture on May 12, 1965.
43 Lacan, 1968–1969: XVIII 3–4.
44 Miller, 1979/2006a: 51.
45 Cf. Eidelsztein, 1979/2008: 24.
46 Miller, 1979/2006a: 51.
47 Lacan, 1966–1967: lecture on June 21, 1967.
48 Cf. Soler, 1988/2007.
49 Lacan, 1965–1966/1989: lecture on January 26, 1966.
50 Lacan, 1967–1968: lecture on January 17, 1968.
51 Ibid.: lecture on February 7, 1968.
52 Ibid.: lecture on January 10, 1968.
53 "[T]he problem of the formation of the psychoanalyst is really nothing other than, through a privileged experience, to allow there to come to birth, as I might say, subjects for whom this division of the subject is not simply something that they know but something in which they think" (Lacan, 1965–1966/1989: lecture on May 11, 1966).
54 Lacan, 1969–1970: 38.

55 Ibid.: 52
56 Lacan, 1967: 6.

References

Eidelsztein, A. (2008). *Las estructuras clínicas a partir de Lacan, Volume 1*. Buenos Aires: Letra Viva. (Original work published 1979)

Eidelsztein, A. (2020). La sustitución de la transferencia de Freud por el Sujeto Supuesto Saber de Lacan, su concepto más desconocido. *El rey está desnudo*, 14.

Freud, S. (1905 [1904]). On Psychotherapy. In S. Freud, A. Freud, A. Strachey, and A. Tyson (Eds.), *The Standard Edition of the Complete Psychological Works of Sigmund Freud, Volume VII*. Trans. J. Strachey, pp. 257–270. London: The Hogarth Press.

Freud, S. (1912). Recommendations to Physicians Practising Psycho-Analysis. In S. Freud, A. Freud, A. Strachey, and A. Tyson (Eds.), *The Standard Edition of the Complete Psychological Works of Sigmund Freud, Volume XII: The Case of Schreber, Papers on Technique and Other Works*. Trans. J. Strachey. London: The Hogarth Press.

Freud, S. (1916 [1915–1916]). The Premises and Technique of Interpretation. In S. Freud, A. Freud, A. Strachey, and A. Tyson (Eds.), *The Standard Edition of the Complete Psychological Works of Sigmund Freud, Volume XV: Introductory Lectures on Psycho-Analysis (Parts I and II)*. Trans. J. Strachey, pp. 100–112. London: The Hogarth Press.

Freud, S. (1923 [1922]). Two Encyclopedia Articles: "Psycho-Analysis" and "The Libido Theory". In S. Freud, A. Freud, A. Strachey, & A. Tyson (Eds.), *The Standard Edition of the Complete Works of Sigmund Freud. Volume XVIII: Beyond the Pleasure Principle, Group Psychology and Other Works*. Trans. J. Strachey, pp. 235–262. London: The Hogarth Press.

Lacan, J. (1953). The Function and Field of Speech and Language in Psychoanalysis. In J. Lacan, *Écrits: The First Complete Edition in English*. Trans. B. Fink, pp. 197–268. New York and London: W.W. Norton.

Lacan, J. (1960–1961). *The Seminar of Jacques Lacan, Book VIII: Transference*. Ed. J.-A. Miller. Trans. B. Fink. Cambridge: Polity Press.

Lacan, J. (1961–1962). *The Seminar of Jacques Lacan, Book IX: Identification*. Trans. C. Gallagher. Unpublished. Retrieved from http://hdl.handle.net/10788/159

Lacan, J. (1964–1965). *The Seminar of Jacques Lacan, Book XII: Crucial Problems for Psychoanalysis (1964–1965)*. Trans. C. Gallagher. Retrieved from http://esource.dbs.ie/handle/10788/161

Lacan, J. (1966–1967). The Seminar of Jaques Lacan, Book XIV: The Logic of Phantasy. Trans. C. Gallagher. Unpublished. Retrieved from http://hdl.handle.net/10788/163

Lacan, J. (1967). Proposition of 9 October on the Psychoanalyst of the School. Ed. R. Grigg. *Analysis No. 6*, 1–13. Retrieved from https://lacancircle.com.au/wp-content/uploads/2017/11/Proposition_of_9_October.pdf

Lacan, J. (1967–1968). *The Seminar of Jacques Lacan, Book XV: The Psychoanalytic Act 1967–1968*. Ed. C. Gallagher. Retrieved from www.lacaninireland.com:http://hdl.handle.net/10788/164

Lacan, J. (1968–1969). *The Seminar of Jacques Lacan, Book XVI: From an Other to the Other*. Trans. C. Gallagher. Unpublished. Retrieved from http://hdl.handle.net/10788/165

Lacan, J. (1969–1970). *The Seminar of Jacques Lacan, Book XVII: The Other Side of Psychoanalysis*. Ed. J.-A. Miller. Trans. R. Grigg. New York and London: W.W. Norton.

Lacan, J. (1981). *The Seminar of Jacques Lacan, Book XI: The Four Fundamental Concepts of Psychoanalysis*. Ed. J.-A. Miller. Trans. A. Sheridan. New York and London: W.W. Norton. (Original work published 1964)

Lacan, J. (1989). The Seminar of Jacques Lacan, Book XIII: The Object of Psychoanalysis. Trans. B. Fink. *Newsletter of the Freudian Field*, 3 (1/2). Retrieved from http://hdl.handle.net/10788/162 (Original work published 1965–1966)

Le Gaufey, G. (2001). *Anatomía de la tercera persona*. Buenos Aires: Edelp. (Original work published 1998)

Miller, J.-A. (2006a). Elementos de epistemología. In J.-A. Miller, *Recorrido de Lacan*. Buenos Aires: Manantial. (Original work published 1979)

Miller, J.-A. (2006b). La transferencia. El sujeto supuesto saber. In J.-A. Miller, *Recorrido de Lacan*. Buenos Aires: Manantial. (Original work published 1981)

Miller, J.-A. (2011). *Donc. La lógica de la cura. Los cursos psicoanalíticos de Jacques Alain Miller*. Buenos Aires: Paidós. (Original work published 1993–1994)

Milner, J.-C. (1995). *A Search for Clarity: Science and Philosophy in Lacan's Oeuvre*. Trans. E. Pluth. Evanston: Northwestern University Press.

Nasio, J.D. (2017). *¡Sí, el psicoanálisis cura!*Buenos Aires: Paidós.

Soler, C. (2007). *Finales de análisis*. Buenos Aires: Manantial. (Original work published 1988)

Chapter 8

Interpreting

The Analytic Reading

How Do We Interpret Today?

In the second chapter of *The Interpretation of Dreams*, when Freud presented his method of interpretation, he began by differentiating it from two classical systems of oneiromancy. The first, symbolic interpretation, is characterized by taking the dream as a whole and substituting its content, initially enigmatic, with some other "comprehensible" or even prophetic content. The new content is obtained from a "clever idea" or "direct intuition" of the interpreter.[1] This method is useless for psychoanalysis: it is not possible to transmit or reproduce. It was important for psychoanalysis to propose a method, something that aspired to rationality. Freud's idea was that interpretation could not be left to the "peculiar gifts"[2] of the interpreter, but that anyone who knew the method could perform it. In the end, this symbolic interpretation was discarded because the interpreter could not rationally explain how they came to an interpretation.[3]

The second method of deciphering "treats dreams as a kind of cryptography in which each sign can be translated into another sign having a known meaning."[4] Once the elements have been substituted, the interpreter is responsible for reconstructing the structure of the dream. This type of interpretation is not very useful either, since there is no guarantee that the books functioning as reading keys are trustworthy. Neither of them provide legitimate arguments to explain the symbolic equivalences. In short, both methods are "an insuperable source of arbitrariness and uncertainty."[5] The oneiric element may evoke the most diverse whims in the interpreter, either through the path of intuition or the fixed key. "It cannot be doubted for a moment that neither of the two popular procedures for interpreting dreams can be employed for a scientific treatment of the subject."[6]

The novelty of the Freudian method was that knowledge of the dream was displaced. The dreamer, not the interpreter, had knowledge of the dream content, but with a major caveat: he does not know what he knows. Freud inverted the popular procedures by asking the dreamer for his own ideas about the dream and constructing from them the key to reading the text.

DOI: 10.4324/9781032696423-8

Be that as it may, throughout the history of psychoanalysis, these two methods—initially discredited by Freud—have been confused with the proper analytic method. From the beginning of Freud's work, reading keys based on psychopathological hypotheses were already surreptitiously at work. What should we look for in the text? Trauma, sexual trauma, childhood sexual trauma, childhood sexual fantasies, and so on, until finally the hermeneutic psychoanalytic device was identified: the Oedipus complex. Leaving aside the major differences between these hypotheses (many of them still important to think about in some cases), it can be said that this movement represented the return by different means of the deciphering method, a universal key to the reading of texts. For decades, psychoanalysis was a machine for Oedipalizing texts, and Oedipalizing texts, for us, is Oedipalizing lives. Finally, knowledge returned to the place which it had cost so much to leave: that of the doctor (the psychiatrist, psychologist, psychoanalyst, or whatever you wish to call it). This is why an analyst such as Racker could affirm with great certainty that, as years went by and knowledge accumulated, analysts would require less and less time to interpret.[7] Having an analytic session was submitting to a hermeneutic wave of castrating fathers, phallic mothers, repressed homosexuality, and penis envy. It cannot have been easy to have been a patient at that time, especially for people who were not male, heterosexual, or genital (mature).

We psychoanalysts have not been completely cured of this hermeneutic mania. It is my impression that the use of the Oedipal device by some psychoanalysts exceeded the psychic dimension. The entire world, if such a thing exists, can be explained by the ambivalent figures of mom and dad. By Oedipalizing, I mean not only the reduction of symptoms in a broad sense, to a familial signification, but also the reduction of the family to its most conservative dimension. I do not deny the importance of primordial Others in subjective constitution and in the formation of particular symptoms. The family is not the origin of complexes but the place where they reproduce and acquire their symptomatic character. What I would like to question is the appropriateness of Oedipal explanations of problems of gender, politics, history, and the like, and also their alleged universal functioning.

In *Soñar con Freud* (*Dreaming with Freud*), Marinelli and Mayer clearly show how the use of symbolism, initially rejected by the inventor of psychoanalysis as a criterion for interpretation, has gained importance in analytic theory and practice over the years.[8] The vast majority of the many additions made to *The Interpretation of Dreams* were linked to symbolism. The research in the first psychoanalytic journals and schools were dedicated to this topic. Analysts also wanted to possess knowledge. It is no wonder that symbolism, instead of being an auxiliary method used exclusively when a thought or image did not generate any association, as Freud proposed on several occasions, became a common way of intervening for psychoanalysts.[9] Finally, the dispute is played out in the field of knowledge. It was not, is not, and will not be easy for psychoanalysts to assume the position most appropriate for our practice: learned ignorance.

It seems to me that the practice of the first method criticized by Freud is more relevant to current technical problems, the one relying on clever ideas or direct intuitions arising from the peculiar gifts of the interpreter. Today, this kind of practice is often theoretically justified by the pseudo-Lacanian quote, "at the moment of the act, the analyst does not think." This phrase, like any other, can be interpreted in many ways. In any case, I am interested in a certain reception of it that has led to irrational and non-transmissible practices.

Chamorro provides a clear example of this in his book *¡Interpretar!* (*Interpreting!*). The problems begin also with the fateful phrase from Seminar XXII:

> Lacan says that there are two analysts, one who intervenes in the act and does not think, and one who, after the act, discusses with his colleagues if that was analytic intervention or not in the context of what, to Lacan, is a school.[10]

It is noteworthy that Chamorro omits the "*at least* two," preventing the possibility of the analyst assuming a position other than either thinking or not thinking. I have already worked on another possible reading of Lacan's proposal. What I am interested in highlighting now is that, for Chamorro, the fact that the analyst does not think means interpretation is an act devoid of meaning. It is, in his view, a matter of introducing nonsense that produces nonsense in the analysand.[11]

He also says, "interpretation cannot be anticipated, it cannot be explained."[12] The comma is misleading, because anticipating and explaining are very different actions. In principle, I agree that interpretation, understood here as an intervention in analysis, cannot be prepared in advance, but this does not mean that it does not have a conjectural basis. The analyst cannot anticipate when or how to intervene. However, what he says in this case has to do with what *is* said about it. I also agree that interpretation cannot be an explanation, though this does not mean it cannot be explained. An interpretation must be explainable.[13] This was Freud's idea when he proposed the method. In Chamorro's view, interpretation is about saying anything that generates a void of meaning and "makes the patient uncomfortable," not as an effect but as an end in itself.[14]

The two examples he gives in the first chapter of his book will serve to demonstrate his position. The first example he provides of a good intervention is that of cutting the session when the patient's phone rings: "it is the irruption of the strange, catching the unforeseen surprise factor of the unconscious."[15] It is difficult to imagine that the sound of a cell phone could affect anyone in their position of enunciation. I cannot understand how a person—and I am not referring so much to the analyst as to the analysand—could understand a phone call as an irruption of the unconscious. What it means for my subjectivity that my phone rang, with rare exceptions, is a question no one can ask. The second example is just as surprising:

> Today we were discussing a case during a small meeting, and someone said: "[m]y father was a wolf in sheep's clothing; he seemed good on the outside but inside there was a wolf." In his discourse, he was talking about problems of life, problems with his father, and suddenly there was a wolf and a sheep. Since we live off metaphors, I would have interpreted "owooooo." What is "owooooo"? It is an interpretive way of making the wolf present in its real sense and removing the figurative meaning of the metaphor.[16]

The intervention proposed by Chamorro, consistent with his theses on interpretation, is absolutely senseless. He could also have said "meeeee" or started humming the tune to Michael Jackson's "Thriller" or acted based on any number of ideas like the ones I am freely associating to right now. Furthermore, I do not understand how the analyst's howling would make the real sense of the wolf present and remove the figurative meaning of the metaphor. Actually, a psychoanalyst howling alone is a beautiful metaphor. A more reasonable intervention might be to keep listening to see what signifiers are attached to that popular expression. At the same time, what is the meaning of "good on the outside, but inside there was a wolf"? What is that inside and that outside? Chamorro's position is extreme, and I do not believe it represents the typical behavior of analysts.

In general, the hypothesis that the analyst intervenes without thinking based on his ideas and intuitions is established in the connection between the pseudo-Lacanian proposal that the analyst does not think at the moment of the act and Freud's evenly suspended attention, a connection which I believe to be incorrect. This is Schejtman's case when he states that:

> in this "at least two," the position of the psychoanalyst who directs the treatment and the one who conceptualizes it (the clinician) are not confused. This is something Freud was able to advance, in a way. If we read again that stunning text entitled "Recommendations to Physicians Practicing Psycho-Analysis," we will see that there Freud was completely establishing the position of the analyst as "avoiding speculation or brooding over cases while they are in analysis, and in submitting the material obtained to a synthetic process of thought only after the analysis is concluded": this is the very basis for evenly suspended attention, which, for the analyst, is the consequence of the fundamental rule proposed for the analysand—free association.[17]

Although Schejtman suggests that interventions take place in a state of evenly suspended attention, he then specifies that the analyst must not think during analysis itself but rather "between sessions."[18] The proposal is interesting, but it is not clear how what is thought outside analysis is related to intervening in a state of evenly suspended attention. It is true that, during an analytic session, it can be difficult for the analyst to establish a conjecture about the case. However, it should be clarified that intervention during analysis must be somehow related to the conjecture established between sessions. Why, then, is it stated that the analyst makes interventions from a position of evenly suspended attention?

The "incommensurable split" between analyst and clinician, between the truth *of* the act and the knowledge *about* the act, does nothing more than prevent the unfolding of what, in my opinion, are the most important questions for analytical work in our time: what is the connection between the analyst and the clinician? How does theory *pass* into experience, and experience into theory? How is theoretical (conceptual) and conjectural (case-by-case) knowledge used to analyze? How can we extract not only knowledge but good questions from experience to produce novel and relevant theories? The analyst can "not think" at the moment of the act, but she undoubtedly functions within the context of something thought, and it is on this last point we need to focus. Furthermore, thinking is not necessarily speculating or reflecting; it could be practical, fast, and conclusive thinking. Perhaps this could be called intuition, closer to writing—how and when it is said—than to reading—what is said.

The idea that the analyst must intervene from a position of evenly suspended attention can be found in Freud. From this position, the analyst can use his unconscious as a receiving organ for the analysand's unconscious. The issue is that, while the idea of communication between unconsciouses implies a selection of the material by the analyst's unconscious, evenly suspended attention brings the impossible task of not understanding, of paying attention to the whole text in the same measure, even if either analyst or analysand believes, for whatever reason, that there are parts that are more meaningful than others. It is "*an effort of incomprehension* to respect the other's alterity" and to enable the production of the textuality of the analytic text.[19]

The fact is that some analysts believe that, from a position of evenly suspended attention, the analyst can interpret with her unconscious. My idea is exactly the opposite: to be able to interpret—that is, to select something from the material—the analyst must step away from the position of evenly suspended attention. Curiously, this is also one of Freud's ideas. The reading I propose, then, is one of Freud against Freud. The analyst does not intervene with his unconscious but *from* the unconscious, which is not his own or anyone's unconscious. Freud confused the procedures he himself had differentiated: the production of textuality of the analytic text and its reading. In conclusion, I think that many analysts believe that they make interventions from the unconscious, even if they do not state it directly, and that, in order to make interventions from the unconscious, they must have completed their analysis.

López has worked in detail on this issue in *El inconsciente del analista* (*The Analyst's Unconscious*). Even though I disagree with many of his ideas, the book is excellent in that it is a good reading of the enunciative position of many analysts regarding the way in which they actually claim to intervene. The central idea of the book is that the analyst's unconscious is a valuable resource for the selection of material for interpretation, but that, in order for this to be possible, it is necessary for him to have radically transformed his relationship with truth and knowledge. The analyst needs to have finished his analysis. He says:

> The problem is that if the unconscious cannot be a source for interpretation and the doctrine must also be left aside at the moment of the act, that is, if the analyst cannot make use of any of his inclinations to intervene, the art of interpretation would seem to come from divine inspiration.[20]

What López does not consider is that, in addition to doctrinal knowledge and the knowledge resulting from the analyst's unconscious, there is *textual knowledge*. My proposal, which follows Freud and Lacan, is that the knowledge the analyst and the analysand must extract in order to read and write is in the very text that they themselves produced. You have to read literally (*à la lettre*), Lacan used to say. As López himself points out, and I will quote him, the reading operation is carried out from "the letter of the discourse, in its texture, its uses, and its immanence to the matter in question."[21] Analytic reading and writing are immanent in the text and, as such, dispense with any external reference, even the analyst's "unconscious" ideas. In truth, there is no such thing as an unconscious idea. Ideas are not unconscious, because the unconscious is not something that emerges on its own. It requires a reader. In any case, this idea can be read in conjunction with others to bring about the realization of the unconscious. Lastly, what the text "evokes" for the analyst need not be what the text says without saying it. In order to inhabit the immanence of the text, it is necessary to review some reading criteria which can and should be made explicit.

Like Schejtman, López holds that the analyst must position herself in a state of evenly suspended attention in order to evaluate and select the material. To this end, he shares some references meant to demonstrate that Freud was consistent throughout his teachings on the subject. The first reference is from 1909:

> Our task is not to understand right away a clinical case; we can only achieve it after having received enough impressions of it. For the time being, we will provisionally leave our judgment in suspense, and pay equal attention to everything there is to observe.[22]

Then, he shares another reference, from 1922:

> Experience showed that the most appropriate behavior for the physician practicing analysis was to surrender himself with evenly suspended attention to his own unconscious mental activity, avoiding as much as

possible any reflection or production of conscious expectations, and without intending to fix anything in particular that he heard in his memory; in this way, he would realize the patient's unconscious with his own unconscious.[23]

Far from finding continuity, I find a contradiction. If we read literally, the first reference is characterized by its temporal references: "right away" and "for the time being." The text says that the analyst must not understand *right away*, which means that, at some point, the analyst will need to understand. The suspension of judgment is *for the time being*. Sooner or later, the analyst will need to exit the state of evenly suspended attention in order to select the material. The second reference highlights the persistence of this position: the selection of material is made without stepping away from evenly suspended attention. It is made with the analyst's unconscious. The method of production of the text is confused here with that of reading and writing. Furthermore, even though evenly suspended attention and free association are correlated positions, they are not symmetrical. Both the analysand and the analyst must suspend their judgment, but, while the analysand does so to let her ideas emerge, the analyst does so to open the text for reading. The analyst's ideas are irrelevant to the case except when, together with the analysand's ideas, they are part of the reading of the material. The analyst does not associate freely, does not evoke; he equivocates and produces evocations through his reading and writing.

Lacan said it clearly: "[y]ou can, in certain cases, know what you are doing and where you are at, without always understanding what is at stake, at least not immediately."[24] Psychoanalysts repeat in a chorus that we need not understand, and we do it so much that abstaining from understanding seems like an easy task! What is not usually said is that epistemic abstention, unlike erotic abstention, cannot be sustained indefinitely. At some point, the analyst must step out of the state of evenly suspended attention in order to form a conjecture and give the case a direction. Our "nonaction has a limit, otherwise we would never intervene at all."[25]

In short, through both Oedipal knowledge and unconscious knowledge, analysts have strayed far from textual knowledge:

> in ruling out any foundation of his relationship with the subject in speech, the analyst can communicate nothing to him that the analyst does not already know from his preconceived views or immediate intuition—that is, nothing that is not subject to the organization of the analyst's own ego.[26]

Analysts who believe they intervene with knowledge extracted from their clinic or intuitively from their unconscious actually do so from their ego, with the important disclaimer that they do not know it. No one comes out of their own analysis with a third ear, or with any other attribute that enables listening and selection with the unconscious.[27] There is no communication between uncon-sciouses. There are only failed communications that lead to its realization.

The Freudian Method

The Freudian procedure is divided into two clearly distinguishable moments that start from a fundamental premise: "[w]e must not concern ourselves with what the dream appears to tell us, whether it is intelligible or absurd, clear or confused, since it cannot possibly be the unconscious material we are in search of."[28] The immediate meaning of the text of the dream must be sus-pended until the textuality required for reading is developed. The first part of the method is breaking up the text of the dream into its minimal elements and asking the analysand for associations with each one of them. In a way, this part of the method resembles symbolic interpretation, with the significant difference that it is the dreamer and not the interpreter who must present his ideas about these elements. This moment corresponds to what I called the function of *enabling*: the production of a text that can be interpreted by a psychoanalyst. Again, interpretation cannot be thought about without the constitution of the textuality of the analytic text.

In a second moment, the analyst interprets the text promoted by associa-tions. It is here that difficulties arise. Freud does not explicitly tell us what his reading criterion is, although it is evident that he has one, as little formalized as it may be. He sometimes even says that there is no need for interpretation, that the unconscious will reveal itself based on free association alone.[29] The idea that the unconscious spontaneously "emerges" through free association is very common among psychoanalysts. In truth, the unconscious is an effect of reading and writing.

"The dream of Irma's injection," the paradigmatic interpretation of Freu-dian dreams, is a clear example of this problem. The great difficulty is that Freud does not fully distinguish his associations from his conjectures. The fact that he himself is the object of his own investigation complicates the matter. For example, in one of his "associations" he says: "[i]t seemed as if I had been collecting all the occasions which I could bring up against myself as evidence of lack of medical conscientiousness."[30] I believe that this is not an associa-tion but a transversal reading of all the associations made up to that moment ("all the occasions"), a first idea of what will be the main conjecture about the dream, as will be seen later. At another point, he says:

> [t]he content of the preceding part of the dream had been that my patient's pains were due to a severe organic affection. I had a feeling that I was only trying in that way to shift the blame from myself.[31]

The difference between association and reading is noticeable here. The suspi-cion does not refer to an idea but to a conjecture established based on other elements in the text—that is, from other associations. For some reason, which I attribute to, among other things, the fact that this is a "self-analysis," Freud cannot make a clear distinction between these two moments in the analysis of this dream and, in the end, believes that its meaning *emerged* from his ideas.[32] But the truth is that Freud associates, reads, and forms a conjecture:

> But when I came to consider all of these, they could all be collected into a single group of ideas and labelled, as it were, "concern about my own and other people's health-professional conscientiousness" [...] It was as though he had said to me: "You don't take your medical duties seriously enough. You're not conscientious; you don't carry out what you've undertaken."[33]

Associating, reading, conjecturing: what remains unclear, if we believe that the unconscious emerges on its own, is how Freud arrives at this conjecture. For now, it is possible to say that interpretation produces a new meaning about the text which can be linked to the emotional life of the dreamer. In this case, the dream "speaks" of its fears regarding his medical integrity. Another fact to note is that Freud understands the "hidden" sense as a thought or a series of thoughts, even as something that the dream tells the dreamer: "you don't take your medical duties seriously enough," and so on. The text has a topic, a theme, a subject; this is what a conjecture must establish.

I must say that the interpretation Freud presents does not seem correct to me, especially because the "label" of the dream refers to a conscious concern about his daily life. In my reading, which I will not be able to solidly argue, the true interpretation of the dream appears in footnote 29:

> In a letter to Fliess on June 12, 1900 (Freud, 1950a, Letter 137), Freud describes a later visit to Bellevue, the house where he had this dream. "Do you suppose", he writes, "that some day a marble tablet will be placed on the house, inscribed with these words?—In This House, on July 24th, 1895 the Secret of Dreams was Revealed to Dr. Sigm. Freud. At the moment there seems little prospect of it."[34]

"The dream of Irma's injection" does not speak so much about Freud's worry about his professional integrity as it does about his desire to invent a new social bond: psychoanalysis. The subject, the topic of the text, is the ambitious desire of a Jewish doctor to conquer "Rome." The dream tells Freud he must trust his "formula" of the sexual unconscious, beyond the resistance of his family, his friends, his colleagues, and even his patients, who refuse to open their mouths. The dream works as "a vector of meaning in real time," a desiring orientation, the truth of a future.[35] This is its prophetic character. The dream tells him: "that's where it's at!" And so, it was.

Now, how does Freud read? It is often said that psychoanalysis focuses on details in the text, on what seems insignificant, but this is not entirely true. Freud distinguishes interpretation *in detail* from interpretation *as a whole*, but this is in response to a first moment, to the separation of the text into its minimal elements and the corresponding associations.[36] The second moment, that of reading itself, does not distinguish between detail and non-detail because, while the text is being constituted, everything is of the same importance. The value of one element of the text is established based on other elements. It is true that a detail can become fundamental, and that any element of the text, such as a footnote, can be of the utmost importance in establishing the conjecture. Schiller's words, quoted by Freud, express this clearly:

> Looked at in isolation, a thought may seem very trivial or very fantastic; but it may be made important by another thought that comes after it, and, in conjunction with other thoughts that may seem equally absurd, it may turn out to form a most effective link. Reason cannot form any opinion upon all this unless it retains the thought long enough to look at it in connection with the others. On the other hand, where there is a creative mind, Reason—so it seems to me—relaxes its watch upon the gates, and the ideas rush in pell-mell, and only then does it look them through and examine them in a mass.[37]

Conjecture allows for the connection of ideas that otherwise do not seem to be linked. It does not matter if the ideas are trivial or not. It is not about the detail as such, but about the possibility that an irrelevant element is transformed into an essential one based on its relationship to any other element, and that, in this way, the hierarchical order of the textual economy is inverted. For this, it is necessary, first, that the analyst not understand too quickly; ideas must be "retained" in order for her to see how they are linked to each other. The text must be opened so that the value of each of the elements can become known. In Lacan's terms, a signifier only acquires its value in covariance with other signifiers.

Once the two moments in interpretation are distinguished, and once it has been made clear that it is not necessarily a question of looking for details, it is necessary to wonder how we arrive at a conjecture—that is, on what basis we establish a connection between the elements of the text. There is no better way to introduce this problem than referencing one of Freud's interpretations *à la lettre*. It is "the dream about Elise L."

> A lady who, though she was still young, had been married for many years had the following dream: She was at the theatre with her husband. One side of the stalls was completely empty. Her husband told her that Elise L. and her fiancé had wanted to go too, but had only been able to get bad seats—three for 1 florin 50 kreuzers—and of course they could not take those. She thought it would not really have done any harm if they had.[38]

This is the text of the dream. Such brief and opaque material can hardly be interpreted. First, it is necessary to open the text. This would be the "first part" of the interpretation, the patient's associations:

> The first thing the dreamer reported to us was that the precipitating cause of the dream was touched on in its manifest content. Her husband had in fact told her that Elise L., who was approximately her contemporary, had just become engaged. The dream was a reaction to this information. [...] Where did the detail come from about one side of the stalls being empty? It was an allusion to a real event of the previous week. She had planned to go to a particular play and had therefore bought her tickets *early*—so early that she had had to pay a booking fee. When they got to the theatre it turned out that her anxiety was quite uncalled-for, since *one side of the stalls was almost empty.* It would have been early enough if she had bought the tickets on the actual day of the performance. Her husband had kept on teasing her for having been in too much of a hurry.—What was the origin of the 1 florin 50 kreuzers? It arose in quite another connection, which had nothing to do with the former one but also alluded to some information from the previous day. Her sister-in-law had been given a present of 150 florins by her husband and had been in a great hurry— the silly goose—to rush off to the jewellers' and exchange the money for a piece of jewellery.—Where did the "three" come from? She could think of nothing in connection with that, unless we counted the idea that her newly-engaged friend, Elise L., was only three months her junior, though she herself had been a married woman for nearly ten years.—And the absurd notion of taking three tickets for only two people? She had nothing to say to that, and refused to report any further ideas or information.
>
> But all the same, she had given us so much material in these few associations that it was possible to guess the latent dream-thoughts from them.

The way Freud encourages associations and text production is very interesting. First, he separates the material into different elements and then asks *where each of them comes from.* The question is not why something is said, or what it means, not even what comes to mind, but where it comes from; that is, it refers to another place, another scene which has been condensed and disguised.

Once the text is constituted, it can be read.[39] It must draw our attention, says Freud, that, "periods of time occur at several points in the information she gave us about the dream, and these provide a common factor between the different parts of the material." In this case, the topic is related to *rush* or *haste*: she bought the tickets early, took them hastily, and had to pay more for them; her sister-in-law rushed to buy the jewelry; and so on. If we add, here, the association that connected the marriage of Elise, three months younger than her, to a high-quality man and the criticism expressed of the sister-in-law (it is silly to rush so much), we find ourselves presented almost spontaneously with the following construction [...] "Really it was absurd of me to be in such a hurry to get married! I can see from Elise's example that I could have got a husband later too."

It is possible to draw numerous conclusions from this beautiful example. The first is that it is necessary to divide the interpretation into two different moments: that of the production of the textuality of the text and that of the reading and writing of it. The second is that reading means *establishing a common relation between the different parts of the text*. In this example, the relation is found through the temporal references that, notably, do not appear in the telling of the dream. The third is that construction arises almost spontaneously. This is fundamental because it takes us back to the problem of the analyst's intuition. The spontaneity Freud highlights does not refer to reading in general but to its conclusion. The localization of temporal repetitions is not spontaneous: it requires the effort of reading. What emerges almost intuitively is the "solution" to the dream. In this case, and because it is a model, the text is so brief that the reading seems simple, but let us imagine a much longer text, going on page after page. It is evident that the localization of repetitions, to name one example, is not easily given: it requires careful and effortful reading. An oblique reading, which we are not used to. What comes "intuitively" is the conclusion, which can only be reached once the common relation between elements is established. We go from slow thoughts to quick ones. The fourth and last conclusion is that Freud's reading of this dream is *à la lettre*; it dispenses with any reading code or his own ideas. As Lacan said, the true Freudian genius

> owes nothing to any intuitive insight—it's the genius of the linguist who sees the same sign appear several times in a text, begins from the idea that this must mean something, and manages to [...] [enable] the entire chain of the text to be reconstituted.[40]

There is nothing beyond the text, neither outside nor inside. Reading is sticking to the textual surface, to its signifying dimension, in order to trace a diagonal oriented by insistences.

The Work of the Text

Freud's idea is that the dream narrative is the result of the distortion of a series of thoughts:

> [w]e have introduced a new class of psychical material between the manifest content of dreams and the conclusions of our enquiry: namely, their latent content, or (as we say) the "dream-thoughts," arrived at by means

of our procedure. It is from these dream-thoughts and not from a dream's manifest content that we disentangle its meaning.[41]

The solution to the dream is not in the latent thoughts, but it is realized *from them*. The first moment of interpretation, the opening of the material, helps us reach the latent thoughts; the second, to read in them the "solution" to the dream.

Setting aside the metapsychological explanations of this process, what I am interested in highlighting is the hypothesis that latent thoughts are disguised through the use of a series of linguistic resources, of rhetorical tropes such as metaphor, allegory, hyperbole, synecdoche, antonomasia, ellipsis, emphasis, irony, and so on. The unconscious is like a skilled author who

> has seen in advance which passages might expect to give rise to objections from the censorship and has on that account toned them down in advance, modified them slightly, or has contented himself with approximations and allusions to what would genuinely have come from his pen.[42]

This kind of writing requires an attentive reader to read between the lines. Truth is reached through detours.

Of the work that produces the dream, I will highlight two fundamental operations: condensation and displacement. The manifest text of the dream is "an abbreviated translation" of latent thoughts.[43] Condensation happens because certain latent thoughts are completely omitted, others come in parts, and some—which have something in common—are fused into a unit. We can suppose that the manifest text will have omissions, part-to-whole analogies, and ambiguous words. Condensation creates "nodal points" where many latent thoughts and intermediate common elements are joined. This mechanism dismantles the possibility of thinking about a one-to-one relationship between the manifest content and the latent content. The connection between the elements on both sides is deeply complex: a manifest element corresponds simultaneously to several latent ones, and vice versa. The elements of the manifest content "are constructed out of the whole mass of dream-thoughts and each one of those elements is shown to have been determined many times over in relation to the dream-thoughts."[44]

The work of displacement is manifested in the substitution of a latent thought by an "extrinsic" reference—that is, by a link that ignores the meaning of the elements. Connection through phonic similarity is typical of this operation. Another fundamental fact is that, through displacement, the "psychic accent" of the dream is transferred to a trivial element. According to Freud, the dream presents as diversely focused. Displacement "strips the elements which have a high psychical value of their intensity, and [...] by means of overdetermination, creates from elements of low psychical value new values."[45] For this reason, it is essentially impossible to know where the importance of the text lies.

Coming back to our example, it is noteworthy that, within the telling of the dream about Elise, temporal details that were fundamental to its comprehension were omitted, and the accent of the dream was transferred from "marrying" to "going to the theater." This displacement happens through arbitrary association and can be the result of any relationship; in this case, it came from the temporal proximity of the narration of both events. The text is organized through temporality.

It is not my intention to, nor could I, demonstrate the entire scope of the Freudian description of the dream work. I will have to leave aside fundamental questions such as the means of representing logical relations and abstract thoughts. What I am interested in pointing out is that, for Freud, "If we attempted to read these characters according to their pictorial value instead of according to their symbolic relation, we should clearly be led into error."[46] Another possible translation of this phrase could be: "[o]ne would undoubtedly make a mistake if one read these signs according to their image value instead of according to the relationship between signs."[47] The analytic text must be read as a rebus or as a pictographic script. It is about reading the elements based not on their evident meaning but rather on their status as signifiers—that is, on the value they acquire in covariance with each other. Interpretation undoes the dream work, producing *openings and displacements* in the text based on signifiers and making possible the appearance of "a serious, intelligible message," in accordance with the emotional life of the dreamer.[48]

While I have only mentioned dream work here, Freud states that the operations of condensation and displacement are characteristics of all "conscious thought," and so we can assume that any given analytic text must be read with this premise in mind. Lacan took this idea to its limits, especially in "The Instance of the Letter," where he says, "in the analysis of dreams, Freud intends to give us nothing other than the laws of the unconscious in their broadest extension."[49] In this article, situated "between writing and speech" (as any analytic text), Lacan uses the Saussurean algorithm of the sign to read "linguistically" Freud's ideas about unconscious thought.[50] The Lacanian subversion of the sign will consist, first of all, in rejecting any kind of referentiality. The sign does not refer to any reality. Furthermore, the elements of sign, signifier, and signified do not have a reciprocal relationship. They are different things, separated by a barrier resisting signification. According to Lacan, the signifier does not represent meaning and does not have to "to justify (*répondre de*) its existence in terms of any signification whatsoever."[51] The signifier occupies a primordial position in the creation of meaning; it enters it, it produces it in its covariance. At the same time, signifiers are subjected to the double condition of being reduced to differential elements and composed according to the laws of a closed order. The topology of the signifying chain is organized as "links by which a necklace firmly hooks onto a link of another necklace made of links." In this sense, discourse is aligned on "several staves of a musical score."[52] The signifying chain is polyphonic.

Meaning insists in the chain, between signifiers, but none of them is the signification. Therefore, to the extent that we share the code with other speakers, there is the possibility of using language to say something *very different* from what it says.

Lacan will call the material support that concrete discourse takes from language and the essentially localized structure of the signifier *the letter*, and he will hold that displacement and condensation are actually the two fundamental operations of language: metonymy and metaphor. Metonymy is the connection between words, and metaphor is the substitution of one word for another. In the polyphonic structure of discourse, the first belongs to the diachronic dimension of language, and the second to its synchronic dimension. In truth, this difference only serves propaedeutic purposes, and it makes no sense to say whether a word is metaphorical or metonymic. Each signifier is at the same time metonymy and metaphor only in relation to other signifiers.

In the end, Lacan formalized the operations of unconscious thought through the tools provided by structural linguistics. This allowed him to situate the signifier as the fundamental element of psychoanalytic work, and metaphor and metonymy as linguistic mechanisms present in all language, beyond the dream work: "[this] linguistic structure [...] enables us to read dreams."[53] Reading and writing are transforming the word into a signifier and the signifier into a letter.

Reading à la lettre

The reading of any element of the text is in principle doubtful because it is not known whether it should be taken in a positive or negative sense, or if it should be interpreted historically, symbolically, or literally. There is never an element that functions as such as a clue. In psychoanalysis, there is no such thing as *one* clue. For something to be a clue, at least another clue is necessary. In these terms, the clue is a localized signifier, not a sign. The way in which a signifier is read will depend on its connection with other signifiers. A signifier is transformed into a letter as long as it is found in covariance. "In analytic discourse [...] you give a different reading to the signifiers that are enunciated (*ce qui s'enonce de signifiant*) than [to] what they signify."[54] This *different reading* must then be based not on the connection between the signifier and "its" meaning—which is given by common sense or by the analyst's knowledge (as doctrine or as an idea)—but on the relationship between signifiers "inside" the text.

> What concerns us now is in what way the signifier will operate in this situation. What needs to be done? Resorting to texts, knowing how to read and construct. When things are reproduced with the same elements, but ordered differently, it is necessary to record them as they are, without looking in them for far analogies, mentions of extrapolated interior events which we would suppose in the subject. It is not about, as we say

in ordinary language, the symbol of something *cogitating*, but something altogether different—they are laws where structure is manifested, not of the real, but of the symbolic, and which interact with each other. They operate, in a way, in themselves independently.[55]

Perhaps the most appropriate analogy for the reading of a case is that of a *puzzle*. In a case, we suppose that, from the start, the pieces are out of order, as if the text had been cut and re-pasted arbitrarily. One can begin taking up the fragments that make up the framework. Once this process is finished, one can take the other pieces and place them in a series, combine them correctly following some pattern (colors, shapes, etc.). The fundamental point is that a single stray piece does not say anything in itself; it must be placed in relation to other pieces, which might be at the other end of the table. Once most pieces are placed, we can begin to see a shape that was—and was not—there before putting the pieces together. We must not forget that the analytic *puzzle* is missing the central piece and that it cannot be said that it was already there.[56]

The analyst's "reasoned" interventions do not come from any reading key outside of or preceding the text, nor from any of the interpreter's ideas.[57] They use the pieces of the material. The key to reading is provided by the text. In any valid interpretation, according to Lacan, it is enough to "stick to the text to understand it."[58] As long as the analyst separates himself from the discourse, his intervention will belong progressively to his own knowledge, transforming what he says into a suggestion separate from any criterion of truth. There is no reason not to take the text as it is presented, "under the pretext of something or other that is supposed to be ineffable, incommunicable, affective."[59]

Reading to the letter implies suspending the immediate signification of the text to attend to its flaws, its ruptures, its contradictions, "its elusions, distortions, elisions, and even holes and syncopes."[60] The analyst must read "the slips, the holes, the disputes, the repetitions of the subject."[61] As Vernazza said, analytic reading "is less about reading between the lines to look for meaning than [...] to look for that which moves meaning and which, precisely for this reason allows for its redefinition."[62] When Lacan says that meaning insists in the chain, but it is not made up of its elements, he does nothing but highlight the fact that interpretation occurs between signifiers. While slips, jokes, dreams, and mistakes are not in themselves manifestations of the unconscious, they are *shortcuts* to it in the sense that they open more easily the question of meaning: what did you mean by what you said?

Analytic interpretation is neither a revelation—we do not reveal to the patient something that was hitherto hidden—nor a deciphering—a one-to-one correspondence between the analyst's knowledge and the patient's unconscious knowledge. The analyst's reading is closer to deciphering because, "it is related to the signifying operation," but with the major difference that the subject is, "as such already determined and inscribed in the world as caused by a certain effect of the signifier."[63] What we must read is not within the analysand, but the analysand is within the text—as is the analyst. Also, what interests us about knowledge are "precisely these points which, for us, give rise to questions in the name of truth."[64] The unconscious is realized based on what limps in language: discontinuities, slips, hesitations, forgetfulness, ignored repetitions, and so on. Lacan's idea is that "we must be attentive to the unsaid that dwells in the holes in discourse, but the unsaid is not to be understood like knocking coming from the other side of the wall."[65] The unsaid is located not beyond what is said (in affectivity, in reality, or in some unknown complex) but in the fractured immanence of the text. To sum up, truth "is here posed as having to be searched for in the faults (*failles*) of statements."[66]

An appropriate way to approach the Lacanian proposal of reading is through his "return to Freud." The best way to read Freudian texts, according to Lacan, is applying "the critical method he himself praised:"

> My "return to Freud" simply means that readers are concerned with knowing what Freud means, and the first condition for this is that they read him seriously. And this is not enough, because since a great part of secondary and higher education is concerned with preventing people from knowing how to read, a whole educational process is necessary to allow them to learn to read a text again [...] knowing how to read a text, understanding what it means, realizing in what "way" it is written (in a musical sense), in what register, implies many other things and, above all, penetrating the internal logic of the text in question.[67]

I cannot agree with Lacan when he says that reading Freud means knowing what he meant. It would be more appropriate to maintain, following Lacan, that reading implies locating the partial, contingent, and historical truths that the Freudian text carries. He himself held that there is nothing further from analytic interpretation than a psychology of the author.[68] Psychoanalysts do not interpret people; we interpret texts. And the text does not tell us about the psychology of that person, it tells us how that person participates in the intelligence of the symbolic, the imaginary, the real. We must pay attention to the text, to its internal logic and its tone.

Foucault understood very well the mode of reading proposed by Lacan. In his lecture "What Is an Author?" he expressed in a very suggestive way the implications of Lacan's "return to Freud" and his critical method:

> it is always a return to a text in itself, specifically, to a primary and unadorned text with particular attention to those things registered in the interstices of the text, its gaps, and absences. We return to those empty spaces that have been masked by omission or concealed in a false and misleading plenitude. In these rediscoveries of an essential lack, we find

the oscillation of two characteristic responses: "[t]his point was made—you can't help seeing it if you know how to read;" or, inversely, "No, that point is not made in any of the printed words in the text, but it is expressed through the words, in their relationships and in the distance that separates them." It follows naturally that this return, which is a part of the discursive mechanism, constantly introduces modifications and that the return to a text is not a historical supplement that would come to fix itself upon the primary discursivity and redouble it in the form of an ornament which, after all, is not essential. Rather, it is an effective and necessary means of transforming discursive practice.[69]

I would like to highlight three of Foucault's ideas about the Lacanian reading method:

1 He returns to the text itself in its nakedness and, at the same time, to its holes, absences, and gaps.
2 He maintains that what the text says *is on the surface*, and is not in any of the particular words but in what is said through them, *between the words.*
3 He affirms that reading is not a supplement or addition to meaning, nor is it an aesthetic accessory. It is a way of transforming the text itself.

More than listening or observing, a psychoanalyst reads. In short, "commenting on a text is like doing an analysis."[70]

The problem of reading takes us again to the fatal phrase "at the moment of the act, the analyst does not think." I could not find this quote in Lacan's work. I suspect that it is the result of an *overly* forced reading of another phrase said by Lacan: "[i]t must then be advanced that the psychoanalyst in psychoanalysis is not a subject, and that by situating his act in the ideal topology of the object a, it can be deduced that he operates by not thinking."[71] Basically, what we can extract from this quote is that whoever occupies the place of the subject in analysis is the analysand, while the analyst occupies the place of the object *a*, cause of the analytic work. From the place of *a*, the analyst does not think. Again, it all depends on how we understand the word "thought" in this context. Everything indicates that thought here refers to Lacan's reform of Cartesian *cogito: I think where I am not, therefore I am where I do not think.* It is important to remember that Lacan equates the signifying chain to thinking (*Gedanke*), since, "Freud uses the term to designate the elements at stake in the unconscious, that is, in the signifying mechanisms [metaphor and metonymy] I just pointed to there."[72] Where I think, where I play the game of the signifying mechanisms of metaphor and metonymy, I cannot situate myself as a being.

Therefore, the one who "thinks" in analysis, who allows himself to be caught up in thought, is the analysand. That the analyst should not think in the moment of the act means, in this context, that she should not freely associate or intervene according to her own ideas. She should not let herself be led by her thoughts nor propose any knowledge outside the knowledge without a subject (textual knowledge) articulated in the analysis. And what does the analyst do with knowledge without a subject? Lacan says it clearly in the same text: "[t]hat there is an unconscious means that there is knowledge without a subject. The idea of instinct crushes this discovery: but it survives *because this knowledge never proves to be anything but legible.*"[73] The analyst and the analysand read this knowledge without a subject to realize the unconscious.

Interpretation and Construction

The first thing an analyst does is enable the production of a type of textuality and construct with the analysand the analytic text. As Freud said, this can occur in different ways: through memories, fantasies, dreams, ideas, and "indications of repetitions," both within and outside of the consulting room.[74] "It is out of such raw material—if we may so describe it—that we have to put together what we are in search of." Now, who produces what is desired? Analysts or analysands? What does it mean that what is desired is produced?

Analytic work requires *action* on the part of the analysand and the analyst. Saying the analyst enables, desires, reads, and writes places the analytic task wholly on one side. To be more precise, we must say that the analyst fosters the conditions and participates, together with the analysand, in the realization of the analytic functions. They happen between these two positions, if they are well occupied. The analyst's task is *being spoken* analytically by the analysand. The analysand's task is speaking according to the rules of the analytic game. In addition to being spoken, the analyst also needs to "make out what has been forgotten from the traces which it has left behind or, more correctly, to *construct* it." According to Freud, the analyst must produce a conjecture about "what is forgotten"—let us call this *subject*—from clues provided by the analytic text.

> The time and manner in which he conveys his constructions to the person who is being analysed, as well as the explanations with which he accompanies them, constitute the link between the two portions of the work of analysis, between his own part and that of the patient.

Here, the construction—which I prefer to call reading or conjecture—is "only a preliminary labour." This is so for two reasons. The first is that the construction of the conjecture does not coincide with its communication. The what does not tell us about the how or the when. All of this depends on the disposition and specific characteristics of the analysand. The analyst may have sufficient elements to establish a conjecture, but at the same time decide that it is not yet appropriate to incorporate it into the material. For example, the analysand may be "too far" from a conjecture, and so the work would consist of setting up the conditions so it can be received. We could say that the players must be in the right position before the analyst takes his shot. Or perhaps the analysand is "close" enough to a conjecture, but the analyst believes it necessary to wait for the right moment, using the contingencies of analysis to achieve a greater impact. A high card is wasted if it is not played at the right time. This is why it is advisable to differentiate between analytic reading and writing.

The second reason why construction is part of the preliminary work is that the incorporation of the conjecture occurs in an open, living, porous, mutating text. Interpretation involves not only reading but also writing the material. Reading is writing. In this sense, reading-writing makes possible the production of hitherto unpublished material and, therefore, the opening up of new readings. Freud put it as follows:

> The analyst finishes a piece of construction and communicates it to the subject of the analysis so that it may work upon him; he then constructs a further piece out of the fresh material pouring in upon him, deals with it in the same way and proceeds in this alternating fashion until the end.

This would seem to lead to infinite analysis, since the text tends to open with each new reading-writing. However, effective reading-writing produces new material as it *crosses out* a different part of the text. That is, in order to produce new material, the conjecture must cross the text transversally. So, where many seemingly different elements appear, the conjecture "unites" them under a subject that both was and was not there before the conjecture was offered. It simultaneously produces something new and reduces the text. A true interpretation opens and closes the text in one fell swoop.

According to Freud, the term construction is much more appropriate than that of interpretation, which is limited to operations on the singular elements of the material. We could say that, in order to make a construction, we need first to interpret. It is clear that the analyst says many things before and after proposing a conjecture if he poses it explicitly. In any case, there are many types of interventions: those that intend to produce textuality in the analytic text, those allowing the analysand to speak, those that gradually expose connections between different elements in the material, and those that present a conjecture, directly or indirectly. All of these can be *analytic writing*, just like the speech of the analysand.

Freud believed, much more than is currently accepted, that the analyst should establish a conjecture and propose it to the patient. History shows this clearly. What is more, he often insisted on his hypotheses despite patients' initial refusal to accept them. It is surprising how much Freud interpreted—in a wider sense, intervened—in his analyses. The deadly silence, the wordplay, and the super short sessions of some Lacanians (the well-known persecutory analyst) have made us forget the importance of analytic constructions, clinical hypotheses, and the necessity that the analyst think about her cases and direct the treatments according to what is thought.

It is now time to ask ourselves how reading is incorporated into the analytic text; about the how and the when, about its limits, its *modes*, its materiality, and its effects and purposes.

What does it mean to write in psychoanalysis?

Notes

1 Freud, 1900 (1899)/1953: 97.
2 Ibid.
3 "An example of this procedure is to be seen in the explanation of Pharaoh's dream propounded by Joseph in the Bible. The seven fat kine followed by seven lean kine that ate up the fat kine—all this was a symbolic substitute for a prophecy of seven years of famine in the land of Egypt which should consume all that was brought forth in the seven years of plenty" (ibid.). The Pharaoh's dream is actually two consecutive dreams in one night: "When two full years had passed, Pharaoh had a dream: He was standing by the Nile, when out of the river there came up seven cows, sleek and fat, and they grazed among the reeds. After them, seven other cows, ugly and gaunt, came up out of the Nile and stood beside those on the riverbank. And the cows that were ugly and gaunt ate up the seven sleek, fat cows. Then Pharaoh woke up. He fell asleep again and had a second dream: Seven heads of grain, healthy and good, were growing on a single stalk. After them, seven other heads of grain sprouted—thin and scorched by the east wind. The thin heads of grain swallowed up the seven healthy, full heads. Then Pharaoh woke up; it had been a dream" (*New International Version Bible*, 2011: Genesis 41:1–7). It is curious that Freud omits what is surely the most relevant characteristic of the dream: repetition. In this sense, it can be said that Joseph does not interpret only in terms of his personal idea but also based on repetition (seven ugly skinny Xs "devour" seven fat beautiful Xs) and substitution (heads of grain for cows).
4 Ibid.
5 Ibid.: 98, footnote 1.
6 Ibid.: 99.
7 "While, for example, in past times, the analyst had to listen for hours and even weeks to the analysand's associations before being able to give them an appropriate interpretation, the analyst today usually realizes much sooner what the analysand needs to know and is able to leverage that in the way an analyst generally can in order to interpret many times during a session, which is progress in the possibilities of more intense and even quicker elaborations of the unconscious conflicts" (Racker, 1959/1981: 38).
8 Cf. Marinelli and Mayer, 2011.
9 "The touchstone with which the progress of this budding science was measured was, to psychoanalysts, to gather dreams and symbols which could form a typology [...] The evidence of the pertinence of interpreting dreams in a psychoanalytic way would be supported by new and impersonal material. Now added to the gathered clinical observations, there were accumulated testimonies which came neither from the clinic nor the office, but from literature, myth and folklore" (ibid.: 78–79).
10 Chamorro, 2011: 8. Note the author's clarification that the discussion with colleagues must take place within the framework of a school.
11 "Psychoanalytic intervention seeks to escape meaning. And in any case it will be an intervention devoid of meaning so that the one who interprets the meaning of the intervention is the patient and not the analyst" (Ibid.: 12).
12 Ibid.: 16.

13 With some exceptions, interpretation does not need to be explained to analysands but does to the "scientific community."
14 "[W]e have to make [the patient] uncomfortable with our interventions" (Chamorro, 2011: 15).
15 Ibid.: 14.
16 Ibid.: 16.
17 Schejtman, 2013: 28.
18 Ibid.
19 Cosentino, 2022.
20 López, 2020: 26.
21 Lacan as quoted by López, 2020: 48.
22 Freud as quoted by López, 2020: 71.
23 Ibid.
24 Lacan, 1958–1959: 26.
25 Lacan, 1953: 258.
26 Lacan, 1955: 281.
27 "The only object that is within the analyst's reach is the imaginary relation that links him to the subject qua ego; and although he cannot eliminate it, he can use it to adjust the receptivity of his ears, which is, according to both physiology and the Gospels, the normal use made of them: having ears *in order not to hear* (*entendre*), in other words, in order to detect what is to be understood (*entendu*). For he has no other ears, no third or fourth ear designed for what some have tried to describe as a direct transaudition of the unconscious by the unconscious." (Lacan, 1953: 211).
28 Freud, 1916c (1915–1916): 114.
29 "We must wait till the concealed unconscious material we are in search of emerges of its own accord" (ibid.).
30 Freud, 1900 (1899)/1953: 112.
31 Ibid.: 114.
32 "I have now completed the interpretation of the dream. While I was carrying it out I had some difficulty in keeping at bay all the ideas which were bound to be provoked by a comparison between the content of the dream and the concealed thoughts lying behind it. And in the meantime the 'meaning' of the dream was borne in upon me" (ibid.: 118).
33 Ibid.: 120.
34 Ibid.: 121.
35 Dufourmantelle, 2012/2020: 50.
36 Cf. Freud, 1900 (1899)/1953: 96–97.
37 Ibid.: 103.
38 Freud, 1916c (1915–1916). The following quotes are taken from this text, pp. 122–124, until otherwise indicated.
39 In truth, this way of putting it is not entirely correct because the analytic text is never fully constituted. Analysts impose arbitrary limits in order to make a partial and momentary reading.
40 Lacan, 1955–1956: 10–11.
41 Freud, 1900 (1899)/1953: 277.
42 Freud, 1916a (1915–1916): 139.
43 Freud, 1916b (1915–1916): 171.
44 Freud, 1900 (1899)/1953: 284.
45 Ibid.: 307.
46 Ibid.: 277.
47 Translation proposed by C. Cosentino (1998).
48 Freud, 1900 (1899)/1953: 135 (footnote 2).

49 Lacan, 1957: 427.
50 Ibid.: 412.
51 Ibid.: 416.
52 Ibid.: 419.
53 Ibid.: 424.
54 Lacan, 1972–1973: 37.
55 Lacan, 1956–1957/2008: 309.
56 Freud used this analogy to think about the interpretation of dreams: "A coloured picture, pasted upon a thin sheet of wood and fitting exactly into a wooden frame, is cut into a large number of pieces of the most irregular and crooked shapes. If one succeeds in arranging the confused heap of fragments, each of which bears upon it an unintelligible piece of drawing, so that the picture acquires a meaning, so that there is no gap anywhere in the design and so that the whole fits into the frame—if all these conditions are fulfilled, then one knows that one has solved the puzzle and that there is no alternative solution" (1923 [1922]: 116). Tomás Pal also used the metaphor of the puzzle to think about psychoanalysis.
57 "What do we do then in substituting for this wild interpretation our reasoned interpretation? [...] in this reasoned interpretation, nothing other than from a reconstituted sentence, to grasp the point where there is a flaw which is the one where, qua sentence, and not at all qua meaning, it allows there to be seen what is not working and what is not working, is desire" (Lacan, 1968–1969: XII 13).
58 Lacan, 1951: 101.
59 Lacan, 1955–1956: 208.
60 Lacan, 1955: 278.
61 Lacan, 1953–1954/1991: 245.
62 Vernazza, 2021: 25.
63 Lacan, 1967–1968: lecture on November 29, 1967.
64 Ibid.
65 Lacan, 1953: 253.
66 Lacan, 1966–1967: lecture on June 21,1967.
67 Lacan, as cited by Caruso, 1969/1976.
68 "When it comes to our patients, please give more attention to the text than to the psychology of the author—the entire orientation of my teaching is that" (Lacan, 1954–1955: 233).
69 Foucault, 1969/1998: 312.
70 Lacan, 1953–1954/1991: 73.
71 Lacan, 1969/2012: 397.
72 Lacan, 1957: 430.
73 Lacan, 1969/2012: 396.
74 Cf. Freud, 1937: 258. All following quotes until the end of the chapter are taken from "Constructions in Analysis," pp. 258–261.

References

Caruso, P. (1976). *Conversaciones con Lévi-Strauss, Foucault y Lacan.* Barcelona: Anagrama. (Original work published 1969)

Chamorro, J. (2011). *¡Interpretar!*Buenos Aires: Grama.

Cosentino, J.C. (1998). Ficha de estudio. "El trabajo del sueño": introducción. Ficha I. Psicoanálisis Freud: cat. II. Faculty of Psychology, UBA.

Cosentino, M. (2022). Textualidad y encuentro. Del imperativo de neutralidad a la hospitalidad. *Revista Universitaria de psicoanálisis*, 22, 51–60. Retrieved from

www.psi.uba.ar/investigaciones/revistas/psicoanalisis/trabajos_completos/revista22/cos
entino.pdf

Dufourmantelle, A. (2020). *Inteligencia del sueño: fantasmas, apariciones, inspiración*. Buenos Aires: Nocturna. (Original work published 2012)

Foucault, M. (1998). What Is an Author? In D. Preziosi (Ed.), *The Art of Art History: A Critical Anthology*, pp. 299–314. New York: Oxford University Press. (Original work published 1969). Retrieved February 22, 2024, from https://books.google.com. ar/books/about/The_Art_of_Art_History.html?id=maRgjgEACAAJ&redir_esc=y

Freud, S. (1916a [1915–1916]). The Censorship of Dreams. In S. Freud, A. Freud, A. Strachey, and A. Tyson (Eds.), *The Standard Edition of the Complete Psychological Works of Sigmund Freud, Volume XV: Introductory Lectures on Psycho-Analysis*. Trans. J. Strachey, pp. 136–148. London: The Hogarth Press.

Freud, S. (1916b [1915–1916]). The Dream-Work. In S. Freud, A. Freud, A. Strachey, and A. Tyson (Eds.), *The Standard Edition of the Complete Psychological Works of Sigmund Freud, Volume XV: Introductory Lectures on Psycho-Analysis*. Trans. J. Strachey, pp. 170–183. London: The Hogarth Press.

Freud, S. (1916c [1915–1916]). The Manifest Content of Dreams and the Latent Dream-Thoughts. In S. Freud, A. Freud, A. Strachey, and A. Tyson (Eds.), *The Standard Edition of the Complete Psychological Works of Sigmund Freud, Volume XV: Introductory Lectures on Psycho-Analysis*. Trans. J. Strachey, pp. 113–125. London: The Hogarth Press.

Freud, S. (1923 [1922]). A Seventeenth-Century Demonological Neurosis. In S. Freud, A. Freud, A. Strachey, and A. Tyson (Eds.), *The Standard Edition of the Complete Works of Sigmund Freud, Volume XIX: The Ego and the Id and Other Works*. Trans. J. Strachey, pp. 69–108. London: The Hogarth Press.

Freud, S. (1937). Constructions in Analysis. In S. Freud, A. Freud, A. Strachey, and A. Tyson (Eds.), *The Standard Edition of the Complete Psychological Works of Sigmund Freud, Volume XXIII: Moses and Monotheism; An Outline of Psycho-Analysis and Other Works*. Trans. J. Strachey, pp. 255–270. London: The Hogarth Press.

Freud, S. (1953). *The Standard Edition of the Complete Psychological Works of Sigmund Freud, Volume IV: The Interpretation of Dreams (First Part)*. Eds. A. Freud, A. Strachey, and A. Tyson. Trans. J. Strachey. London: The Hogarth Press. (Original work published 1900 [1899])

Lacan, J. (1951). Intervention on Transference. In C. Bernheimer and C. Kahane (Eds.), *In Dora's Case Freud-Hysteria-Feminism*, pp. 92–104. New York and Chichester: Columbia University Press.

Lacan, J. (1953). The Function and Field of Speech and Language in Psychoanalysis. In J. Lacan, *Écrits: The First Complete Edition in English*. Trans. B. Fink, pp. 197–268. New York and London: W.W. Norton.

Lacan, J. (1954–1955). *The Seminar of Jacques Lacan. Book II: The Ego in Freud's Theory and in the Technique of Psychoanalysis*. Ed. J.-A. Miller. Trans. S. Tomaselli. New York and London: W.W. Norton.

Lacan, J. (1955). Variations on the Standard Treatment. In J. Lacan, *Écrits: The First Complete Edition in English*. Trans. B. Fink, pp. 269–302. New York and London: W.W. Norton.

Lacan, J. (1955–1956). *The Seminar of Jacques Lacan. Book III: The Psychoses*. Ed. J.-A. Miller. Trans. R. Grigg. New York and London: W.W. Norton.

Lacan, J. (1957). The Instance of the Letter in the Unconscious or Reason Since Freud. In J. Lacan, *Écrits. The First Complete Edition in English*. Trans. B. Fink, pp. 412–441. New York and London: W.W. Norton.

Lacan, J. (1958–1959). *The Seminar of Jacques Lacan, Book VI: Desire and Its Interpretation*. Ed. J.-A. Miller. Trans. B. Fink. Cambridge: Polity Press.

Lacan, J. (1966–1967). The Seminar of Jaques Lacan, Book XIV: The Logic of Phantasy. Trans. C. Gallagher. Unpublished. Retrieved from http://hdl.handle.net/10788/163

Lacan, J. (1967–1968). *The Seminar of Jacques Lacan, Book XV: The Psychoanalytic Act 1967–1968*. Ed. C. Gallagher. Retrieved from www.lacaninireland.com:http://hdl.handle.net/10788/164

Lacan, J. (1968–1969). The Seminar of Jacques Lacan, Book XVI: From an Other to the other. Trans. C. Gallagher. Unpublished. Retrieved from http://hdl.handle.net/10788/165

Lacan, J. (1972–1973). *The Seminar of Jacques Lacan. Book XX: On Feminine Sexuality. The Limits of Love and Knowledge*. Ed. J.-A. Miller. Trans. B. Fink. New York and London: W.W. Norton.

Lacan, J. (1991). *The Seminar of Jacques Lacan. Book I: Freud's Papers on Technique*. Ed. J.-A. Miller. Trans. J. Forrester. New York and London: W.W. Norton. (Original work published 1953–1954)

Lacan, J. (2008). *El Seminario IV: La relación de objeto*. Buenos Aires: Paidós. (Original work published 1956–1957)

Lacan, J. (2012). El acto psicoanalítico. Reseña del seminario 1967–1968. In J. Lacan, *Otros escritos*, pp. 395–403. Buenos Aires: Paidós. (Original work published 1969)

López, M. (2020). *El inconsciente del analista*. Buenos Aires: Letra Viva.

Marinelli, L., and Mayer, A. (2011). *Soñar con Freud. La interpretación de los sueños y la historia del movimiento psicoanalítico*. Buenos Aires: El cuenco de plata.

New International Version Bible. (2011). Retrieved from www.biblegateway.com/versions/New-International-Version-NIV-Bible/#vinfo

Racker, H. (1981). *Estudios sobre técnica psicoanalítica*. Buenos Aires: Paidós. (Original work published 1959)

Schejtman, F. (2013). Clínica psicoanalítica: Verba, Scripta, Lectio. In F. Schejtman, *Psicopatología: clínica y ética. De la psiquiatría al psicoanálisis*. Buenos Aires: Grama.

Vernazza, D. (2021). *Lacan, el arte de leer*. Buenos Aires: Letra Viva.

Chapter 9

Cutting

Analytic Writing

When?

Originally, psychoanalysis was like any other practice where money was exchanged for knowledge. After some time "listening"—through hypnosis, for example—the physician communicated "the solution" the patients themselves had *unknowingly* provided, and they accepted it, no matter how unlikely it seemed to them. Today, we understand that interpretation cannot be completely alien to the analysand. It must have the weight of an intimate strangeness. However, the ghost of unconscious knowledge still haunts us as property that can be donated, whether it comes from the mouth of the patient or the writings of some renowned psychoanalyst (this is a different problem). It is important to keep in mind the violence psychoanalysts exercise in the name of truth, in the belief that we possess the ultimate knowledge about the subjective position and suffering of our patients.

Freud identified this problem rather early on. "The dream of Irma's injection" begins with Freud's reproach of her for "not having accepted the solution." One aspect of dreams is resistance to truth: "[i]t is your responsibility because you do not want to hear it," Freud says about the dream, exonerating himself from any responsibility for the poor outcome of the treatment.

> It was my view at that time (though I have since recognized it as a wrong one) that my task was fulfilled when I had informed a patient of the hidden meaning of his symptoms: I considered that I was not responsible for whether he accepted the solution or not—though this was what success depended on. I owe it to this mistake, which I have now fortunately corrected, that my life was made easier at a time when, in spite of all my inevitable ignorance, I was expected to produce therapeutic successes.[1]

I am not so sure that this mistake has been fully overcome. Analysts may still be too concerned with producing successes. Analysands' resistance, their failure to accept solutions, their "not wanting" to be cured are proportional to the symbolic pressure analysts exert. Analysands who resist do nothing

DOI: 10.4324/9781032696423-9

more than protect their desire. It is necessary to renounce the exercise of power, along with the seizure and privatization of knowledge, in order to read, write, and participate in it. The analyst reads a knowledge that passes through him, not one that he possesses. How can we transmit something that we do not possess? Do we transmit knowledge, or do we transmit *ourselves*?

Our knowledge need not match the analysand's. And I refer here not to knowledge about the unconscious the analyst is supposed to already have (and which she must renounce as an ethical and technical principle) but to knowledge that can be read in the analytic text. Freud says in "An Outline of Psycho-Analysis,"

> But in all this we never fail to make a strict distinction between *our* knowledge and *his* knowledge. We avoid telling him at once things that we have often discovered at an early stage, and we avoid telling him the whole of what we think we have discovered.[2]

We must carefully choose the moment when we will make our conjecture known to the analysand. For that, we must be patient, wait until it seems appropriate, "which it is not always easy to decide."[3] It is true that those who wait for the perfect moment will wait their entire lives. Just as haste can be a problem in analysis, inhibition in interpreting can also be one, especially for young professionals who fear their words will cause disasters in their patient's subjectivity. These fears are largely disproportionate to reality. I believe they are caused by the position of some professors who shroud themselves in an air of mystery and wisdom. We were taught that we must be extremely careful, that knowing the right words requires many years of analysis, that, if we lack this obscure and non-transmissible knowledge, we will go through life making people unbalanced. This is false: it is not a matter of course that one has so much power over a patient.

Being careful does not mean forgetting that our practice involves getting into the mud and coming out with some stains. Sometimes we need to rush. Certain times are better than others, and analysis offers several opportunities of different kinds—errors, ambiguities, repetitions, lucky coincidences, and so on—to put conjectures into play. *Kairós* is a generous god. Additionally, there are precise criteria:

> As a rule, we put off telling him of a construction or explanation till he himself has so nearly arrived at it that only a single step remains to be taken, though that step is in fact the decisive synthesis. If we proceeded in another way and overwhelmed him with our interpretations before he was prepared for them, our information would either produce no effect or it would provoke a violent outbreak of resistance which would make the progress of our work more difficult or might even threaten to stop it altogether. But if we have prepared everything properly, it often happens

that the patient will at once confirm our construction and himself recollect the internal or external event which he had forgotten. The more exactly the construction coincides with the details of what has been forgotten the easier it will be for him to assent. On that particular matter our knowledge will then have become his knowledge as well.[4]

The arrival of a conjecture never coincides with its direct communication.[5] The analysand needs time to understand, and the analyst does not know how long that will take.[6] In the same vein, the analyst's task is not limited to establishing and sharing a conjecture but also involves *preparing the conditions* for the appearance of the reading-writing together with the analysand. We need analysts who assist rather than analysts who score goals; those who take their time, who adjust quickly to their position in the game, but who also take into consideration the position and timing of the other. In other words, someone who plays the game rather than showing off his game.

In this sense, it can be said that analytic interpretation is neither a revelation nor an invention; it is a reading-writing *in* the analytic text. We do not reveal to our analysand knowledge that we already have and that he does not yet know. The meaning of the symptoms must not be revealed, "it must be assumed by [the analysand]. In this respect, psychoanalysis is a technique which respects the person [...] not only respects it, but cannot function without respecting it," says Lacan.[7]

Analytic interpretation approaches and encloses. It establishes relationships and produces contact between elements in the text in which analyst and analysand participate. In this way, the analyst accompanies the analysand in the reading-writing of the truth that resides in the failures of knowledge.

> This truth which speaks and whose verdict one is waiting for ... one strokes it, one tames it, one pats it on the back! [...] And in order for him to do better one pretends, in short—this is the sense of the rule of free association—[...] not to give a feck about it, to be thinking about something else, in that way it will perhaps let something important appear.[8]

Enabling the analytic text and its particular textuality prepares the ground for the truth to speak. Through its opening, the text gives us the necessary elements to carry out a reading-writing that produces a subject. The truth does not speak on its own: we must make it speak, as Lacan suggests. We must be patient, give it time. We must let the text unfold, open, offer itself to us based on the conditions we propose. Haste is also a frequent clinical problem among analysts. We delay interpretation, but we rush to understand.

If we are still victims of *furor sanandi*, despite countless warnings, it is because we are pressed to answer the suffering of our patients quickly. How could this not be so if we consent to take responsibility for their suffering! This is why patience is a great virtue. Some problems take time to solve.

Urgency makes us fall into our own trap: the belief that we possess knowledge and should donate it. This is often called "responding to demand." Analytic reading-writing is not supported by "I know and I say" or by "you know and you say." It is an "it says" in the multiple voices in the text, according to a knowledge without a subject.

The Analytic Cut

What a psychoanalyst interprets is desire. She neither names it nor expects the analysand to do so. "How can one name a desire? One circumscribes a desire. There are many things in history that provide us with tracks and traces here."[9] Through these "tracks and traces" the text provides, the analyst and the analysand produce reading-writings that enable the analysand to recognize himself in the dimension of desire. Psychoanalysts do not interpret the object of desire, but we read desire's coordinates: its refuges, its masks, its friction, its bindings, its symptomatic lines, and its vanishing points. The analyst "is mistaken" if she believes she must show the analysand that what he desires is this or that object.

The traversal of the fantasy is a journey, it is the detour through the object cause of desire. There is nothing to traverse, but a long way to go. "Everything happens on the steps, in the stages, on the different rungs of the revelation of this desire."[10] Psychoanalysis is always a work in progress.

Reading-writing is a cut that generates a surface. Let us call a cut a significant intervention that produces a partial closure of the text. Saying that an analyst interprets texts and not people does not mean forgetting the body. One of Freud's most brilliant ideas is that the body of interest to the analyst is a textual body, and that subjective suffering is weaved into the signifying automaton. Textual bodies are read and written.

In Lacanian psychoanalysis, the concept of the cut became intimately linked to the interruption of the session. It is well known that Lacan used time as a fundamental tool of analysis and was firmly opposed to any attempt at standardization. His idea is that the fixing of analytic time by the analyst, as a whole or for each session, favors the illusion that "truth's due date can be predicted," as if the truth were already there, establishing again the prejudice that views truth as a possession of the analyst.[11] Another way of saying this is that fixed time sustains the prejudice of the subject supposed to know.

What resulted from this is a different matter: extremely short sessions, people crowded in waiting rooms, and analysands afraid to sigh lest they be expelled from the session and, on top of that, charged for it. Today, some colleagues do not work with variable-length sessions; they hold short sessions exclusively. The reasons for this abbreviation seem to be strictly economic. When the time of the unconscious suspiciously approaches that of capital, we may allude, as Pal did, to a transference of "funds." The fact that several patients are called within minutes of each other shows this clearly. That unconscious time does not coincide with modern chronometric time or with so-called "subjective time" cannot be an excuse to turn each session into a countdown. Analysis cannot take place in an atmosphere of urgency or immediacy. We must open a new temporal space, different from the temporality of everyday life.

Regarding short and ultra-brief sessions, I would like to call to mind the following advice from Freud:

> one comes across patients to whom one must give more than the average time of one hour a day, because the best part of an hour is gone before they begin to open up and to become communicative at all.[12]

I have a similar experience. At the beginning of a treatment, sessions tend to be longer. Analysands need time to articulate their suffering, the context of their lives, their history, and their imagination, but also, to begin to trust their interlocutor, to break through the inhibiting barriers of shame and suspicion. Likewise, it takes time to absorb the analytic rules, to learn to speak analytically, to let go of the pitfalls of reality. Lacan's proposal, as I understand it, is not that sessions must be short, but that they *should tend towards* brevity and concision.[13] It is like this: as analysis progresses, sessions tend to be shorter, and this happens without forcing it. In fact, it has on occasion happened that an analysand, anticipating the session's conclusion, has said to me "we'll stop here today." This speaks not only of my slow pace, but of the spontaneity with which some analyses develop. "It was said" between us, what *needed* to be said was said, and so, does it matter who made the cut?

There are analysands who use the time in service of their neurosis. A typical example is the demand for completeness some suffer when speaking to the analyst. Such analysands want to say everything, as if anything remaining unsaid would be a *misfortune* for the analysis. It is only necessary to point out this demand for totality and remind them of the rules of the game: preparation in advance is not permitted, and trying to say everything is a contradiction. As a rule, analysis involves saying something other than what was intended, it is about letting oneself be carried away by the analytical game.

A concept closely linked to the cut is dialectical punctuation. According to Lacan, the analyst's function is close to that of an ancient scribe[14] or, closer to us, to that of the editor.[15] Both the ancient scribe and the modern editor are tasked with tending to the text, protecting its truth, and finding its truest mode of expression. But the most important thing for us is that, by punctuating the text, the editor inevitably modifies its meaning. As we know, punctuation retroactively gives meaning to what is said. We can only know what the speech will have been once it finds its stopping point. "Punctuation, once inserted, establishes the meaning; changing the punctuation renews or upsets it; and incorrect punctuation distorts it."[16] An analysand may wish to keep speaking in order to avoid or forget the consequences of what was said.

The interruption of the session is less a "go and think about what I've told you" than a "it is necessary for what has been said to resonate," which is why the time before and after the session is so important (unfortunately, virtual sessions have encumbered those resonating commutes). An analyst uses punctuation to locate speech, and this does not necessarily coincide with the cut of the session. It is a cut in the textual surface, "for it shatters discourse only in order to bring forth speech."[17] It is sometimes paramount to wait for the analysand's response to the punctuation, to evaluate whether it was appropriate, depending on the subsequent association. Other times, it is best to interrupt and leave meaning in suspense. It is a gamble, which, like all gambles, can fail. It is clear that one of the analyst's tasks is to evaluate "to which 'part' of this discourse the significant term is relegated."[18]

From Lacan's perspective, the analytic cut is a signifying intervention made on the subject, understood as a topological surface. In the same way that the subject is a product of the signifier, the surface is a product of the cut. In this sense, we can say that the cut does not necessarily coincide with the interruption of the session. It is not a chronological but a topo-logical cut. The analytic text—conceived as a topological surface—is made of demands that are repeated owing to their dissatisfaction. "Repetition is nothing other than the most radical form of the experience of demand," Lacan says.[19] But demand is not something that goes without saying, it is necessary to carry out a reading-writing that locates at least two signifiers as infinitely close, as "the same," as that which always returns to the same place. In this way, the seemingly chronological line of speech becomes a loop. Analysis must produce *double loops*. Lacan said, "it is a signifier which is repeated, even though it happens in a single gesture, for topo-logical reasons which make possible the existence of the double loop created by a single cut."[20]

There is no way to access desire if not through working with demand. Desire is what lies between demands (perhaps we should abandon the trans-cendental "beyond"). It is articulated but it is not articulable; it can only be said elliptically. The analytic task is to transform that inner void produced by the turn of unsatisfied demand into the object cause of desire. In analysis, we turn from drive to desire, and to locate the latter it is necessary that the set of demands be located in their repetition. "It is a matter of establishing what kind of field is precisely established through the return of demand. From there, and with a sufficient set of loops, we aim to unify them through their interpretation."[21] Eidelsztein holds that, if repeated demands are articulated as "one," the object cause of desire appears—that is, there emerges the pos-sibility of half saying it. The cuts that give rise to the double loops produce in their closure the topological surface called a torus (which can be imagined as a donut). From the point of view of transference, it is possible to maintain that "a case" is made by the interlocking of two tori, where what embraces the object *a* in a torus matches the return of demand in the complementary torus: what marks (seals) the object of desire in each of us is the demand of the Other, and not the desire of the Other.[22]

When the loops are closed, there is either an extra loop or one less loop, depending on how one counts. Each double loop implies a closure, but, at the same time, the complete turn of the double loops produces a closure that gives rise to the torus and the object cause of desire.[23]

Repetition is a product of reading: "the act is in the reading of the act," says Lacan.[24] If the analyst is in charge of initiating the opening of the text, it is also her responsibility to ensure that partial closures are produced. In the first place, the analyst encourages the production of a loop through reading at least two repeating signifiers. Then, she looks for the "other scene" as a repetition of this loop, leading to a double loop—that is, the structure of at least four signifiers, which Lacan considers necessary for the realization of the subject. This is what we call interpreting demand. Lastly, a "one" of desire will be read in the closure of all the loops of demand. This act of reading enables a half-saying of desire, a saying it elliptically. "What it is most important to understand in the analysand's demand is what is beyond that demand. The space occupied by not understanding (*la marge de l'incompréhension*) is the space occupied by desire (*la marge du désir*)."[25]

The demand of the Other connotes and suggests the object of desire.

Resonances

It is not enough for a truth to be true for it to be accepted as such. We know this from personal experience. Whether a truth wakes us up or puts us to sleep, "depends on the tone in which it is said."[26] Analytic interpretation must focus on both the content of truth—what is said—and the mode and timing of its enunciation—how and when it is said. The time has come to ask ourselves about the *aesthetics of the cut*.

In Lacan's work, there is a concept that is key to thinking about this problem: resonance. The third section of "The Function and Field of Speech and Language in Psychoanalysis" is entitled "The Resonances of Interpretation and the Time of the Subject in Psychoanalytic Technique," which I have tried to delimit as the questions of when and how. Here, Lacan says that "the analyst can play on the power of symbols by *evoking them in a calculated fashion* in the semantic resonances of his remarks."[27] Calculation, evocation, and resonance. In the same text, the concept of resonance appears several times and for different reasons. As Kripper demonstrates, resonance can be considered a concept owing to the value it has when one considers, "the uses and effects of language in psychoanalytic theory and practice" or, in a more specific sense, interpretation.[28] Lacan uses it in reference to the question of how to read Freud, stating that Freudian concepts must be revised since, in retaining "the ambiguity of everyday language, [they] benefit from the latter's resonances while incurring misunderstanding."[29] Words such as unconscious, desire, love, repetition, and so on are commonly used and carry with them their common meaning and a particular meaning for each person. Every time we hear or read one of these words, each of these meanings can resonate with "us," beyond the specific meaning these words have within a theory. This is why it is necessary to apply some effort in reading and conceptualizing, a rigorous fidelity to the text that allows us to extract meaning particular to *this* text. Another occasion in which this concept appears is when Lacan defines telepathy as "a case of resonance in the communicating networks of discourse."[30] This definition is concomitant with the topological model he uses to think about human relationships:

> links, supports, rings in the same circle of discourse, agents integrated in the same circle of discourse [...] the unconscious is the discourse of the other. This discourse of the other [is] the discourse of the circuit in which I am integrated.[31]

(This is, at the same time, equivalent to the model of the two linked tori.) Telepathy is not a transmission of thoughts from one person to another but a resonance of the same thought in both people. If there are telepathic phenomena between analyst and analysand, it is not because the analyst can listen with his unconscious to the unconscious of the other. Telepathy occurs when they both inhabit the same knowledge without knowing it, they are part of the same text. That something resonates means it evokes something in us in both an ideational and a sensitive sense. Resonance produces a vibrant evocation, as sometimes happens with certain smells, places, melodies, or words.

In order to think about the problem of resonance in interpretation, Lacan uses a concept from the Hindi aesthetic tradition *dhvani*. This concept succinctly refers to sound—the echo, the sound of a drum—to the reverberation words produce in bodies. Lacan defines it as "the property of speech by which it conveys what it does not say."[32]

Most philosophical schools of ancient India, according to Kripper, attributed two types of meanings to words: a primary meaning—denotation—called *vacyartha*, and a secondary meaning—connotation—called *laksyartha*. An example of the first would be the phrase "here is a cow," where the word "cow" denotes a cow. Conversely, an example of the second type of meaning might be "a village on the Ganges," where the word "on" substitutes "on the banks of." The secondary meaning, while not a denotation, is connected to it through a metaphor. In the expression "a lion among men," the same thing occurs; it is clear we are talking not about a literal lion but about a person who shares certain characteristics with the lion: strength, bravery, authority, and so on.

Other philosophers posit the existence of a third meaning of words and sentences that is not reduced to denotations or *stricto sensu* to connotation:

dhvani, poetic meaning. It is "what is suggested but cannot be derived from denotation."[33] All senses, the literal, the figurative, and the poetic, are experienced at the same time. "The literal sense is grasped, the poetic sense is suggested; the first is easily accessible to the reader, the second is only for the cultured reader. Both coexist, like light and darkness in the sunset."[34] The idea that the poetic sense is accessible only to the cultured reader is useful for the clinic. In analysis we learn analytically. It is not that the patient must either be or become someone knowledgeable, intelligent, cultured, having "symbolic fabric," and so on, but, as Freud forewarned, becoming an analysand requires certain preparation. An analysand must learn the rules of the game connected to the production, reading, and writing of the text in which she participates. This is not obvious, and it is the analyst's task to familiarize her with analytic functions. Sometimes, when an analysand wants to recant or clarify what he meant in the face of a slip or ambiguity, I simply tell him that "this is not part of the rules of the game."

Dhvani is an "accomplished failure" so long as it transmits something that is non-transmissible in the literal sense, something that does not coincide with any of its words but lies between them, only resonates with an attentive reader, one who can read between the lines.[35] Lacan's references to the tradition of Hindi philosophy are exemplary. The first says:

> A girl, it is said, is awaiting her lover on the bank of a river when she sees a Brahmin coming along. She approaches him and exclaims in the most amiable tones: "What a lucky day this is for you! The dog whose barking used to frighten you will not be on this riverbank again, for it was just devoured by a lion that roams around here ..."
> The absence of the lion may thus have as many effects as his spring— which, were he present, would only come once, according to the proverb relished by Freud.[36]

The literal meaning of the story is that the barking dog is no longer there, and so there is nothing to fear. However, if the dog is gone, it is because it was killed by a lion. This is what poetic meaning says between the lines: the danger is greater now! The lion's absence can have as many effects as its presence, just like the suggested meaning: "a presence made of absence." The lion also *evokes* the dangers of poetic meaning.

Kripper argues that Lacan uses the term "resonance" in both the figurative and the poetic sense. Lacan's idea is that interpretation must avoid the denotative, informative, or explicative style; it should rather suggest, evoke, and produce resonances that position the reader as the protagonist in the appearance of meaning. Although the function of language is not to inform but to evoke, and every phrase, no matter how denotative, produces resonances, it is advisable that the analyst *suggest* his conjectures rather than report them. Interpretation must be open enough for the reader-interpreter—in this case, the analysand—to participate in the construction of meaning. In this way, asserting that only the analyst interprets is another propaedeutic forcing. Interpretation occurs between analyst and analysand. The interpreter here is also the one who executes the suggestion, as someone might interpret or execute a musical score.

Before continuing these disquisitions on the aesthetics of the cut, let us examine another example Lacan gives at the close of his famous essay:

> When the Devas, the men, and the Asuras were finishing their novitiate with Prajapati, as we read in the first Brahmana of the fifth lesson of the Brihadaranyaka Upanishad, they begged him, "Speak to us."
>
> "*Da*" said Prajapati, god of thunder. "Did you hear me?" And the Devas answered, saying: "Thou hast said to us: *Damyata*, master your-selves"—the sacred text meaning that the powers above are governed by the law of speech.
>
> "*Da*" said Prajapati, god of thunder. "Did you hear me?" And the men answered, saying: "Thou hast said to us: *Datta*, give"—the sacred text meaning that men recognize each other by the gift of speech.
>
> "*Da*" said Prajapati, god of thunder. "Did you hear me?" And the Asuras answered, saying: "Thou hast said to us: *Dayadhvam*, be merci-ful"—the sacred text meaning that the powers below resound (*resonnent*) to the invocation of speech.
>
> That, continues the text, is what the divine voice conveys in the thun-der: Submission, gift, grace. *Da da da.*
>
> For Prajapati replies to all: "You have heard me."[37]

Prajapâti says "Da" three times, but it resonates in each person hetero-geneously, since this "Da" is heard and understood by each person as the first syllable of different words: *Damyata, Datta*, and *Dayadhvam*. For the Devas, the men, and the Asuras, "Da" evokes different things, but still everyone has heard and understood it because "the meaning to which the Creator points is not given by denotation or metaphor, but by suggestion."[38] The analyst, like Prajapâti, does not deliver a meaning but produces symbolic evocations based on calculation. By this I mean that "Da" is not merely nonsense pointing to nonsense: it is a calculated intervention which can evoke different things—but not just anything. "Da" as such is nonsense, but it points to a limited register of evocations. In this case, despite the differences, it always refers to the characteristics of the word.

Kripper says that analytic interpretation can be divided into two moments: first, the analyst suggests and produces evocations; second, she punctuates the analysand's evocation, highlighting its truth value: "when the subject's ques-tion takes the form of true speech, [analysts] sanction it with our answer [...] we do nothing more than give the subject's speech its dialectical punctua-tion."[39] Prajapâti says "you have heard me" and confirms the truth of each evocation. This does not mean that "Da" *must have meant* different things to each of the listeners, "but that *meaning* is suspended from what resonates in them—not from what they hear, but what *is heard* in them."[40] That "Da," as such, does not mean anything does not prevent it from being a delimitation in the field of resonances, an adjustment in the production of evocations. "Da" means nothing, but it does not mean just anything. Kripper concludes that,

> Lacan reduces to a minimum the *via di porre*, to redirect the analysis along the extreme *via di levare*. Interpretation does not "provide meaning" since resonance *evokes meaning*—it provides a saying whose meaning comes from the analysand, not from the analyst—and punctuation *sanctions this meaning*, sanctioning also the text that emerges from the analysand.[41]

Interpretation does not provide meaning. It evokes meanings, locates signifiers, and sifts through the conditions of desire. "Analytical interpretation is not made to be understood; it is made to make waves."[42] It spreads in waves, like when a stone is thrown into a lake or a guitar string is plucked. That said, it is possible to affirm that any strict dichotomy between the logical analyst and the poetic analyst is false in that both skills are required: on the one hand, "logic," understood in this case as the possibility of establishing a reasoned, coherent, and transmissible reading of the case; on the other hand, "poetry," so that the writing of a conjecture is a calculated suggestion awaiting the analysand's evocations and not a donation of meaning. It is uniquely through equivocation that interpretation operates.[43]

The Nonsense of the Signifier

It is common for psychoanalysts to say that analytic interpretation does not add meaning, that it is directed towards nonsense, even that it *is* nonsense. One of the sources of this idea is the Freudian contrast between *via di porre* and *via di levare*. Freud held that psychoanalytic interpretation took the second route: it did not add anything to the raw textual material but rather subtracted and modeled, just as sculptors do with clay, stone, and wood. However, in psychoanalytic history, this theoretical-clinical principle was intersected by the development of the Oedipal hermeneutic device, undoubtedly a return to *via di porre*. This contrast exposes two models for the position of the analyst: one who already knows and who adds his knowledge to the text, or one who does not know and expects to extract knowledge from the text. At the same time, textual knowledge extracted from a case is not applicable to other cases, because in this way we would occupy the position of the one who "already knows" and adds knowledge to the text. I do not mean that analysts do not learn anything from experience, or that each case cannot teach us to read better, but the knowledge we extract from one case cannot be a "reading key" for another.

Another resource for thinking about the nonsense of interpretation is Lacan's work. For example, in Seminar XI, he says that "the effect of interpretation is to isolate in the subject a kernel [...] of *non-sense*."[44] We will see what the scope of this idea is, and what it means that analysis is directed towards nonsense. For the time being, I would like to pause for a few paragraphs on the gloating of some colleagues over what could be called an "ethics of nonsense." Many analysts believe that psychoanalysis should lead analysands to encounter the meaninglessness of life, the non-existence of the Other, the desert of the real. Analysis would, in this case, demonstrate that nothing makes sense, that our suffering is sustained only by "mere" fictions, that the fantasies haunting us are nothing but inventions of human gullibility, and none of that actually exists. There is only nonsense. This reminds me of a meme in which a young man sets up a stage full of monsters (the Other) and then lies on the floor, terrified by what he himself had built. The meme is not funny because it is far from any truth. However, there are colleagues who smirk a little. They tell us that the end of analysis should show the young man that those monsters do not exist, that he invented them himself, that behind the scenes there is nothing. The Other does not exist! The disillusioned believe that psychoanalysis is useful for dismantling fictions and embracing the meaninglessness of reality, but the real lies not behind the fictions but rather *in* them. Otherwise, it is ridiculous that we should lie on the couch for years to find a nihilism resembling the existential conflict of a libertarian more than an ethical premise supported by the unconscious. Miller proposes it in this way:

> Then, the Other does not exist [...] the subject loses all possibility of obtaining a place in the Other, because it is the very place of the Other that is lost. And this is what we need to face. Is it easy, then, to live when the Other does not exist? This means that we cannot count on anyone but ourselves. But this means that we need to sustain ourselves without identifications, at least without the support of the identifications through which the subject has unknowingly adhered until now in the place of the Other. It would also be necessary to sustain oneself without apologies, without excuses, without explanations, without complaints [...] *Never complain, Never explain.* [...] a long time ago we saw that something cynical appears at the end of analysis, a cynical loneliness which comes from the Other is a semblance [...] it is understandable that a state of enthusiasm ensues and that this is accompanied by an affect of depression that comes and goes for a while.[45]

The Millerian clinic produces cynical, rather depressed subjects, who do not apologize, do not make excuses, who neither explain nor complain. You can only count on yourself, say the obediently warned, the entrepreneurs of the self. As can be seen, depending on how we understand that interpretation points towards nonsense, we will have different, even opposite, clinics. Let us remember the case of Chamorro. According to this perspective, interpretation is nonsense producing nonsense. For him, this means the analyst can use anything—even a howl, or a ringing phone—as long as it generates an effect of nonsense in the analysand.

Material can yield several readings, but this does not mean that interpretation can be anything. Lacan says:

> it is false to say, as has been said, that interpretation is open to all meanings under the pretext that it is a question only of the connection of a signifier to a signifier, and consequently of an uncontrollable connection.[46]

This is an apt reply to both Chamorro's interpretations and to another common way of understanding and practicing nonsense in interpretation: the famous Lacanian wordplay. I believe that wordplay is completely useless and even cartoonish, while the only thing it proves is the polysemy of the signifier. It is obvious that words can mean many things. Wordplay is an interpretation when a "wrong" meaning is found in relation to other meaningful elements in the text. This can happen by chance or as the result of a conjecture. The second option is ideal.

Analytic interpretation "is not just any signification," "It is not just any interpretation. It is a significant interpretation."[47] A text enables several readings, but it does not allow infinite ones. One cannot make the text say what one wants, and not all of the text can be interpreted. The appropriateness of an interpretation also depends on the use we want to make of the text. I find no contrast, at least in this sense, between interpretation and use of the text. I mean that we will not use the analytic text to do, for example, literary critique or psychobiography. Otherwise, the term intervention is more appropriate than interpretation because analytic reading is not validating but performative, it does not intend to understand but to produce. Interpretation does not reveal a truth but triggers the truth as such.[48] Every analytic reading is reading-writing.

So, no reading is complete or definitive. The text we read and write admits other readings and writings, and, furthermore, our reading and writing will never be complete. Freud put it in these terms:

> I have already had occasion to point out that it is in fact never possible to be sure that a dream has been completely interpreted. Even if the solution seems satisfactory and without gaps the possibility always remains that the dream may have yet another meaning.[49]

The Freudian concept designating limits of interpretation is the "navel of the dream," the place where the text settles into "the unknown," the mark, the scar of the unreadable that opens the legibility of the text.[50] The navel of the text is what points to its incompleteness, the polysemy, and the limits of what can be interpreted. It is the most concise and thickest point of the signifying chain where meaning stops momentarily, and "the dream-wish grows up, like a mushroom out of its mycelium."[51]

That interpretation points to nonsense means to Lacan that its goal is to locate primordial signifiers. Interpretation has the effect of "bringing out an irreducible signifier."[52] To be more precise, it is a signification that illuminates, beyond itself, "to what signifier—to what irreducible, traumatic, non-meaning—" the subject is subjected to. Just as Freud stated when he said that interpretation dismantled the work of the dream, for Lacan it "reverses the relation by which the signifier has the effect, in language, of the signified." Interpretation is a signification that makes signifiers appear, and signifiers, as such, mean nothing, they make no sense.

On several occasions, I have heard from analysands who in previous analyses only received from their analysts a highlighting of certain words, as if they were machines arbitrarily highlighting isolated elements. Highlighting certain words to transform them into signifiers is an appropriate practice for opening the text, but it cannot be the sole intervention of the analyst. The text must also be closed, and these cuts are necessary. It is also true that the highlighting of a signifier can represent a cut, but only if this signifier is connected to another, and, at the same time, this pair is connected to another.

Analytic reading-writing rations the meaning of the symptom and reduces it to the signifiers that command it. "It is not the effect of meaning that is operative in interpretation, but rather the articulation in the symptom of signifiers (without any meaning at all) that have gotten caught up in it."[53] Interpretive work must locate the signifiers that determine the subject, but this does not mean that interpretation is nonsense or that it can be anything. Interpretation should not be explained, but it must be possible to explain it. It must be "reasoned." These problems derive from the idea that I have been developing throughout the book: at the moment of the act, the analyst does not think. As Lacan says, "[w]e see here that the dilemmas in which the practitioner gets bogged down derive from depreciations by which his thinking fails his action."[54]

Lightning and Truth

How true is it that long interpretation is ineffective? It is likely that an elaborate discourse will end up in detours and produce variations on the same thing and so will lose its impact. It is also true that some discourses, despite their long duration, maintain their vitality. It is difficult to hold that only brief words produce an effect. The truth is that what seems to make an impact is often just a few words, and the conditions surrounding them can be excellent preparation, like jabs before an uppercut or the bridge of a song. The difference is that, in general, we do not know precisely what the lucky strike or the chorus of our song will look or sound like.

Now, I do not see the need for the analyst to remain silent or to only open his mouth to cut the session or to say mysterious and incomprehensible things. Often, analysts must intervene to set up the analytic game or to reset it; at other times, to calm and contain overwhelming anxieties; at yet others, to prepare the groundwork for the incorporation of a conjecture; at others, to exit the imaginary field of transference passions; and so on.

Needless to say, intervention should be brief. Interpretation is brief and abrupt by default, no matter the words it contains. Let us say that, most times, further clarification only serves to obfuscate, and a few words are often more effective than extensive arguments. No possibility is prohibited from the outset. When an analysand tells me that she did not understand what I said because I was enigmatic or too vague, I answer that clarifications—with very few exceptions—are not part of the rules of the game for either of the parties involved, and that there will be another opportunity to work on that idea.

Lacan said that, "in order to decipher the diachrony of unconscious repetitions, interpretation must introduce into the synchrony of signifiers that come together there *something* that suddenly makes translation possible."[55] *Suddenly* might refer to the style of the interpretation, to its brief, abrupt, and unexpected character, or to its "essence"—that is, the fact that interpretation as such suddenly produces a new meaning in the text. On the path to locating the master signifiers, the reading-writing of the material produces new meanings that "narrow" other meanings. The location of the discursive constants limits the multiplicity of meanings that manifest from the opening of the text. The production of new meanings on the way to nonsense is not a contradiction. In the same way, the new meaning produced does not respond so much to a desire to say but to an orientation, a tendency, an intention of the text.

The most beautiful image to illustrate these matters was offered by Lacan: "interpretation, namely this addition by means of which something appears which gives meaning to what you think you know, which makes appear in a flash what it is possible to grasp beyond the limits of knowledge."[56] I would say, as a slight alteration to this metaphor, that interpretation is a lightning bolt: first, lightning appears, illuminating the text fleetingly and surprisingly; then, at some point, we do not know exactly when, we hear the roar and resonance of thunder. The effect of a good reading of the material, in the analysis itself and in supervision, feels like this: "I cannot understand how I did not see this before; it was in front of my eyes the whole time, I only had to read the material using this key." Then, of course, we return to the inherent opaqueness of the material, but with the direction provided by that instant of light.

Interpretation produces truth—partial and contingent—with the corresponding transmutation of the subject, understood in the double sense of both the analysand and the subject matter of the text. However, how do we know if it was "true," appropriate, or effective? Interpretation is measured according to its effects; it is repeated over and over. But what must those effects be with which we can measure it? Some colleagues believe that interpretation is verified to the extent that the analysand continues to associate freely, understanding by this a "shift in the topic" of the conversation—that is, talking about something else, and something else, and something else, and something else. I do not agree with this idea. I will repeat: no one is cured by free association alone.

Can we trust the approval or denial of the analysand? Let us see what Freud says:

> The "Yes" has no value unless it is followed by indirect confirmations, unless the patient, immediately after his "Yes", produces new memories which complete and extend the construction. Only in such an event do we consider that the "Yes" has dealt completely with the subject under discussion.
>
> A "No" from a person in analysis is quite as ambiguous as a "Yes" and is indeed of even less value. In some rare cases it turns out to be the expression of a legitimate dissent. Far more frequently it expresses a resistance which may have been evoked by the subject-matter of the construction that has been put forward but which may just as easily have arisen from some other factor in the complex analytic situation. [...]
>
> An equally valuable confirmation is implied (expressed this time positively) when the patient answers with an association which contains something similar or analogous to the content of the construction.[57]

In the end, according to Freud, "yes" or "no" is not so relevant. The important thing is that the analysand produces new textual material that complements and broadens the conjecture, which brings an association including "something similar or analogous to the content of the construction." Nothing could be further from the patient producing a shift in the topic.[58] On the contrary, it must give us another indication in favor of our conjecture. Lacan states even more clearly:

> [i]t is impossible, in analytic experience, to consider the subject's change of style as being the proof of the correctness of an interpretation. I consider the proof of the correctness of an interpretation to lie in the confirmatory material the subject supplies.[59]

And even this must be qualified, Lacan adds. The thing is that there is nothing, absolutely nothing, that guarantees that the transformations of the subject are produced by interpretations. This is the castration of the analyst: the impossibility of accurately predicting the effects of an interpretation and knowing with certainty whether it produced the changes. We operate in the realm of conjecture, not logical-mathematical or probabilistic calculation. Our work is somewhat artisanal; each case has something different from the others. We do not do serial work; we do not have treatment manuals; and we do not make "typical" interventions. None of this means we do not demand of ourselves "rigor that is in some sense ethical, without which any treatment, even if it is filled with psychoanalytic knowledge, can only amount to psychotherapy. This rigor would require a formalization, by which I mean a theoretical formalization."[60]

Analytic functions—enabling, desiring, reading, and writing—are nothing more than a theoretical proposal for psychoanalysts so that we can better orient ourselves in our practice. The radical renunciation of power that the ethical position of the analyst requires is not achieved solely through personal virtues or personal analysis. Concepts must be refined, *ideaffects* must vibrate, bodies must resonate, and desires must dance.

Let us suspend time, let us perform the ritual, let us mourn.

Is psychoanalysis not a party?

Buenos Aires
December 2021

Notes

1 Freud, 1900 (1899)/1953: 108.
2 Freud, 1940 (1938): 178.
3 Ibid.
4 Ibid.
5 "It is not difficult for a skilled analyst to read the patient's secret wishes plainly between the lines of his complaints and the story of his illness; but what a measure of self-complacency and thoughtlessness must be possessed by anyone who can, on the shortest acquaintance, inform a stranger who is entirely ignorant of all the tenets of analysis that he is attached to his mother by incestuous ties, that he harbours wishes for the death of his wife whom he appears to love, that he conceals an intention of betraying his superior, and so on!" (Freud, 1913: 140).
6 "We cannot predict how long a subject's time for understanding will last, insofar as it includes a psychological factor that escapes us by its very nature" (Lacan, 1953: 255).
7 Lacan, 1953–1954/1991: 29.
8 Lacan, 1975–1976: lecture on June 21, 1976.
9 Lacan, 1964/1981: 262.
10 Lacan, 1954–1955: 211.
11 Lacan, 1953: 256.
12 Freud, 1913: 127–128.
13 Cf. Cosenza, 2003/2009: 59.
14 "A witness blamed for the subject's sincerity, trustee of the record of his discourse, reference attesting to its accuracy, guarantor of its honesty, keeper of its testament, scrivener of its codicils, the analyst is something of a scribe" (Lacan, 1953: 258).
15 Another of Tomás Pal's ideas.
16 Lacan, 1953: 258.
17 Ibid.: 260.
18 Ibid.: 209.
19 Lacan, 1961–1962: lecture on May 30, 1962.
20 Lacan, 1966–1967: lecture on February 22, 1967.
21 Eidelsztein, 2006: 174.
22 Ibid.: 178–179.

23 I would like to point out the intimate link between the "Return to Freud"—that is, the critical method of reading proposed by Lacan—and the problem of the double loop: "[m]y return to Freud has an entirely different meaning insofar as it is based on the subject's topology, which can only be elucidated through a second twist back (*tour*) on itself. Everything about it must be restated on another side so that what it hones in on can be closed, which is certainly not absolute knowledge but rather the position from which knowledge can reverse truth effects" (Lacan, 1966: 306).
24 Lacan, 1967–1968: lecture on November 22, 1967.
25 Lacan, 1960–1961: lecture on March 15, 1961.
26 Lacan, 1976–1977: lecture on April 19, 1977.
27 Lacan, 1953: 243.
28 Kripper, 2018: 650.
29 Lacan, 1953: 199.
30 Ibid.: 220.
31 Lacan, 1954–1955: 89.
32 Lacan, 1953: 243.
33 Mohanty, as cited by Kripper, 2018.
34 Ibid.
35 Kripper, 2018.
36 Lacan, 1953: 244.
37 Lacan, 1953: 265.
38 Kripper, 2018: 657.
39 Lacan, as quoted by Kripper, 2018: 658.
40 Kripper, 2018: 658.
41 Ibid.
42 Lacan, 1976: 35.
43 "In no case must psychoanalytic intervention be theoretical, suggestive, that is, imperative: it must be misleading" (ibid.).
44 Ibid.: 250.
45 Miller, 1993–1994/2018: 22.
46 Lacan, 1964/1981: 249–250.
47 Ibid.: 250.
48 Cf. Lacan, 1971: 13.
49 As cited by Laplanche and Pontalis, 1967: 293.
50 Freud, 1900–1901: 525.
51 Ibid.
52 Lacan, 1964/1981: 250–251. All quotes in this paragraph come from this reference.
53 Lacan, 1960: 714.
54 Lacan, 1955: 273.
55 Lacan, 1958: 496.
56 Lacan, 1962–1963: 26.
57 Freud, 1937: 262–263.
58 Just as Chamorro (2011) holds, for example.
59 Lacan, 1953–1954/1991: 56.
60 Lacan, 1955: 269–270.

References

Chamorro, J. (2011). *¡Interpretar!* Buenos Aires: Grama.
Cosenza, D. (2009). *Jacques Lacan y el problema de la técnica en psicoanálisis.* Madrid: Gredos. (Original work published 2003)

Eidelsztein, A. (2006). *La topología en la clínica psicoanalítica*. Buenos Aires: Letra Viva.

Freud, S. (1900–1901). *The Standard Edition of the Complete Psychological Works of Sigmund Freud, Volume V: On Dreams*. Eds. A. Freud, A. Strachey, and A. Tyson. Trans. J. Strachey. London: The Hogarth Press.

Freud, S. (1913). On Beginning the Treatment (Further Recommendations on the Technique of Psycho-Analysis I). In S. Freud, A. Freud, A. Strachey, and A. Tyson (Eds.), *The Standard Edition of the Complete Psychological Works of Sigmund Freud, Volume XII: The Case of Schreber, Papers on Technique and Other Works*. Trans. J. Strachey, pp. 121–144. London: The Hogarth Press.

Freud, S. (1937). Constructions in Analysis. In S. Freud, A. Freud, A. Strachey, and A. Tyson (Eds.), *The Standard Edition of the Complete Psychological Works of Sigmund Freud, Volume XXIII: Moses and Monotheism; An Outline of Psycho-Analysis and Other Works*. Trans. J. Strachey, pp. 255–270. London: The Hogarth Press.

Freud, S. (1940 (1938)). An Outline of Psycho-Analysis. In S. Freud, A. Freud, A. Strachey, and A. Tyson (Eds.), *The Standard Edition of the Complete Psychological Works of Sigmund Freud, Volume XXIII: Moses and Monotheism, An Outline of Psycho-Analysis and Other Works*. Trans. J. Strachey, pp. 141–296. London: The Hogarth Press.

Freud, S. (1953). *The Standard Edition of the Complete Psychological Works of Sigmund Freud, Volume IV: The Interpretation of Dreams (First Part)*. Eds. A. Freud, A. Strachey, and A. Tyson. Trans. J. Strachey. London: The Hogarth Press. (Original work published 1900 [1899])

Kripper, A. (2018). De la resonancia a la metonimia. La teoría temprana del sentido en Lacan. *Revista Signa*, 27, 647–663.

Lacan, J. (1953). The Function and Field of Speech and Language in Psychoanalysis. In J. Lacan, *Écrits: The First Complete Edition in English*. Trans. B. Fink, pp. 197–268. New York and London: W.W. Norton.

Lacan, J. (1954–1955). *The Seminar of Jacques Lacan, Book II: The Ego in Freud's Theory and in the Technique of Psychoanalysis*. Ed. J.-A. Miller. Trans S. Tomaselli. New York and London: W.W. Norton.

Lacan, J. (1955). Variations on the Standard Treatment. In J. Lacan, *Écrits: The First Complete Edition in English*. Trans. B. Fink, pp. 269–302. New York and London: W.W. Norton.

Lacan, J. (1958). The Direction of the Treatment and the Principles of Its Power. In J. Lacan, *Écrits: The First Complete Edition in English*. Trans. B. Fink, pp. 489–542. New York and London: W.W. Norton.

Lacan, J. (1960). Position of the Unconscious. In J. Lacan, *Écrits: The First Complete Edition in English*. Trans. B. Fink, pp. 703–721. New York and London: W.W. Norton.

Lacan, J. (1960–1961). *The Seminar of Jacques Lacan, Book VIII: Transference*. Ed. J.-A. Miller. Trans. B. Fink. Cambridge: Polity Press.

Lacan, J. (1961–1962). The Seminar of Jacques Lacan, Book IX: Identification. Trans. C. Gallagher. Unpublished. Retrieved from http://hdl.handle.net/10788/159

Lacan, J. (1962–1963). The Seminar of Jacques Lacan, Book X: Anxiety: 1962–1963. Trans. C. Gallagher. Unpublished. Retrieved from http://hdl.handle.net/10788/160

Lacan, J. (1966). On a Purpose. In J. Lacan, *Écrits: The First Complete Edition in English*. Trans. B. Fink, pp. 303–307. New York and London: W.W. Norton.

Lacan, J. (1966–1967). The Seminar of Jaques Lacan, Book XIV: The Logic of Phantasy. Trans. C. Gallagher. Unpublished. Retrieved from http://hdl.handle.net/10788/163

Lacan, J. (1967–1968). *The Seminar of Jacques Lacan, Book XV: The Psychoanalytic Act 1967–1968.* Ed. C. Gallagher. Retrieved from www.lacaninireland.com:http://hdl.handle.net/10788/164

Lacan, J. (1971). The Seminar of Jacques Lacan. Book XVIII: On a Discourse That Might not be a Semblance. Trans. C. Gallagher. Unpublished. Retrieved from http://hdl.handle.net/10788/167

Lacan, J. (1975–1976). The Seminar of Jacques Lacan, Book XXIII: Joyce and the Sinthome (Parts 1 and 2). Trans. C. Gallagher. Unpublished. Retrieved from http://hdl.handle.net/10788/172;http://hdl.handle.net/10788/173

Lacan, J. (1976). Conférences et entretiens dans des universités nord-américaines (*Lectures and interviews at North American universities*). *Scilicet*, 6/7, 5–63.

Lacan, J. (1976–1977). Seminario XXIV: Lo no sabido que sabe de la una-equivocación se ampara en la morra. Unpublished.

Lacan, J. (1981). *The Seminar of Jacques Lacan, Book XI: The Four Fundamental Concepts of Psychoanalysis.* Ed. J.-A. Miller. Trans. A. Sheridan. New York and London: W.W. Norton. (Original work published 1964)

Lacan, J. (1991). *The Seminar of Jacques Lacan. Book I: Freud's Papers on Technique.* Ed. J.-A. Miller. Trans. J. Forrester. New York and London: W.W. Norton. (Original work published 1953–1954)

Laplanche, J., and Pontalis, J.-B. (1967). *The Language of Psychoanalysis.* Trans. D. Nicholson-Smith. London: Karnac Books.

Miller, J.-A. (2018). *Donc. La lógica de la cura. Los cursos psicoanalíticos de Jacques Alain Miller.* Buenos Aires: Paidós. (Original work published 1993–1994)

Index

For Product Safety Concerns and Information please contact our EU
representative GPSR@taylorandfrancis.com
Taylor & Francis Verlag GmbH, Kaufingerstraße 24, 80331 München, Germany